Pipers at the
Gates of Dawn

PIPERS AT THE GATES OF DAWN

The Wisdom of Children's Literature

JONATHAN COTT

Random House   New York

Library of Congress Cataloging in Publication Data
Cott, Jonathan.
Pipers at the gates of dawn.
Bibliography; p.
Includes index.
1. Children's literature—History and criticism—
Addresses, essays, lectures.   I. Title.
PN1009.A1C667   1983   809'.89282   82-15152
ISBN 0-394-50464-X

Manufactured in the United States of America
9   8   7   6   5   4   3   2

BOOK DESIGN BY LILLY LANGOTSKY

"Now it passes on and I begin to lose it," he said presently. "O, Mole! the beauty of it! The merry bubble and joy, the thin, clear, happy call of the distant piping! Such music I never dreamed of, and the call in it is stronger even than the music is sweet! Row on, Mole, row! For the music and the call must be for us."

The Mole, greatly wondering, obeyed. "I hear nothing myself," he said, "but the wind playing in the reeds and rushes and osiers."

—"The Piper at the Gates of Dawn"
from *The Wind in the Willows*
by Kenneth Grahame

Piping down the valleys wild,
Piping songs of pleasant glee,
On a cloud I saw a child,
And he laughing said to me:

"Pipe a song about a Lamb!"
So I piped with merry cheer.
"Piper, pipe that song again."
So I piped: he wept to hear.

"Drop thy pipe, thy happy pipe,
Sing thy songs of happy cheer."
So I sung the same again,
While he wept with joy to hear.

"Piper, sit thee down and write
In a book, that all may read."
So he vanished from my sight,
And I plucked a hollow reed,

And I made a rural pen,
And I stained the water clear,
And I wrote my happy songs
Every child may joy to hear.

—William Blake

Acknowledgments

I am deeply grateful to Michele Napear who originally suggested that I write this book; to the John Simon Guggenheim Memorial Foundation for a fellowship that allowed me to do it; to Jason Epstein, vice president and editorial director of Random House, for signing up the book and for his instructive essay "'Good Bunnies Always Obey': Books for American Children," which pointed out the path to follow; to Jonathan Galassi for his excellent, perspicacious editing; to Jean McNutt for her invaluable help with and contributions to the manuscript; to Angeline Moscatt and the staff of the Central Children's Room of the New York Public Library for their interest in my project; to Professor Francelia Butler for her continual encouragement and inspiration; to Susan Bergholz and John Donovan, Executive Director of the Children's Book Council, for their advice and help; to Professor Brian Sutton-Smith and Dr. Howard Gardner for their insights into the work of Dr. Seuss; and to Ann B. Weissmann for her translation of Astrid Lindgren's memoirs.

I would also like to thank the following persons who, in various ways, helped make this book possible: Rob Baker, Joan C. Barker, Diane Breitweiser, Jim Bruce, Fabiano Canosa, Portia Clark, Jean Cott, Cathy Crane, Madeleine de Bekassy, Michael di Capua, Kate Ezra, Catchia Goggin, Margaret Gorenstein, Alex Halsey, Thea Hardigg, Ty Hendrick, Barbara Hodes, Debbie Hurst, Ruth Jarmofsky, Daniel and Susan Juda, Lorraine Kisly, Robert Kraus, Lillian Langotsky, Christine and Gilles Larrain, Elizabeth Latshaw, Dialta Lensi-Orlandi, Sally McCartin, Harold and Henrietta Napear, Nancy Paulsen, Joan Robins, Robin Roth, Trudie Schafer, Justin G. Schiller, Evelyn Shrifte, Carol Schwartz, Arthur and Aurora Steig, Jeanne Steig, Jeremy Steig, Alexandra Stewart, Michael Stone, Dr. Douglas van der Heide, Nigel and Victoria Waymouth, Martin Weaver, Jane and Jann Wenner, Anna Wintour, Laurie Witkin.

Special thanks to Mr. William Shawn and the editors of *The*

New Yorker, in which the profiles of Astrid Lindgren and of Iona and Peter Opie were first published; to D. M. Dooling and the editors of *Parabola,* in which the conversation with Chinua Achebe and excerpts from the chapter on P. L. Travers originally appeared; and to Jann Wenner and the editors of *Rolling Stone,* in which a shortened version of the section on Maurice Sendak was featured (later reprinted in my book *Forever Young*).

Contents

Introduction

I often find myself wandering through the Central Children's Room of the New York Public Library. Located in the Donnell Library Center in Manhattan, this treasure house consists of a circulating and reference collection, an enclosed alcove of rare children's books (about 2,500 eighteenth- and nineteenth-century volumes of fiction, poetry, and works on folklore and toys), and the office of the supervising librarian. This last enclave contains, among other things, autographed copies of three of my favorite childhood books—Wanda Gág's *Millions of Cats*, Munro Leaf's *The Story of Ferdinand*, and Ludwig Bemelmans' *Madeline*—and various pieces of Mary Poppins memorabilia, including an old-fashioned wooden Dutch doll that served as the model for drawings of the cosmic nanny (donated by the author, P. L. Travers), and a magnificently green, parrot-headed umbrella, one of Mary Poppins's distinguishing accouterments (donated by one of the author's editors).

Although from time to time I pester the librarian into giving me a short tour of her office, I never fail to meander through the aisles of three-foot-high bookshelves, bending over as I walk and grazing with a finger the rows of mostly plastic-enclosed volumes, hoping to light upon a new (to me) children's novel or picture book—one that might have been kept out for months (forgotten under a pile of old space-age toys and video cassettes), but that has now been returned to its (sort of) proper place. And here I often stop, open the book in order to smell it (one of the things I've loved to do ever since I was little, and still do with all books), read a sentence or two, decide whether or not to borrow the volume, then continue on my quest.

Occasionally, children passing by will glance quizzically at me. Mostly, however, I tend to find them sitting on the floor, blissfully absorbed in a book with their noses barely an inch or two from the page. But one day a critical-looking little girl came up to me and, in the contumelious tone of voice of the Caterpillar in *Alice's Adven-*

tures in Wonderland, intoned: "What are *you* doing here?" I didn't know how to respond, mumbled something or other about "doing research," and shuffled nervously away (pretending to myself that I'd gotten lost). It was at that very moment I decided to write a book that would answer my young inquisitor's question.

In 1967 I went to live in London, traveling up once a week by train to a university where I was supposed to be studying contemporary

Illustration by Maurice Sendak for George MacDonald's *The Golden Key*

British poetry. With a few exceptions, however, most of the British poets I was then reading seemed conventional and unexciting. London in the late sixties, on the other hand, was exhilarating, turbulent, and continually surprising—with "music in the cafés at night and revolution in the air," as Bob Dylan once sang. My university, moreover,

was on continual student strike; and with classes and seminars can-
celed, it began to dawn on me that I had been in school for too many
years (nineteen including kindergarten). At the same time I was
suffering from a broken heart, and also sensed that I was undergoing
a kind of *crise de vingt ans*—the results of which were that I stopped
almost all reading and writing and began wandering aimlessly around
the streets of London with a bad case of acedia, staring, as if color-
blind, as red traffic lights turned to green, to red, to green.

At that time, eccentric, vertiginous behavior was actually considered quite normal and, in some circles, *de rigueur*. Fortunately for
me, an empathic friend decided to step in and direct me away from
World's End and toward the more supernal regions of existence. To
this purpose, my friend one day presented me with a copy of the
fairy tales of George MacDonald—the great nineteenth-century Scottish visionary preacher and writer—whom I had never heard of before.
The first story I read was "The Golden Key," which tells of a boy and
girl named Mossy and Tangle who start out searching for the country
from which the shadows come. Separated from each other, they both
encounter the Old Man of the Sea, the Old Man of the Earth, and
the Old Man of the Fire—the last of whom is a naked child sitting
on moss and arranging balls of various colors and sizes into mysterious
formations and sequences. All three of these figures—who are, perhaps, Mossy and Tangle in their various and transforming states of
awareness—guide the children through a journey of death and rebirth
(for MacDonald, death is "only more life")—what Gnostics call "a
migration into newness." And at the end, having opened the door of
a cave with their golden key, Mossy and Tangle discover a winding
stair within. "The key vanished from his fingers. Tangle went up.
Mossy followed. The door closed behind them. They climbed out of
the earth; and, still climbing, rose above it. They were in the rainbow.
Far abroad, over ocean and land, they could see through its transparent
walls the earth beneath their feet. Stairs beside stairs wound up
together, and beautiful beings of all ages climbed along with them."

Carl Jung has mentioned that in ancient Egypt, when a man was
bitten by a snake, a priest-physician was called in. Taking a manuscript from the temple library, he would begin to recite the story of
Rā and his mother Isis to the sick man, and in this way raise the personal ailment into a "generally valid situation," thereby mobilizing
the patient's unconscious forces so as to affect his nervous system.
Bruno Bettelheim, too, has commented on how Hindu medicine men
would often ask their patients to contemplate a fairy tale in order that

they might "find a way out of the inner darkness which beclouded their minds." Such was the effect on me of "The Golden Key." And immediately I rushed off to buy everything by George MacDonald that I could find, unable to get over the fact that his greatest writings (*At the Back of the North Wind, The Princess and Curdie, Sir Gibbie*) were intended for children. If this were so, I thought, then perhaps I should reread the classics of children's literature that I had remembered liking when I was young—*The Wind in the Willows, The Wizard of Oz, The Tale of Mrs. Tiggy-Winkle, Swallows and Amazons, Babar the King*. I was astonished at how wonderful these books were; and even though I was occasionally discomforted when someone, having asked me what book I had in my pocket, looked aghast when I pulled out a copy of *Heidi* or *Finn Family Moomintroll*, I soon realized that my then-present condition of "second childhood" was not one of senility and depression but of renewal and awakening.

Quasi-scholar that I was (or at least was supposed to be), I next wondered what earlier children's literature was like, for aside from Lewis Carroll and Edward Lear I knew almost nothing about Victorian children's books. Happily, I chanced upon *Children's Books in England: Five Centuries of Social Life* by F. J. Harvey Darton. Originally published in 1932, this extraordinary and beautifully written work (reprinted in 1982 by Cambridge University Press in an excellent, thoroughly revised third edition by Brian Alderson) revealed to me that this literature had its origins in bestiaries, fables, romances, rhymed treatises, primers, and the invention of the horn- and chapbook; that it only began to become a commercial publishing enterprise in the early-to-mid-eighteenth century; and that its greatest flowering occurred during the Victorian period. So off I went to the British Library and proceeded, with Harvey Darton as my guide, to spend two months reading scores of books by writers such as Catherine Sinclair, Mark Lemon, Mrs. Juliana Horatia Ewing, Mrs. Mary Louisa Molesworth, Mary de Morgan, Charles Kingsley, and Thomas Hughes, among others.

And in the midst of all my reading (which went on, or back, to include seventeenth- and eighteenth-century books as well), what I began to discover was that children's literature was a body of work that not only simply consoled, as it instructed and delighted, but also clearly presented different types of social attitudes and behavior. And it did not merely reflect a specific social scene but it also became a kind of magnifying glass focused on the operations and processes of society at large. As I once noted in another context, this "magnifying" effect can easily be seen in many fairy tales, in the medieval *Reynard the Fox,* in the numerous early chapbook versions of *The World Turned Upside Down* (in which a child turns into a parent, a soldier into a nurse), in *Gulliver's Travels* (which children early on adopted as their own), in juvenile animal stories such as the eighteenth-century *Biography of a Spaniel* and *Keeper's Travels,* in Victorian political satires like *Petsetilla's Posy* and *The Rose and the Ring,* and, most obviously, in the mirror world of Lewis Carroll.

But even in many overtly didactic works for children—with the possible exception of the life-denying "Joyful Deaths" tradition promulgated by the Puritans, who considered children to be "brands of Hell"—the ineradicable nature of childhood energy insists on attaining a power that no "improving" or "cautionary" force can destroy. For in the attempt to admonish and chastise reprehensibly "childish" behavior, these minatory works cannot help but evoke what Herbert Marcuse once termed "the words, the images, the music of another reality, of another order repelled by the existing one and yet alive in memory and anticipation." Just the simple depiction of scurrying little mice in Dorothy Kilner's eighteenth-century *The Life and Perambulations of a Mouse,* of prankster children in Catherine Sinclair's early-Victorian *Holiday House,* or, in this century, of Beatrix Potter's mischievous rabbits, Gelett Burgess's ill-mannered Goops, and Palmer Cox's trickster Brownies allows the reader to fantasize the subversion of the restricting moral and social order and to envisage a reality more open and connected to the instinctual forces of childhood. And as the novelist and critic Alison Lurie has reminded us, works like *Huckleberry Finn, Alice's Adventures in Wonderland, The Story of Ferdinand,* and *The Cat in the Hat* are truly "on the subversive side. . . . Most of the lasting works of juvenile literature," she writes, "express feelings not generally approved of or even recognized by grown-ups; they make fun of honored figures and piously held beliefs; and they view social pretences with clear-eyed directness, remarking—as in Andersen's famous tale—that the emperor has no clothes" ("On the Subversive Side").

Consolation and *critique*: these are what children's literature, as I first encountered it as an adult, seemed to be about. And this was confirmed for me in an amazing little story from the Ekoi tribe in Nigeria that I discovered one day in Paul Radin's *African Folktales*:

> Mouse goes everywhere. Through rich men's houses she creeps, and she visits even the poorest. At night, with her bright little eyes,

she watches the doing of secret things, and no treasure chamber is so safe but she can tunnel through and see what is hidden there.

In olden days she wove a story child from all that she saw, and to each of these she gave a gown of a different color—white, red, blue, or black. The stories became her children and lived in her house and served her because she had no children of her own.

It has been told that a noted eighteenth-century Talmudic scholar, afraid of losing his faith, came to seek the advice of the Hasidic master the Maggid of Mezeritch. As Elie Wiesel recounts in *Souls on Fire,* the Maggid "did not engage the man in lengthy philosophical discussions, but instead asked him to repeat with him, over and over again, the very first prayer every Jewish child learns by heart. And that was all." Similarly, we are told by the Jungian psychologist Marie-Louise von Franz that among the Australian aborigines, when the rice crop shows signs of failure, the women go into the ricefield, bend down, and relate to it the history of its origins; the rice, now understanding why it is there, begins again to grow.

In a sense, then, my turning to children's books as an over-satiated adult reader induced in me the kind of "intense attention" that, the critic Helen Vendler has suggested, the greatest literature should induce, making us enter, in her words, a state of "receptivity and plasticity and innocence," and, in Shelley's words, purging "from our inward sight the film of familiarity which obscures from us the wonder of our being." Simply, I had begun again to begin to read! And, as if for the first time, words seemed to glisten and sparkle, like the light on clear mountain streams. Rereading *The Tale of Peter Rabbit,* for instance, I began to recall and re-sense how, when I was little, the word "parsley" and its *taste* had once seemed to me to be one and the same. For children's literature reawakens in us our sense of remembering, which, in fact, is often stored in, and brought to new life by, our senses.

Inevitably, one thinks of Proust's involuntary memory epiphanies, brought on by the taste of the madeleine and by the feeling under his feet of the unevenness of the pavement. One thinks, also, of Jean Cocteau who, returning to his childhood street and trailing his finger along the wall as he had done as a child, could summon up no sense of his past. But realizing that he had been smaller then, he decided to bend down, close his eyes, and again trace the wall—but this time at the level of a little person. And "just as the needle picks up the melody from the record," Cocteau tells us, "I obtained the melody of the past with my hand. I found everything: my cape, the leather of my satchel, the names of my friends and those of my teachers, certain expressions I had used, the sound of my grandfather's voice, the smell of his beard, the smell of my sister's dresses and of my mother's gown."

In a similar way, children's books can enable us to recapture and re-enter our earliest worlds: a sudden word or phrase or description—or a beloved illustration—may cast light on a darkened past. And, as the psychologist Ernest Schachtel writes, "each genuine recovery of forgotten experience and, with it, something of the person that one was when having the experience, carries with it an element of enrichment, adds to the light of consciousness, and thus widens the conscious scope of one's life." For like Wordsworth's conception of childhood, children's literature is "the fountain-light of all our day . . . a master-light of all our seeing." (In a similar but more mysterious light, the French philosopher Gaston Bachelard has written: "Each childhood is a night light in the bedroom of memories.")

As many writers have demonstrated, one can draw upon this light and direct it onto one's later work—and in one's subconscious, needless to say, it may often, unnoticed, shine forth on its own. It has been suggested, for example, that the mosaic and primer format of William Blake's *The Marriage of Heaven and Hell* may have been influenced by John Newbery's *A Little Pretty Pocket-Book*—the "historic milestone" in children's literature that I discuss in my opening chapter. And it has also been claimed that the color sequence in Rimbaud's famous "Vowels" sonnet ("*A noir, E blanc, I rouge, U vert, O bleu*") is based not only on alchemic experimental procedures but also on a colored alphabet used extensively among French children during the Second Empire. And as another French author, Jean-Paul Sartre, recollects in his autobiography *The Words*: "At about the age of ten, I read with great pleasure *Les Transatlantiques*, which tells about a little American boy and his sister, both of them very innocent. I identified myself with the boy, and through him loved Biddy, the little girl. I thought for a long time of writing a story about two lost children who were discreetly incestuous. Traces of this fantasy can be found in my writings."

It is interesting to note that a child's favorite books are often consciously the models for, or the most important influence on, his or her later beliefs and ways of living. A journalist I know told me that when he was young he was so taken by the character of Walter R. Brooks's Freddy the Pig—portrayed as a writer and detective—that he decided to combine both professions and become a reporter! According to another reporter, Ray Connolly, John Lennon was, as a child, "an early and avid reader, his favorite books being *Alice in Wonderland, The Wind in the Willows*, and the *Just William* series by Richmal Crompton, stories of a naughty but very funny small boy. John undoubtedly cast himself in William's image, as did so many other boys at that time." (In many ways, John Lennon might truly be seen as William *redivivus*, with that character's irrepressible sense of leadership, intense fantasy life, almost brutal candor, and anarchistic rejection of almost all establishment values, standards of decorum, and modes of speech.) In addition, several of my women friends—as I mention in my chapter on Astrid Lindgren—have suggested to me that their independent spirits and attitudes were encouraged early on by their love for the character of Pippi Longstocking. And my own basically pacifist values seem to me to have been influenced by *The Story of Ferdinand*, the tale of the bull who likes to sit under a cork tree smelling the flowers.

It is also worth remembering that the poems and stories we *first* hear and read may well be the basis for many of our important literary forms, practices, and traditions. Lullabies and fairy tales have often been cited as the genesis of all songs and stories. Northrop Frye, moreover, has suggested that charms and riddles are the "generic seeds or kernels" of our larger, more sophisticated literary genres. And, of course, charms like "Ladybird, ladybird,/Fly away home,/Your house is on fire/And your children all gone" and riddles like "White bird featherless/Flew from Paradise,/Pitched on the castle wall . . ." are preserved in nursery rhymes—those little pieces of verse that adults, remembering them from their childhood, pass on to *their* children or grandchildren who, in turn, remember to pass them on again. (In the end are their beginnings.)

"It is grown people who make the nursery stories," wrote Robert Louis Stevenson; "all children do is jealously preserve the text." But is this last assertion really true anymore? In our current electronic revolution, children—at least in America, Japan, and, to a lesser extent, in Europe—have increasingly been turning (and turning on) to television, video games, and computer programs. It has been estimated that the average American adolescent has already in his or her life watched 17,000 hours of television. And Mary Alice White, a psychologist who heads the Electronic Learning Laboratory at Columbia University's Teacher's College, reports that the average American child already spends twenty-eight *voluntary* hours each week with electronic learning tools compared with twenty-five *mostly involuntary* hours with printed learning materials. And discussing a recent experimental program in selected New York City public schools—one that integrates computers into virtually the entire curriculum—Fred M. Hechinger writes in *The New York Times* that "planners say they are aware of the danger of dehumanization through excessive or ill-advised computerization," but "point out that, in addition to computers, the classroom will still rely on books, pencils, toys, art materials, hamsters, and goldfish."

"I am thinking in a Fortran way," says one New York City high school student of her work with computer languages. And it is all too easy to be contemptuous of and to discount the possibility that many children may well become more competent in mathematics and writing skills by mastering computer programs and word processors than they would with traditional teaching methods. (The psychologist Howard Gardner has even speculated that "the ways in which one teaches history—with its time frames—or geometry—with its spatial components—might differ depending on the media with which children happen to have been raised *and* the media in which lessons are conveyed"—*Art, Mind, and Brain.*) But it is becoming increasingly evident that for many elementary school—and many more high school—students, storytelling and reading are fast becoming lost arts. As a sixteen-year-old tenth grader at North Mesquite High School in Texas is reported to have said: "If a kid wants to spend his money playing [in a video game arcade], I don't see why he shouldn't be able to. It's his money. If we weren't here, we'd probably be home watching TV. What's the difference?" And if he weren't watching TV, he might well be reading a "Young Adult" novel like *Dinky Hocker Shoots Smack,* while his sister, in her turn, might be absorbed in a "Teen Romance" like *Superflirt.* As a marketing executive recently said about these romances: "They're a publisher's dream. The market may be insatiable."

The psychologist Jan H. van den Berg has stated that today, "maturity means living pluralistically. It is simply not permissible to deny the child its inner contrasts." And it is obvious that children in America and Western Europe are growing up sooner than they used to (puberty sets in at least three years earlier now than it did a century ago—a result, it is thought, of improved nutrition). More than ever before, kids are street-wise, TV-wise, and R-rated-movies-wise. (Films like *Star Wars* and *E.T. The Extra-Terrestrial* are, of course, children's literature in a different guise.) But an information-processing society that neglects to pass on the *real* wisdom of tales and rhymes from one generation to another—whether around a campfire or at bedtime—will eventually become desiccated, distempered, and self-destroying. And it is the adults who need the tales and rhymes as much as the children, lest there be no more Wise Women or Wise Men. We must, as the depth psychologist James Hillman has asserted, "restory the adult . . . in order to restore the imagination to a primary place in consciousness in each of us, regardless of age."

In his "Immortality" Ode, Wordsworth states that "our birth is but a sleep and a forgetting"; and the older we get, the harder it is for us to wake up. Children's literature—and what is that but tales and rhymes writ and drawn large or small?—helps us to wake up. It brings us back to experiencing our earliest and deepest feelings and truths. It is our link to the past and a path to the future. And in it we find ourselves.

Pipers at the Gates of Dawn consists of my reflections about and encounters with six extraordinary creators of children's literature, and with a man and woman who, together, have studied in depth not only the roots and blossomings of this literature but also the lore, games, and language of the "savage tribe" of schoolchildren.

Commenting on the evolutionary process of *neotony* ("the slowing down of developmental rates and the consequent retention to adulthood of traits that mark the *juvenile* stages of our ancestors"), the scientist Stephen Jay Gould comments: "I believe that the analogy between childhood wonder and adult creativity is good biology, not metaphor." And it should not seem surprising that the creators in this book have all attested to their experience that one writes not so much for the child one used to be as for the child one always is. In the words of P. L. Travers: "You do not chop off a section of your imaginative substance and make a book specifically for children for—if you are honest—you have, in fact, no idea where childhood ends and maturity begins. It is all endless and all one." (Etienne Delessert's *How the Mouse was Hit on the Head by a Stone and So Discovered the World*—a book, published in 1971, that was subjected to the scrutiny and final approval of twenty-three five- and six-year-old children, and which, for some bewildering reason, inspired the great psychologist Jean Piaget to praise "the remarkable professional integrity that led [Delessert] conscientiously to adapt himself to his young readers instead of simply trusting to his intuition"—is a classic example of the benightedness and banality of this kind of collusive and cosseting literary procedure—e.g., "'Who is night?' asks the mouse. 'I am the night,' a deep voice answers. 'I already know you,' says the mouse. 'You are as black as ink. I saw you underground in my parents' house'.")

C. S. Lewis once said that "a children's story is the best art form for something you have to say." And it seems to me that the masterpieces of children's literature are simply masterpieces of literature in miniature, conveyors of wisdom and wonder. The subjects of this book are, in my opinion, creators of such masterpieces—almost all of which (the works of Dr. Seuss are the exceptions) I discovered only when I was an adult. And, in a sense, these books discovered *me*, for I came across them either by chance or at the recommendation of friends who liked reading them to their kids or remembered them as favorites from their childhoods. And by reading these books, I enlarged my own sense of childhood.

"The Authors are in Eternity," said William Blake. And so, too, are the heroes and heroines of children's literature; for characters like Dr. Seuss's Cat in the Hat, Maurice Sendak's Rosie, William Steig's Dominic, Astrid Lindgren's Pippi Longstocking, Chinua Achebe's Leopard, and P. L. Travers's Mary Poppins seem always to have existed. This last writer has even suggested that Mary Poppins might have invented *her*, rather than the other way around; and I have felt that in meeting each of these authors I have somehow come into closer contact with both the characters in their books and the characters of the writers themselves. Like the Mole in *The Wind in the Willows* who, on encountering a river for the first time, felt "bewitched, entranced, fascinated," so, too, have I felt about my eight subjects (or should I say rulers?) whose works have both instructed and delighted me, and with whom I was fortunate enough to have spent time exploring the lives of their stories and the stories of their lives. "By the side of the river," writes Kenneth Grahame, "[the Mole] trotted as one trots, when very small, by the side of a man who holds one spellbound by exciting stories; and when tired at last, he sat on the bank, while the river still chattered on to him, a babbling procession of the best stories in the world, sent from the heart of the earth to be told at last to the insatiable sea."

THE GOOD
DR. SEUSS

PHOTOGRAPH © ANTONY DI GESU

$\mathcal{O}$n June 18, 1744, the following advertisement appeared on the back page of the *Penny London Morning Advertiser*:

This Day is publish'd According to Act of Parliament (Neatly bound and gilt)
A LITTLE PRETTY POCKET-BOOK, intended for the Instruction and Amusement of little Master Tommy and pretty Miss Polly; with an agreeable Letter to each from *Jack the Giant-Killer*; as also a Ball and Pincushion, the Use of which will infallibly make Tommy a good Boy and Polly a good Girl.
To the Whole is prefix'd, A Lecture on Education, humbly address'd to all Parents, Guardians, Governesses, etc.; wherein Rules are laid down for making their Children strong, hardy, healthy, virtuous, wise, and happy . . .
Printed for J. Newbery, at the *Bible and Crown*, near Devereux Court, without Temple Bar. Price of the Book alone 6d., with Ball or Pincushion 8d.

In England up until the eighteenth century, most reading matter for children consisted of grammars, primers, catechisms, lesson and courtesy books, and other edifying works emphasizing religious, moral, and scholastic concerns. But what boys and girls loved most of all, of course—then as now—were the fables, romances, ballads, and old wives' tales that children shared with adults as part of an irrepressible oral and popular literary tradition. "Keepe them from reading of fayned fables, vayne fantasies, and wanton stories and songs of love, which bring much mischiefe to youth," advised Hugh Rhodes in his *Boke of Nurture* (1545), foreshadowing similar types of warnings that were to be promulgated during the following four centuries by innumerable educators, moralists, and critics.

After the excrescence in the seventeenth century of the malignant "Joyful Deaths" tradition of life-denying Puritan children's books ("Are the Souls of your Children of no Value?" asked the children's author James Janeway. "They are not too little to die, they are

A Little Pretty
POCKET-BOOK,
Intended for the
INSTRUCTION and AMUSEMENT
O F
LITTLE MASTER *TOMMY*,
A N D
PRETTY MISS *POLLY.*
With Two Letters from
J A C K the GIANT-KILLER;·
A S A L S O
A BALL and PINCUSHION;
The Ufe of which will infallibly make *Tommy*
a good Boy, and *Polly* a good Girl.

To which is added,
A LITTLE SONG-BOOK,
B E I N G
A *New Attempt* to teach Children the Ufe of
the *Englifh Alphabet*, by Way of Diverfion.

L O N D O N:
Printed for J. NEWBERY, at the *Bible and Sun*
in St. *Paul's Church-Yard.* 1767.
[Price Six-pence bound.]

Title page and frontispiece for an early edition of John Newbery's *A Little
Pretty Pocket-Book* (originally published in 1744)

not too little to go to Hell"), it is a comfort to be able to point to the
publication of *A Little Book for Little Children* (c. 1705) by a certain
"T. W."—a short reading and spelling book, meant to instruct "in a
plain and pleasant way," which featured verses, riddles, and tiny
woodcuts illustrating, for example, the famous nursery rhyme beginning: "A was an Archer, and shot at a frog,/B was a Blindman, and
led by a dog." Then, in the early 1740s, there appeared Thomas
Boreman's *Gigantick Histories* (a series of two-inch high books for
children that, among other things, told the story of Gog and Magog,
the two giants of the Guildhall, and described the Tower of London,
St. Paul's, and Westminster Abbey), as well as works such as T.
Cooper's *The Child's New Play-thing* (which featured alphabet
rhymes, fables, songs, proverbs, and shortened versions of medieval
tales about St. George and Guy of Warwick), and Mary Cooper's
Tommy Thumb's Song-Book (the first nursery rhyme collection for
children).

Although it drew heavily on the innovative form and content of
its predecessors, *A Little Pretty Pocket-Book* is today regarded as an
historic milestone in the development of children's literature. Its
creator was a clever entrepreneur. Born in 1713, John Newbery was
the son of a Berkshire farmer, and when he was about sixteen he was

apprenticed to a printer whose widow he eventually married and with whom he moved to London in 1744. From then until his death in 1767, he designed, produced, marketed, and sold about thirty books for children—all issued anonymously or under alliterative pseudonyms (Abraham Aesop, Tommy Trapwit, Tom Telescope). Some of the books, it is surmised, were written by persons such as Oliver Goldsmith, Christopher Smart, and, perhaps, Newbery himself. Conjointly with his publishing ventures, Newbery was merchandising gingerbread for children, as well as nostrums and remedies—Cephalic Snuff, Dr. Hooper's Female Pills, and Dr. James's Fever Powder for adults. (In Newbery's children's novel *Goody Two-Shoes* the heroine's father, we are informed, dies for lack of Dr. James's Powder!)

A Little Pretty Pocket-Book was Newbery's first publication; like most of those that followed, it was small (about four by two-and-a-half inches) and attractively attired with a cover of Dutch floral paper. Unlike Boreman's or the Coopers's books, Newbery's little volume was "profusely illustrated," as we would say today (it contained fifty-eight rough woodcuts in a text of ninety pages); in content, it was a kind of gallimaufry, consisting of a letter from Jack the Giant-Killer, an advertisement, an alphabet, verses about games and play, proverbs, four Aesopian fables, and a "Poetical Description of the Four Seasons." Following the educational theories of John Locke (who vowed that children should "play themselves into what others are whipp'd for"), Newbery insisted that learning be made pleasurable, not onerous. It was obviously an idea whose time had officially come. For with this book—which was in its twelfth edition by 1767—Newbery single-handedly created (or discovered) the children's book market. And, as with most pioneers, he ingenuously set the patterns—in terms of subjects, themes, and approaches—that children's book creators and publishers would later develop.

Among Newbery's publications were alphabet, spelling, and riddle books; collections of fables and poems; histories; novels—especially the popular *The History of Little Goody Two-Shoes*; a ten-volume compendium of knowledge for boys and girls known as *The Circle of Sciences*; a science text containing fact and fiction entitled *The Newtonian System of Philosophy*; and possibly the first children's magazine, *The Lilliputian Magazine*. His books are filled with amusingly named characters like Tommy Trip, Zig Zag, and Giles Gingerbread; and with friendly animals like Tippy the lark, Jouler the dog, and Willy the lamb. But aside from his informal publishing approach, John Newbery could barely disguise his Lockean-derived notion that amusement and delight were simply the sugar-coated ingredients of a cachet (think of Giles Gingerbread, who learned his letters by eating them!), the medicinal purpose of which was to foster an acceptance of a conservative social order and a mercantile ideology. And Newbery's books do nothing less than idolize, as they help define, middle-class values. He advised young boys to learn to read well so that they might be rewarded with a "Coach and Six"; to young girls he promised that virtuous behavior would result in their becoming "Ladies of the Manor." The qualities and virtues he valued and promoted were those of dutifulness, moderation, self-control, rationality, sobriety, prudence, and industry. His motto: "Trade and Plumbcake forever, Huzza!"

Almost two hundred years later, in 1936, a cartoonist, illustrator, and writer named Theodor Geisel was walking along Madison Avenue, carrying the manuscript of a children's book that had already been rejected by twenty-seven publishers, when he ran into a Dartmouth schoolmate, one year his junior. Marshall McClintock had just the day before become juvenile editor of Vanguard Press, and this fortuitous reunion resulted in the publishing of *And To Think That I Saw It on Mulberry Street* (1937), a book credited to Geisel's nom de plume "Dr. Seuss" (Seuss was Geisel's middle, and his mother's maiden, name; the "Dr." his self-appointed title, saving his real name for his "still forthcoming"—as he laughingly puts it— Great American Novel).

John Newbery—great admirer of pseudonyms and of commercial enterprise that he was—would have undoubtedly admired the panache with which Theodor Geisel entered the publishing marketplace. But he would have been appalled by Dr. Seuss's first children's book, and would certainly have identified himself with the father of the book's imaginative hero, Marco:

> When I leave home to walk to school,
> Dad always says to me,
> "Marco, keep your eyelids up
> And see what you can see."
>
> But when I tell him where I've been
> And what I think I've seen,
> He looks at me and sternly says,
> "Your eyesight's much too keen.
>
> "Stop telling such outlandish tales.
> Stop turning minnows into whales."

"Now, what can I say/When I get home today?" Marco asks himself. And in the course of his walk home from school, he notices a now-immortalized dumpy horse and wagon—"That *can't* be my story. That's only a *start*"—and transforms it into what, added detail by added detail, eventually becomes a howdah-caparisoned blue elephant marching astride two crocked-looking yellow giraffes pulling a seven-piece brass band and attached pixilated-old codger-inhabited trailer to the admiring salutes and cheers of flag-waving governmental dignitaries—the entire police-escorted parade entourage showered by brightly colored confetti emptied from red and white baskets by two jaunty men on the top of a low-flying, whirring motor plane. . . . But when Marco gets home and his frowning, prosaic father asks him what he has seen that day, he gives his only possible reply: " 'Nothing,'

How a plain horse and wagon on Mulberry Street . . .

Grows into a story that no one can beat . . .

I said, growing red as a beet,/'But a plain horse and wagon on Mulberry Street'."

"Useless trumpery" is the way John Locke condemned fairy tales, ballads, and chapbook romances in the eighteenth century; his disciple John Newbery might have applied the same epithet to Marco's Mulberry Street hallucinations, as well as to the book that preserves them. But just as *A Little Pretty Pocket-Book* opened up new possibilities for children's literature in its time, so did *Mulberry Street* in ours. One could say that while Newbery created the children's book industry in England, Dr. Seuss—two centuries after its inception—has, astonishingly, been able to create his own microcosmic publishing universe: Walk into most children's bookstores today and you will find sections devoted to "Fairy Tales," "Picture Books," and "Dr. Seuss." He has become a genre, a category, an institution; more than eighty million of his books have been sold around the world.

"What exactly is it that makes this stuff immortal?" asked Rudolf Flesch (author of *Why Johnny Can't Read*) about Dr. Seuss's work. "There is something about it," Flesch tried to explain. "A swing to the language, a deep understanding of the playful mind of a child, an undefinable something that makes Dr. Seuss a genius pure and simple."

And To Think That I Saw It on Mulberry Street immediately provides several other answers to Flesch's question, striking as it does the characteristic Seussian chord and rhythm, and ringing their changes. There is, first of all, the unflagging momentum, feeling of breathlessness, and swiftness of pace, all together acting as the motor for Dr. Seuss's pullulating image machine that brings to life—through rhymes and pictures—what William James describes as our earliest experiences of the world ("The baby, assailed by eyes, ears, nose, skin, and entrails at once, feels that all is one great blooming, buzzing confusion"), as well as what, more specifically, Selma G. Lanes calls "Marco's rapidly expanding universe." All of this expansiveness expresses itself through Seuss's unique, children's-drawing style of illustration and through a theme-and-variations technique (the theme is usually that of searching for, discovering, or inventing something *new*) that the author uses in many of his books, including *Scrambled Eggs Super!* (in which the hero cook searches for new and different birds whose eggs will create a unique mélange) and *On Beyond Zebra* (in which the hero creates a new alphabet beyond the letter Z with invented animals representing each new letter). It is a technique that features the use of visual exaggeration. "I think that when ideas

The Woset from *There's a Wocket in My Pocket!*

are first differentiated by children," says Brian Sutton-Smith—professor of education and folklore at the University of Pennsylvania—"they have to be caricatured. There has to be an exaggerated form of a thing in order to get it out of the background, in order to differentiate the figure from the ground—whether you're talking about an idea or a picture. You can't, for example, do jigsaws unless you make the edges really clear. And Dr. Seuss uses exaggeration all the time."

In *Mulberry Street*, Dr. Seuss's illustrations are less exaggerated than they would become several years later—as in the books mentioned above—but you can already observe incipient signs of this tendency in the way he portrays the bibulous faces of his animals—zebras, reindeer, giraffes, and elephants. (His creatures, as poet and critic Karla Kuskin aptly observes, all have "slightly batty, oval eyes and a smile you might find on the Mona Lisa after her first martini.") Indeed, more than any other children's-book artist—except perhaps

The Collapsible Frink
from *Dr. Seuss's Sleep Book*

The Curious Crandalls from *Dr. Seuss's Sleep Book*

Two-headed Amphisbaena from a twelfth-century bestiary
The "su" as drawn by Father André Thevet, 1558
From a book of grotesques by C. Jamnitzer, 1610

The Luan, an auspicious bird;
one of the ancient Chinese shen,
or mountain gods

The Stoop and the Booba, from six-year-old Sybil Corbet's *Animal Land
where there are no People*, 1897

for Edward Lear (think of the Dong with a Luminous Nose and the Quangle Wangle)—Dr. Seuss has created the most extraordinary variety of ingeniously named, fantastical-looking animals and composite beasts. (One might have imagined that it could *only* have been Dr. Seuss who had thought up and named the zedonk—the animal produced when a male zebra mates with a female donkey!) Looking at preternatural creations such as Seuss's Foona-Lagoona Baboona and the Nutches—as well as his elephant-bird (*Horton Hatches the Egg*) and fish-cow (*McElligot's Pool*)—one is reminded of the zoomorphic creatures joyfully imagined by artists in all parts of the world. Seuss-like animals are suggested by, for example, the tao-tieh of the Chinese Bronze Age, and by the hybrid creatures known as the shen —the ancient Chinese mountain gods; by the ant-lion (lion in front, ant in back) and the eales or yales (with tails like an elephant's and the jowls of a boar) of the fourth-century *Physiologus*, medieval bestiaries, and Topsell's seventeenth-century *The Historie of Fourefooted Beastes*; and by the imaginary animals of the sixteenth-century Father André Thevet and of the six-year-old English girl, Sybil Corbet, who, in 1897, published them in a book entitled *Animal Land where there are no People*.

Also extremely characteristic of Seuss's work—in this and almost all of his other books—is his habitual use of anapestic tetrameter verse. Geisel claims that in 1936, when he was returning from Europe on an ocean liner, he became entranced by the rhythm of the ship's engines: "Da da *da*, da de *dum* dum de *da* de de *da*." The words that to him seemed to match the boat's beat were: "And to think that I saw it on Mulberry Street"—the line that set him off writing and illustrating the book, and was a promise of the musical energy and excitement to be found in all of Dr. Seuss's poetry. For the anapest line embodies movement and swiftness, as in: "Oh, he flies through the air with the greatest of ease" and "O who rides by night thro' the woodland so wild?"

This last line is Sir Walter Scott's translation of the opening words of Goethe's famous "The Erl-King" (Scott used anapestic tetrameter to imitate Goethe's anapest-weighted *Knüttelvers*). It is a poem, both in the original German and in Scott's translation, that acts on its readers and listeners like a dream, with its forceful depiction of a father embracing his dying son as they ride feverishly through the woods. Yet what is worth mentioning here is that, as their journey progresses, the son and his father engage in a dialogue much like that between Marco and *his* father:

"O father, see yonder! see yonder!" he says;
"My boy, upon what dost thou fearfully gaze?"
"O, 'tis the Erl-King with his crown and his shroud."
"No, my son, it is but a dark wreath of the cloud." . . .

"O father, my father, and did you not hear
  The Erl-King whisper so low in my ear?"
"Be still, my heart's darling—my child, be at ease;
  It was but the wild blast as it sung thro' the trees." . . .

"O father, my father, and saw you not plain
  The Erl-King's pale daughter glide past thro' the rain?"
"O yes, my loved treasure, I knew it full soon;
  It was the gray willow that danced to the moon." . . .

Although the poem resonates on many levels, it might be taken to suggest that the denial of one's powers of fantasy and imagination (both share the same image-generating roots) is a form of death. John Newbery and his contemporaries, one remembers, wished to crush children's imaginative powers and the literature that nourished them. One eighteenth-century writer even boasted that writing for children required one "to restrain a lively imagination," a "sort of heroic sacrifice of gratification to virtue, which I cannot doubt is acceptable to the Supreme Being."

In this century, of course, many artists, educators, and psychologists have adamantly taken a stand strongly in favor of fantasy ("Whenever we are caught in a literal view," states the depth psychologist James Hillman, "a literal belief, a literal statement, we have lost the imaginative metaphysical perspective to ourselves and our world"). But such disparate figures as Einstein and Lenin have also affirmed the importance of fantasy. As the former once said: "When I examine myself and my methods of thought, I come to the conclusion that the gift of fantasy has meant more to me than any talent for abstract, positive thinking." And as the latter stated: "It is incorrect to think that fantasy is useful only to the poet. This is an insipid prejudice! It is useful even in mathematics—even differential and integral calculus could not have been discovered without it. Fantasy is a quality of the highest importance." And it was another Russian— the children's poet and educator Kornei Chukovsky—who spoke of the child's "rights" to fairy tales and nonsense verse. "Fantasy," he said, "is the most valuable attribute of the human mind, and it should be diligently nurtured from earliest childhood." And he offered the following little case study:

> The well-known children's author, T. A. Bogdanovich, was brought up by another children's author, Aleksandra Annenskaia. Under the influence of the "enlightenment" of the Sixties [of the nineteenth century], she so zealously protected the little girl from the *skazka* [the folk tale] that she even hesitated to hire a *niania* for her, fearing that the nurse would tell the child fairy tales. Only educational books were read to the child—mainly books on botany and zoölogy. But, at night, when the governess finally fell asleep, the child, at last free from the constant supervision, filled her room with all kinds of creatures. Monkeys scampered all over her bed. A fox and her babies suddenly appeared on her table. Strange birds nested in her clothes left folded near her bed, and she talked to these visitors for a long time.

And this last nighttime scene might well be the prototype for the plot of *There's a Wocket in My Pocket!*—a book featuring the appearance of some of Dr. Seuss's most outrageous bedtime companions.

"It is central to the Seuss formula," writes Selma G. Lanes in *Down the Rabbit Hole*, "that the action of all his books with children as protagonists takes place either (1) in the absence of grownups, or (2) in the imagination"—usually in both at the same time, one might add. In *If I Ran the Circus*, the young hero Morris McGurk finds that "the most wonderful spot" for imagining his circus is behind Sneelock's Store "in the big vacant lot"—confirming Iona and Peter Opie's suspicion that "the places [children] like best for play are the secret places 'where no one else goes'." As the Opies write in *Children's Games in Street and Playground*: "The literature of childhood abounds with evidence that the peaks of a child's experience are not visits to a cinema, or even family outings to the sea, but occasions when he escapes into places that are disused and overgrown and silent. To a child there is more joy in a rubbish tip than a flowering rockery, in a fallen tree than a piece of statuary, in a muddy track than a gravel path."

Imagination, said Wordsworth, "Is but another name for absolute power/And clearest insight, amplitude of mind,/And Reason in her most exalted mood." He also knew that it was an "awful Power" which "rose from the mind's abyss/Like an unfathered vapour," usurping the light of the senses. In the story "The Glunk that got Thunk," for example, from *I Can Lick 30 Tigers Today! and Other*

Stories, the heroine uses her Thinker-Upper to create the monstrous and obstreperous green Glunk and finds that she can't easily "unthunk" him. "Our true element extends without shores, without boundaries," asserts the Italian writer Italo Calvino, affirming what both artists and scientists have always known. (As the hero of *On Beyond Zebra* says: "In the places I go there are things that I see/ That I *never* could spell if I stopped with the Z.") But imagination, in the mind of an obliquitous or greedy person (like the king in *Bartholomew and the Oobleck* who brings down ruin from the sky in the form of an all-entangling, sticky, gluey, viscous slime), can be a dangerous power. Yet it is a necessary one. Imagination allows for and creates the possibility for things to happen and to change, freeing us from the genetic programming of specific behavior patterns (and making life less boring in the process). As Brian Sutton-Smith remarked in a conversation with me:

> I think that Dr. Seuss is packaging flexibility and possibility, and it's a new kind of thing in children's literature, which used to be much more staid. His books reflect a recognition—at least implicitly by intelligent people—that flexibility of thinking and brightness and associations and combinations, etc., are what mental development is about these days—it's as much a part of achievement as anything else. The notion that you can capture people's souls just by pressing the basics on them is nonsense and terrifying and stupid. . . . Seuss breaks barriers. What happens is that some person like him comes along who's intuitively a bit more in touch with the younger generation, he's nearer to his childhood and he expands the danger zones a little; and because kids love it, gradually parents come to accept it. It's the *adults* who have to be comforted.

And as Theodor Geisel has often said: "Adults are only obsolete children, so the hell with them!"

"You're going to see the good Doctor?" asked the cabdriver cheerily as we drove up the La Jolla hills to Theodor Geisel's home. "He's full of character and brings joy—unlike most doctors!" the driver adds. "My children love his books, and so do I."

It was July of 1980, and a typically beautiful southern California morning—sunshine, warm breezes, and a perfect blue sky— the kind of weather that makes you feel as if you've finally arrived in Dr. Seuss's mythical city of Solla Sollew, "where they *never* have troubles! At least, very few" (*I Had Trouble in Getting to Solla Sollew*).

The good Doctor met me at the gate, with a twinkle in his eye and sporting a white beard that reminded me of the high-spirited, white-bearded figure pictured in the trailer in *Mulberry Street*, who oversees the wondrous, multispangled parade scene with exorbitant delight. I told Geisel about the cabdriver's exuberant characterization of him, which he appeared pleased by, saying modestly and with a smile, "I'm probably just a good tipper."

He led me through the front door of his spacious, pink-stucco house built around a converted watchtower overlooking La Jolla and the Pacific—a house he shares with his second wife, Audrey, and Sam (short for Samantha), a twelve-inch Yorkshire terrier almost as tiny as a Who. Geisel took me into the living room, and we sat down and began to chat.

He pointed through the window to the dozens of sailboats out on the Pacific below, saying, "Those are some of my retired friends down there, but retirement's not for me! [Geisel was seventy-six when I saw him in 1980.] For me, success means doing work that you love, regardless of how much you make. I go into my office almost every day and give it eight hours—though every day isn't productive, of course. And just now," he added, putting on a pair of glasses, "I've slowed down because of my second cataract operation. It was impossible for me to mix a palette—I didn't know which colors were which. With my cataract I had two color schemes—red became orange, blue became slightly greenish: my left eye was like Whistler and the right one was like Picasso—seeing things straight and clear in primitive colors."

"I was just thinking of your book *I Can Read with My Eyes Shut!*" I said, "with those lines: 'If you keep/your eyes open enough,/ oh, the stuff you will learn! . . . Keep them wide open . . ./at least on one side'."

"That book was dedicated to my surgeon, by the way," Geisel replied, smiling. "Now I have to learn to focus my pen—it'll take about a month. . . . I realized I was getting blind when I was at the Hilton Hotel in Las Vegas. It has this tremendous runway, and forty naked women on Harley-Davidsons came right by us; my friend asked me what I thought of the women, and I could only see the motorcycles!"

"Your first published book was called *The Seven Lady Godivas*," I mentioned.

"It came out in 1937, in the Depression," Geisel said, "and nobody bought any copies at all—they were remaindered at Schulte's cigar store at a quarter a piece; today they go for about three hundred dollars. It's a book that proved that there were seven Lady Godivas who happened to be engaged to the seven Peeping brothers. The seven daughters weren't frivolous or anything like that . . . they just happened not to have clothes on, and they couldn't marry the Peeping brothers until each of the girls had discovered a horse truth: you shouldn't put the cart before the horse, you shouldn't change horses in midstream, et cetera. . . . The book was embarrassing to many librarians—it got onto the children's bookshelves, and they had to take it out."

"I'd imagine children would have loved it!" I commented.

"They did! That was the problem."

"You once said that your career began at the zoo. What did you mean by that?" I asked.

"When I was young," Geisel explained, "I used to go to the zoo a lot, and when I returned home I would try to draw the animals. . . . You see, my father, among other things, ran a zoo in Springfield, Massachusetts. He was a guy who became president of a Springfield brewery the day Prohibition was declared (this was wartime prohibition). So he became very cynical and sat for days in the living room saying 'S.O.B., S.O.B.' over and over—he didn't know what to do with himself. But he had been honorary head of the Parks Department, and there had been a mix-up with the books and he had to straighten them out. At that time the superintendent left the park system, so my father took the job permanently. And at a salary of five thousand dollars a year he became a philanthropist. He built tennis courts, trout streams, three golf courses, bowling greens—he changed people's lives more than he would have done if he'd been a millionaire; he used WPA funds and government money to put people to work. So he ended up as a very worthwhile guy."

"Imagine what you might have conceived in that position!" I said.

"I would have been fired if I'd had that job!"

"Would your father have been critical or approving of Marco's imaginative powers in *Mulberry Street*?" I wondered.

"My mother would have loved it," he said. "My father would have been critical. But he was a remarkable man. Let me tell you a story: My father's hero was a person named Cyril Gaffey Aschenbach, who had been captain of the first Dartmouth football team that beat Harvard. When I lived in New York City, I mentioned to my father that Cyril lived near me. So one night we all had dinner together. My father would ask all night long: Tell me how you scored that winning touchdown. And Cyril would say: 'Look at these sconces, they're two hundred and fifty years old'—all he talked about was antiques. So when my father was heading back to Springfield, he said, 'I'm going to send you an antique that will shut Cyril Gaffey Aschenbach up forever!' He found a dinosaur footprint—a two-hundred-and-fifty pound slab showing three toes—which is hanging outside next to the swimming pool—you can see it through the window. It was found around Holyoke, Massachusetts, near a shale pit. My father sent it to me in New York in a truck, but on the way down he stopped off at Yale and had it appraised—and he found out that it was a hundred and fifty million years old.

"My father, as you see, had an unusual sense of humor. And every time I've moved I've taken that footprint with me: It keeps me from getting conceited. Whenever I think I'm pretty good, I just go out and look at it. Half the people I show it to think I've made it myself."

"The Glunk might have made a similar footprint," I suggested.

"I think they're related," Geisel was happy to agree. He pointed to a shelf across the room on which were resting various baked-clay imaginary animals. "They were made a couple of hundred miles from Kabul, Afghanistan," he told me, "at a place the American diplomats call Dr. Seussville—they've had this craft going on for a thousand years. Someone at the embassy sent me these weird animals—a lot of two-headed beasts."

"'Where *do* you suppose he gets things like that from?/His animals all have such very odd faces./I'll bet he must hunt them in rather odd places!'" I said, quoting from *If I Ran the Zoo*. "What is it with you and the animals?" I asked him.

"Let's just say I find them more compatible than most people," he said, smiling.

In reading a number of articles about Geisel, I'd discovered that he had been drawing "his" animals since his childhood days at the zoo; had done animal cartoons for Dartmouth's humor magazine *Jack-o-lantern*, which he edited for a while, as well as for magazines such as *Judge*, *Vanity Fair*, and *Saturday Evening Post*; had doodled winged horses in his class notebooks at Oxford; had painted pictures of donkeys for a month in Corsica after leaving academia; had used animals for his political cartoons for *P.M.* magazine—depicting a Nazi as a dachshund, Pierre Laval as a louse on Hitler's finger—as well as for his famous advertising cartoons that accompanied his "Quick, Henry! The Flit!" insect-spray caption; and had created many bizarre animals for Standard Oil billboards, including the Moto-Munchus, the Oilio-Gobelus, and the Zerodoccus. As a child once wrote to him: "Dr. Seuss, you have an imagination with a long tail!"

"My style of drawing animals," Geisel now explained, "derives from the fact that I don't know how to draw. I began drawing pictures as a child—as I mentioned before—trying, let's say, to get as close to a lion as possible; people would laugh, so I decided to go for the laugh. I can't draw normally. I *think* I could draw normally if I wanted to, but I see no reason to re-create something that's already created. If I'd gone to art school I'd never have been successful. In fact, I did attend one art class in high school. And at one point during the class I turned the painting I was working on upside down—I didn't exactly know what I was doing, but actually I was checking the balance: If something is wrong with the composition upside down, then something's wrong with it the other way. And the teacher said, 'Theodor, real artists don't turn their paintings upside down.' It's the only reason I went on—to prove that teacher wrong.

"I'm fascinated by all kinds of animals. When I was at Oxford, I read *The Travels of Sir John Mandeville*, which describes weird animals and a race of people who lived in a desert; they had enormous feet, which they put up in the air over their heads to give them shade. I was bogged down in Old High German, and Mandeville sort of opened up a door for me. That's one reason I left Oxford—in order to go in that direction.

"I met a professor there who suggested that I leave Oxford and come study with him in Paris. He was a Jonathan Swift scholar, and I thought he had a bright, original mind. So I packed up and went to the Sorbonne. I had fifteen minutes with him in his study, and I almost went crazy; instead of the wild, exciting things I expected to be studying, he asked me to investigate whether Swift wrote anything between the ages of sixteen and a half and seventeen—something like that—and I was to research all the obscure libraries in England, Scotland, and Ireland to find out. And, I said, supposing I found out that he didn't write anything? Well, the professor said, you will have had a lovely time in Paris and in traveling. That was when I booked myself on a cattle boat to Corsica—it was my final revolt against academicism."

"I wanted to bring up a slightly 'academic' point of my own"—I hesitated—"about the possibility of *Mulberry Street* and Goethe's

'The Erl-King' being somewhat similar, for both of them are about a father and a son and about the exigencies and power of the imagination."

"It's interesting you say that," Geisel replied, as he broke into German: "_Wer reitet so spät durch Nacht und Wind?/Es ist der Vater mit seinem Kind. . . ._ I was brought up in a German-speaking home, I minored in German in college, and I learned 'The Erl-King' —I still remember those first two lines—when I was still in high school. It could tie up, though I never thought of it before. It's very odd that you discovered that . . . I've learned something. Back to the psychiatrist's couch!"

"I was wondering what books you read as a child," I said. "I've brought along a few pages from two books about freedom-loving creatures that I thought might have influenced you a bit—Palmer Cox's _Brownies: Their Book_ and Gelett Burgess's _Goops and How To Be Them._"

"Both books were very popular when I was a kid," Geisel replied. "My parents bought them and I read and loved them, though I haven't seen them for years. They bring back a lot. The Goops were a little too moralistic for me, but I loved the Brownies—they were wonderful little creatures; in fact, they probably awakened my desire to draw.

"I also remember liking Wilhelm Busch's _Max and Moritz_; and when I was six or seven years old I read Peter Newell's _The Hole Book_, which I remember very well. It had a die cut through the whole thing, from the cover to the end, and it began: 'Tom Potts was fooling with a gun/(Such follies should not be),/When—bang! the pesky thing went off/Most unexpectedly!' And it followed the course of that bullet, which went through a hot-water boiler—and the house got flooded—then through ropes people were swinging on . . . it just raised hell. And it ended with what was then considered to be one of the funniest things in the world: The bullet hit a cake made by a bride, and the cake was so hard that the bullet flattened out . . . which was very fortunate, because otherwise it would have gone completely around the world and come back and killed Tom Potts on the spot!"

"Aside from Newell and Cox—and, best of all, Carroll, Lear, and Busch," I added, "you've consistently written some of the greatest comic verse for children. Peter Slade, in his book _Child Drama_, states that 'after the age of six or so, this gift of rhythm appears naturally in child work, but the adult has to toil hard "for it" and often does not attain it. Those who are most successful in doing so are, for the most part, those who have actually retained it from childhood. We call them great artists.' And I wanted to know how you've managed to keep your rhythmic and rhyming impulses intact."

"It's so ingrained in me," Geisel replied, "that I now have trouble writing prose. I find that if I'm writing a short letter, it comes out in verse. It's become a normal method of expression.

"I hate making speeches, incidentally, but several years ago I solved my problem: In 1977, for a commencement address at Lake Forest College, I read an epic poem of fourteen lines entitled 'My Uncle Terwilliger on the Art of Eating Popovers.' The kids in the graduating class are probably still cheering because they thought I'd speak for hours. *The New York Times* picked it up and said that there should be a law that no commencement speech should be longer than that. And the *Reader's Digest* even 'digested' it by cutting out the three short introductory paragraphs."

"Is it easy or hard for you," I asked, "to write the kind of verse in your books—like the following stanza, say, from *On Beyond Zebra* —a stanza, by the way, that sounds like a perfect description of the apartment situation in New York City:

> The NUH is the letter I use to spell Nutches
> Who live in small caves, known as Nitches, for hutches.
> These Nutches have troubles, the biggest of which is
> The fact there are many more Nutches than Nitches.
> Each Nutch in a Nitch knows that some other Nutch
> Would like to move into his Nitch very much.
> So each Nutch in a Nitch has to watch that small Nitch
> Or Nutches who haven't got Nitches will snitch."

"It's hard," Geisel said, laughing. "I'm a bleeder and I sweat at it. As I've said before: The 'creative process' consists for me of two things—time and sweat. And I've also said that too many writers have only contempt and condescension for children, which is why they give them degrading corn about bunnies. The difficult thing about writing in verse for kids is that you can write yourself into a box: If you can't get a proper rhyme for a quatrain, you not only have to throw that quatrain out but you also have to unravel the sock way back, probably ten pages or so. . . . You find that you're not driving the car, your *characters* are driving it. And you also have to remember that in a children's book a paragraph is like a chapter in an adult book, and a sentence is like a paragraph."

"In 1925," I mentioned, "the Russian children's poet Kornei Chukovsky wrote an important book that in English is called *From*

Two to Five, and in it he formulated a set of rules for the composing of verse for children. I wanted to find out what you thought of these rules."

"I'd love to hear what they are!"

"Chukovsky's first rule is that poems for children must be *graphic*, and by that he meant that every stanza must suggest an illustration, since children think in terms of images."

"I agree," Geisel said, "and one should add the importance of eliminating the nonessentials."

"Two," I continued, "there must be a rapid change of images—movement and change."

"He's talking about progression," Geisel responded, "and I agree entirely."

"Three, that this verbal painting must be lyrical—so that a child can sing and clap to the verse."

"I'll go along with that," said Geisel.

"Four, that there be a moving and changing of rhythm."

"Definitely a change of pace," Geisel allowed. "I'll get going at a certain pace and meter, and I'll turn the page and then have one line in prose to break up what I've been doing and then start building up again from there."

"Five, that there be a heightened musicality of poetic expressiveness."

"What does that mean?"

"He's referring to what he calls the flow and fluidity of sound—the avoidance of cluttered-up clusters of consonants, for example."

"O.K.," Geisel assented.

"Six, that there be frequent rhyming."

"Yes."

"Seven, that the rhyming words carry the meaning."

"That's *very* true," Geisel insisted. "I find that a lot of authors will use convenience rhymes and not positive thought rhymes. And the child's interest disappears entirely."

"Eight," I continued, "that every line must have a life of its own, with no internal pauses."

"Yes."

"Nine, that the author not crowd the poem with adjectives—*more verbs and fewer adjectives*."

"He's definitely right about the adjectives," Geisel explained. "If I'm supplementing the words with pictures and if I can substitute the adjectives with a picture, I'll leave them out of the text."

"Ten, that the predominant rhythm be that of the trochee."

"That could be true in Russian," Geisel suggested, "it could come out of the way the Russian language sounds. In most of my work I use anapests. But in any case, I think the subject matter is more important than what meter you use."

"Eleven, that the verse be suitable for play and games."

"All of my books," said Geisel, "are informally dramatized in schools. And recently, the Children's Theater Company in Minneapolis did a wonderful adaptation of *The 500 Hats of Bartholomew Cubbins*—an amazing production."

"Twelve, that verses for children have the skill, the virtuosity, the technical soundness of poetry for adults."

"I think so," Geisel agreed.

"And thirteen," I concluded, "that through your verse you try to bring children within reach of adult perceptions and thoughts."

"I don't know how far you can bring them to it," said Geisel, "but you can try to initiate them. . . . I like this guy, and I think that what he says holds up."

About the first years of his life, Tolstoy wrote: "Was it not then that I acquired all that now sustains me? And I gained so much and so quickly that during the rest of my life I did not acquire a hundredth part of it. From myself as a five-year-old to myself as I now am there is only one step. The distance between myself as an infant and myself at five years is tremendous." And following Tolstoy's notion, Chukovsky states: "It seems to me that, beginning with the age of two, every child becomes for a short period of time a linguistic genius." Throughout his book, the author makes many fascinating observations, among them:

> Two- and three-year-old children have such a strong sensitivity to their language—to its many inflections and suffixes—that the words they construct inventively do not seem at all distorted and freakish but, on the contrary, extremely apt, beautiful, and natural.

> In the beginning of our childhood we are all "versifiers"—it is only later that we begin to learn to speak in prose. The very nature of an infant's jabbering predisposes him to versifying.

> Another quality of children's rhymes and nonsense verse is that they are saturated with joy. They do not show a trace of tears or a whisper of a sigh. They express the child's feeling of happiness with himself and his world which every healthy child experiences so much

of the time. This is the reason that their rhymes and nonsense verse have such a zestful spontaneity.

When the children sing, clap, play, or work out a project, I look on with the greatest pleasure. When they begin to read me poems that have been taught to them in school or in boarding school, I often feel like a real martyr. . . . Together with the works of our classical poets, they have been taught hackneyed lines, absurd rhythms, cheap rhymes. There are times when I could cry with disappointment.

For some mysterious reason the child is attracted to that topsy-turvy world where legless men run, water burns, horses gallop astride their riders, and cows nibble on peas on top of birch trees. . . . The more aware the child is of the correct relationship of things, which he violates in his play, the more comical does this violation seem to him.

He is always in control of his illusions and knows perfectly well those limits within which it is important that he hold them. He is the strongest realist in his fantasies. . . . His main purpose, as in all play, is to exercise his newly acquired skill of verifying his knowledge of things.

It is high time to promote these "nonsense" verses into the category of educationally valuable and perceptive works of poetry. . , . With the help of fantasies, tall tales, fairy tales, and topsy-turvies of every type, children confirm their realistic orientation to actuality.

All of these observations make it clear that Chukovsky would undoubtedly have greatly approved of the works of Dr. Seuss, who has never severed his connection with the child's ways of being in and conceiving the world. As Goethe wrote: "Every child is to a certain extent a genius and every genius to a certain extent a child. The relationship between the two shows itself primarily as the naïveté and sublime ingenuousness that are a fundamental characteristic of true genius."

Geisel's illustrative style, for example, has its roots in the naïve and sublimely ingenuous manner with which young children create their own drawings. Unlike the child, however—about whom André Malraux once wrote: "his gift controls him, not he his gift"—Geisel is always in command of his idiosyncratic style. As he once told Michael J. Bandler: "Schools send me hundreds of drawings each year, and I find most kids draw as I do—awkwardly. I think I've refined my childish drawing so that it looks professional. But kids exaggerate the same way I do. They overlook things they can't draw, their pencils slip, and they get some funny effects. I've learned to incorporate my pencil slips into my style." As he later told me: "Technically, I'm capable of doing more complicated things. But every time I try to do something sophisticated in a children's book, it fails—it doesn't attract kids. This is due to the fact that I work the way they work. A child's idea of art is a pen-and-ink drawing filled in with flat color, with no modulation and no subtlety. *McElligot's Pool*, which has modulation of tones, isn't as successful as the books with hard black outlines and flat color. That's just the way kids see things."

The Cat in the Hat

And concerning the little stories very young children themselves make up, Brian Sutton-Smith, in his essay "The Child's Mind as Poem," has noted certain recurring features in these stories—their verselike quality (rhythm, alliteration, and rhyme); their simplified syntax and use of nonsense; their expressive as opposed to referential features (melody preceding meaning); their use of exaggeration and of emphatic and pantomimic effects; and their reliance on theme-and-variation, repetitive, and cyclical forms of organization. And Sutton-

Smith concludes his discussion by affirming that "the child's mind is like a poem."

One might even suggest that the child's mind is indeed like many a Dr. Seuss book, for his poetic style—although more controlled—has its roots in these characteristic modes of children's storytelling; simply and unselfconsciously, Dr. Seuss has retained a fresh perceiving system, naturally communicating an understanding of children's energies, needs, and desires.

Nowhere is this more obvious than in *The Cat in the Hat* (1957). "It's the book I'm proudest of," Geisel told me, "because it had something to do with the death of the *Dick and Jane* primers. In 1954 John Hersey wrote an article in *Life* that suggested something to the effect that we should get rid of the boredom of Dick and Jane and Spot and hand the educational system over to Dr. Seuss! William Spaulding, who was then the textbook chief at Houghton Mifflin, read the article and asked me if I'd like to try to do a primer, and he sent me a list of about three hundred words and told me to make a book out of them.

"At first I thought it was impossible and ridiculous, and I was about to get out of the whole thing; then decided to look at the list one more time and to use the first two words that rhymed as the title of the book—*cat* and *hat* were the ones my eyes lighted on. I worked on the book for nine months—throwing it across the room and letting it hang for a while—but I finally got it done. Houghton Mifflin, however, had trouble selling it to the schools; there were a lot of Dick and Jane devotees, and my book was considered too fresh and irreverent. But Bennett Cerf at Random House had asked for trade rights, and it just took off in the bookstores."

It is not hard to guess what John Newbery would have thought of Dr. Seuss's first primer. In one of his prefaces to his own primer, *A Little Pretty Pocket-Book*, Newbery assumes the character of a moralizing Jack the Giant-Killer and in this guise addresses a letter to Little Master Tommy that begins:

My dear Tommy,
Your Nurse called upon me Today, and told me that you was [sic] a good Boy; that you was dutiful to your Father and Mother, and that, when you had said your Prayers in the Morning and the Evening, you asked their Blessings, and in the Day-time did every Thing they bid you. She says, you are obedient to your Master, loving and kind

to your Play-fellows, and obliging to every body; that you rise early in the Morning, keep yourself clean, and learn your Book; that when you have done a Fault you confess it, and are sorry for it. And though you are sometimes naughty, she says you are very honest and good-humoured; that you don't swear, tell Lies, nor say indecent Words, and are always thankful when any body gives you good Advice; that you never quarrel, nor do wicked Things, as some other Boys do.

This Character, my Dear, has made every body love you; and, while you continue so good, you may depend on my obliging you with every thing I can. I have here sent you a *Little Pretty Pocket-Book*, which will teach you to play at all those innocent Games that good Boys and Girls divert themselves with: And, while you behave so well, you shall never want Play I assure you. . . .

And just as Theodor Geisel, during his one and only art class, turned his painting upside down, so Dr. Seuss, in *The Cat in the Hat*, created one of the great *bouleversements* in the history of children's reading.

"The sun did not shine./It was too wet to play./So we sat in the house/All that cold, cold, wet day" is the way the book begins, as two children—brother and sister—and a surprised goldfish in a bowl suddenly hear the *bump* that announces the dramatic arrival of the Cat in the Hat, who, in the absence of the children's mother, tells them: "I know it is wet/And the sun is not sunny./But we can have/Lots of good fun that is funny!" To which the goldfish—a combination superego and what Geisel calls "my version of Cotton Mather"—warns: "No! No!/Make that cat go away!/Tell that Cat in the Hat/You do NOT want to play./He should not be here./He should not be about./He should not be here/When your mother is out!" And the rest of the book is an unloosening of all sanctions and rules concerning "proper" children's behavior, as, in one rambunctious scene after another, the Cat and his blissed-out assistants—Thing One and Thing Two—run amok, create pandemonium, and tear the house apart—only to put everything back together just moments before the arrival home of Mother, who, like Marco's father, asks: "Did you have any fun?/Tell me. What did you do?"

> And Sally and I did not know
> What to say.
> Should we tell her
> The things that went on there that day?
> Should we tell her about it?

Now, what SHOULD we do?
Well . . .
What would YOU do
If your mother asked YOU?

Like Coyote of many American Indian tribes and like Rabbit of
Afro-American folklore, the Cat in the Hat is nothing less than an
archetypal trickster hero, whose manifestation is perfectly suited—
as is Bugs Bunny—for mid-twentieth-century children's appreciation
and delight. As Brian Sutton-Smith describes this type of character:
"The trickster figure does not just sit down and plan out logical
maneuvers; he uses the most outrageous trickery. He does not simply
make his way in the world independent of others' support; he baldly
mocks authority figures and breaks all societal rules, which forces him
to remain autonomous. Nonsense humor and the creation of ribald,
regressive trickster figures give the child a more flexible grasp on what
is and what is not possible."

John Hersey has called *The Cat in the Hat* a "gift to the art of
reading" and a "harum-scarum masterpiece." Selma G. Lanes, in
Down the Rabbit Hole, has perceptively written of Seuss's "clever
and relentless piling on of gratuitous anxiety until the child is fairly
ready to cry 'uncle' and settle for any resolution, however mundane,
that will end his at once marvelous, exquisite, and finally unbearable
tension. . . . The anxiety in Seuss's books," she adds, "always arises
from the flouting of authority, parental or societal. . . . The child can
sit back and experience genuine pleasure, knowing that the anxiety
building up in him is vicarious and that no punishment will follow
Seuss's forbidden pleasures." And Alison Lurie, in her essay "On the
Subversive Side," has seen *The Cat in the Hat* as being part of the
subversive tradition of children's literature represented by books such
as *Huckleberry Finn* and *Alice's Adventures in Wonderland*. As she
writes: "It is the particular gift of some writers to remain in one sense
children all their lives: to continue to see the world as boys and girls
see it, and take their side instinctively. One author who carries on
this tradition today in America is Dr. Seuss, who like Twain and
Carroll has adopted a separate literary personality."

"It's interesting," I mentioned to Geisel, "that after Samuel
Clemens and Charles Dodgson, you are the most famous and most
popular pseudonymous writer for children."

"I never thought of that," he replied. "Twain and Carroll are
both a couple of phonies, masquerading under false colors. It's not

bad company at all. I'm very flattered to be included. When I received an honorary Doctor of Humane Letters from Dartmouth in 1955, the president of the college, in his conferral speech, said that this would make an honest man of me, and no longer would I have to masquerade under a phony doctorate."

"You seem quite recusant yourself, and I think a lot of your books *are* subversive," I added. "Don't you?"

"I'm subversive as hell!" Geisel replied. "I've always had a mistrust of adults. And one reason I dropped out of Oxford and the Sorbonne was that I thought they were taking life too damn seriously, concentrating too much on nonessentials. Hilaire Belloc, whose writings I liked a lot, was a radical. *Gulliver's Travels* was subversive, and both Swift and Voltaire influenced me. *The Cat in the Hat* is a revolt against authority, but it's ameliorated by the fact that the Cat cleans everything up at the end. It's revolutionary in that it goes as far as Kerensky and then stops. It doesn't go quite as far as Lenin."

"Like many of your books," I suggested, "*The Cat in the Hat* is quite anarchistic."

"It's impractical the way anarchy is, but it works within the confines of a book," Geisel agreed.

"Without pushing you further down the revolutionary path," I said, laughing, "I've always wondered about the concluding lines of *Yertle the Turtle*: 'And today the great Yertle, that Marvelous he,/Is King of the Mud. That is all he can see./And turtles, of course . . . all the turtles are free/As turtles and, maybe, all creatures should be.' Why 'maybe' and not 'surely'?"

"I qualified that," Geisel explained, "in order to avoid sounding too didactic or like a preacher on a platform. And I wanted *other* persons, like yourself, to say 'surely' in their minds instead of my having to say it."

"Within the confines of your books," I added, "you've written some very moral and political tales. The two books about Horton the elephant praise the virtues of loyalty and faithfulness. And you once said that the idea for *The 500 Hats of Bartholomew Cubbins* came about when you were 'taking a railroad train through Connecticut, sitting in a smoky, stuffy car, and ahead of me sat a smoky, stuffy Wall Street broker, wearing a derby and reading the *Wall Street Journal*. I was fascinated with his hat, and wondered what his reaction would be if I took his hat off his head. And then, half an hour later, I wondered how he'd react if there was still another hat on his hat.' "

"Yes," Geisel responded, "children's literature as I write it and as I see it is satire to a great extent—satirizing the mores and the habits of the world. There's *Yertle the Turtle* [about the turtle dictator who becomes the 'ruler of all that I can see' by sitting on the backs of hundreds of subject turtles, his throne brought down by the simple burp of the lowliest and lowest turtle],* which was modeled

Yertle the Turtle

on the rise of Hitler; and then there's *The Sneetches* [about Star-Belly Sneetches who ostracize Plain-Belly Sneetches who pay to become Star-Belly Sneetches who then have to become Plain-Belly Sneetches, etc.], which was inspired by my opposition to anti-

* In December 1981, New York City's Mayor Koch called the city's Council President, Carol Bellamy, "a horror show" who can be "just tremendously vicious." They made up in front of the press, but not before Bellamy presented Koch with a copy of *Yertle the Turtle*, saying: "Some days Ed Koch wakes up in the morning and decides he wants to be Yertle for the day. Whenever that happens, I find myself with a terrible case of indigestion."

Semitism. These books come from a different part of my background and from the part of my soul that started out to be a teacher. Every once in a while I get mad. *The Lorax* [about a rapacious Once-ler who despoils the land of its Truffula Trees, leading to the total pollution and destruction of the environment] came out of my being angry. The ecology books I'd read were dull. But I couldn't get started on that book— I had notes but was stuck on it for nine months. Then I happened to be in Kenya at a swimming pool, and I was watching a herd of elephants cross a hill; why that released me I don't know, but all of a sudden all my notes assembled mentally. I grabbed a laundry list that was lying around and wrote the whole book in an hour and a half. In *The Lorax* I was out to attack what I think are evil things and let the chips fall where they might; and the book's been used by ministers as the basis of sermons, as well as by conservation groups."

"Aside from works like *Yertle the Turtle* and *The Sneetches*, which have the power of the great fables," I said, "there's a certain folktale quality to a few of your stories—I'm thinking particularly of "The Big Brag" in *Yertle the Turtle*—about the pomposity and egomania of a bear and a rabbit and of how they are cut down to size by a little worm—and "The Zax" in *The Sneetches*—about two Zaxs who bump into each other in the prairie and who each stubbornly refuse to let the other one pass until, eventually, highways are built over and around them. This last tale is similar to an African tale I recently read about two goats who bump into each other on a bridge and refuse to budge, each of them finally throwing the other into the water below."

"It just proves that there's nothing new," Geisel replied. "People are always reacting to the same stimuli. You could probably find duplications of all of my stuff. But I used to read a lot of Uncle Remus and a lot of Belloc, as I mentioned before, so maybe there's some influence there.

"Anyway, to get back to what we were talking about earlier," Geisel said: "*The Cat in the Hat* was an immediate best seller. And at that point Bennett and Phyllis Cerf of Random House conceived the idea of starting a publishing house just for the lower graders, which we called Beginner Books.

"It's interesting," I interrupted, "that a Zen Buddhist monk once said: 'If your mind is empty, it is always ready for anything; it is open to everything. In the beginner's mind there are many possibilities; in the expert's mind, there are few. . . . That is always the real secret of the arts: always be a beginner' " (Shunryu Suzuki).

"But to create a book," Geisel said, "you have to have an ability and a technique, which you don't have in an empty mind. So maybe we should change 'empty' to 'receptive.' . . . Anyway, when we started Beginner Books we had no idea what we were doing—it was *really* an 'empty' mind. And when we began Beginner Books, we found out that *The Cat in the Hat* was at that time hard for first graders to read. It all depended, of course, on what experts you talked to—how many words a kid could read. But I realized that there was a level below Beginner Books, so we began making things simpler and simpler; and then we set up Bright and Early Books for younger and younger readers. At the moment I'm working on something I call Prenatal Books [laughing], but there are a few little difficulties we haven't yet solved. [N.B.: Theodor Geisel might have been kidding, but recently a number of persons have seriously suggested the educational importance of parents narrating to their womb-enclosed progeny; and many books—cloth and bathtime items among them—are being published for infants six months old and younger!]

"When I first started doing children's books I knew nothing about the market. But, obviously, parents read my earlier books to their kids. Did the parents like them? In his autobiography, Prince Rainer of Monaco says something like: 'My children insist that I read those silly Dr. Seuss books to them—I don't care for them, but my kids do.' In those earlier and regular-sized books I'm writing for people; in the smaller-sized Beginner Books I'm still writing for people, but I go over them and simplify so that a kid has a chance to handle the vocabulary. But, basically, I've long since stopped worrying about what exact ages the books are for—I just put them out. Sometimes the more complex books can be the simplest ones to read because the clues given in the pictures are stronger. You can't base it entirely on words."

Almost all the regular Dr. Seuss books have been widely praised by both children and adults—the most popular being *Horton Hatches the Egg, Horton Hears a Who, Thidwick the Big-Hearted Moose, On Beyond Zebra!, If I Ran the Zoo, If I Ran the Circus, How the Grinch Stole Christmas*—though a book like *Dr. Seuss's Sleep Book* has its devotees (myself included).* Yet aside from *The Cat in the*

---

* The most recent Dr. Seuss book, *Hunches in Bunches* (1982), is about a boy who, unable to make up his mind, follows all kinds of Hunches—one Hunch leading to another—in a thousand different directions at once.

Hat and its brilliant sequel *The Cat in the Hat Comes Back,* most of Dr. Seuss's Beginner and Bright and Early Books have often been overlooked, patronized, and undervalued.

One of the most difficult tasks is to create a book meant to be read by very young children that will prove instructive to the child and also exciting to adults who might be reading over their shoulders. John Newbery's books were pleasing in form and generally rigid and boring in content. Dr. Seuss's books perfectly mate form and content,*

---

* Howard Gardner—the author of books such as *The Arts and Human Development* and *Artful Scribbles: The Significance of Children's Drawings*—is a research psychologist at the Boston Veterans Administration Hospital and the co-director of Harvard Project Zero. In a conversation with me, he expanded on and developed this point about form and content:

"Dr. Seuss really seems to be tuned into both the form and the content that constitute the child's world, and he can approach the world through the child's conscious and unconscious abilities or faculties.

"To fill that out a bit: There are some people who write works that appeal formally to children because they have certain rhythms, certain words, certain structures, certain visual patterns. You can enjoy Dr. Seuss's books, for example, even if you don't understand some of the words, even if you don't know English, and even if you don't follow the plots—some of them are fairly complicated. But there's enough regularity and sequence built into them so that even if you don't get all the words or all the points, it doesn't matter. You don't have to get the moral of *The Sneetches* in order to enjoy it.

"There are also people who can produce works which appeal to kids in terms of content—something little overpowers something big, for example, or somebody goes on an adventure and comes home and becomes secure. Or you can take a book like Robert McCloskey's *Make Way for Ducklings*—the content is something very close to kids (animals, mothers, etc.), but the form isn't the sort of thing kids produce themselves—there isn't that metrical wordplay. And what I think is special about Dr. Seuss is that he's exploited both of these things—form and content—at the same time.

"Now, as far as 'conscious' and 'unconscious' elements are concerned: I think that Dr. Seuss has read his Freud, at least implicitly; I think his works are polymorphously perverse—they play with kids' desire to muck things up, to get dirty, to overpower authority. No kid would talk about this explicitly, but Dr. Seuss is sensitive to the unconscious strivings of kids in the same way that Bettelheim describes fairy tales as being responsive to kids' concerns.

"But Dr. Seuss also writes about things and objects kids are consciously concerned with. In *The Cat in the Hat,* for example, a mother goes away, and what do the kids do then? They play, but all the time are worrying about what their mother will think when she comes back and finds out what they've been doing. So he's right in the center of two very important intersections—the kinds of formal properties of work that children like and the kinds of content they're interested in, and kids' unconscious and conscious concerns.

RED
NED
TED
and
ED
in
BED

From *Hop on Pop*

using nonsense, rhyme, and illustration to strengthen in the child's mind—and to confirm in the adults a sense not of the "required" but of the "possible." (In Dr. Seuss's moral universe, what "should" happen is always connected to the heart's desires—as when Horton the faithful elephant hatches the elephant-bird, "it should be, it *should* be, it SHOULD be like that!"; and what "could" or "might" happen is limited only by one's patience and the powers of one's imagination—as when the hero of *McElligot's Pool* says: "'Cause *you never can tell/What goes on down below!*/This pool *might* be bigger/Than you or I know!")

Dr. Seuss's ABC (one of the freshest additions to this centuries-old genre), *Hop on Pop* (subtitled "The Simplest Seuss for Youngest Use"), and *Fox in Socks* (a volume of mind-boggling tongue twisters) are among the most innovative, amusing, and audacious teaching books I have ever seen. *One Fish Two Fish Red Fish Blue*

"*Sesame Street* could also be described in a similar way, though I don't think the program does very much with the child's unconscious because it's 'pro-social'—as is *Mister Rogers' Neighborhood* . . . they want to make kids behave well so they don't deal very much with kids' aggressive desires. And, in a way, Dr. Seuss can be said to capture not only this kind of *Sesame Street* approach but also things that you find in Saturday morning cartoons, which play a lot more with aspects of a child's unconscious.

"In a way, of course, any good work of art has got to play with those two dimensions I spoke about before. And for society today—at least in the West—Dr. Seuss has been as effective as anybody in doing this."

Fish and *There's a Wocket in My Pocket!* feature some of Dr. Seuss's most remarkable animal creations. And books like *Green Eggs and Ham, Mr. Brown Can Moo! Can You?* and *Marvin K. Mooney, Will You Please Go Now!* remind us that Dr. Seuss is one of the great creators of nonsense verse in the English language—verse in which you can almost hear an unmistakable musical accompaniment.

These last three books—along with *The Cat in the Hat Songbook* (which includes titles like "My Uncle Terwilliger Waltzes with Bears," "Beeper Booper," and "Rainy Day in Utica, N.Y.")—are in fact part of the wonderful tradition of American nonsense songs represented by "Old Aunt Kate," "Chick-a-Li-Lee-Lo," and "Risselty-Rosselty." As Charles Wolfe—an authority on folk music and popular culture—has written: "Most traditional nonsense songs have been classified as children's songs . . . and young children, for whom so much language is meaningless, doubtless delight in wordplay so full of assonance, consonance, and rhythm. Children's authors like Dr. Seuss often capitalize on this delight." And as composer Ruth Crawford Seeger points out in her excellent *American Folk Songs for Children*: "The adult faces numerous pitfalls when 'thinking up' words for children, such as affectation or overconscientious attention to particular uses for a song, or preconceived notions as to child speech, understanding, or enjoyment." Dr. Seuss completely avoids these pitfalls, for he is especially sensitive to what Seeger calls the "sound-meaning" and "touch-meaning" of words, and is able to "play" with words like Chukovsky's two-to-five-year-old linguistic geniuses (and certain poets such as John Skelton and Edward Lear).

Along with "imagination," "play" is the cornerstone of Dr. Seuss's world. And its importance is specifically revealed in one of Seuss's early fairy tale-type prose works, *The King's Stilts* (1939), which seems to illustrate Nietzsche's comment that "in any true man hides a child who wants to play."

The Kingdom of Binn, we are told, is surrounded by mighty Dike Trees that hold back the sea from engulfing the land. But since the roots of these trees are extremely tasty to the rapacious Nizzard birds, King Birtram has gathered an army of a thousand Patrol Cats, who guard the kingdom both day and night. The Changing of the Cat Guard takes place at seven each morning; and once King Birtram reviews the Guard, he rushes off to a special castle closet where he keeps his beloved red stilts, grabs them and begins leaping around the palace grounds on them: "This was the moment King Birtram lived for. When he worked, he really worked . . . but when he played, he really PLAYED!" ("The essence of kingship is childlikeness," wrote Georg Groddeck, adding: "The greatest monarch is the infant.")

The townsfolk do not really understand, but they approve of their king's playful ways, until one day the malicious, curmudgeonly Lord Droon ("Laughing spoils the shape of the face" is his motto) steals the stilts and has them secretly buried. King Birtram grows sadder and sadder and finds it impossible to take care of his Patrol Cats, who in turn become lazy and apathetic. The Nizzards, of course, start ravaging and destroying the roots of the trees, and the kingdom is in danger. But with the help of his courageous page boy Eric ("Quick, Eric! The stilts!" shouts the king—parodying Geisel's "Quick, Henry! The Flit!" insect-spray commercial), he regains his stilts and leads the Patrol Cats to victorious battle. And the book ends with Lord Droon imprisoned and Eric rewarded with his own pair of stilts, on which he races around the kingdom with King Birtram every afternoon: "And when they played they really PLAYED. And when they worked they really WORKED. And the cats kept the Nizzards away from the Dike Trees. And the Dike Trees kept the water back out of the land."

As Erik Erikson reminds us in *Toys and Reasons*, Plato's notion of playfulness recognized the need of young creatures—animal or human—to leap; and Erikson writes: "To truly leap, you must learn how to use the ground as a springboard, and how to land resiliently and safely. It means to test the leeway allowed by given limits; to outdo and yet not escape gravity" . . . and, he adds, to leap into make-believe and yet be able to return to factual reality. ("True make-believe," he comments—as if to describe *Mulberry Street* "may play with facts, but it cannot lie; while fake reality may, up to a point, seem to master the facts, but it never tells the truth"—which is what Beatrix Potter surely must have meant when she commented on "the natural truthful simplicity of the untruthfulness" of *Mulberry Street*.

There are, of course, a great many theorists who have pointed to different (and, I think, equally valid) characteristics of play—the autonomous (Erikson), the cognitive (Piaget), the affective (Berlyne), and the communicational (Bateson), among many others. And today there certainly seems to be a consensus that the kind of adult-supervised or -directed play that is supposed to instill the virtues of adult life has little to recommend it. (One is reminded of *A Little Pretty Pocket-Book*'s moral about the children's money-tossing game called Chuck-Farthing: "*Chuck-Farthing*, like Trade,/Requires great Care;/The more you observe,/The better you'll fare.") As Piaget wrote: "Every

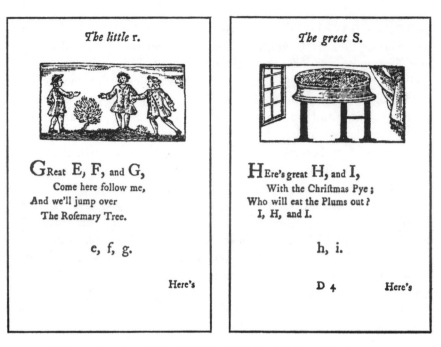

Illustrations from John Newbery's *A Little Pretty Pocket-Book*

From *Dr. Seuss's ABC*

time we teach a child something, we keep him from inventing it himself. On the other hand, that which we allow him to discover for himself will remain with him." And as the hero of *McElligot's Pool* says: "If I wait long enough; if I'm patient and cool,/Who knows *what* I'll catch in McElligot's Pool!"

Along with imagination, play allows us to innovate, test, accept, and reject; to explore and integrate different forms of behavior; and to envisage and to conceive of new ideas, new theories, new creations, new discoveries, and new societies. Imagination and play are at the basis of all our hope. In the words of the psychologist D. W. Winnicott: "One has to allow for the possibility that there cannot be a complete destruction of a human individual's capacity for creative living and that, even in the most extreme cases of compliance and the establishment of a false personality, hidden away somewhere there exists a secret life that is satisfactory because of its being creative or original to that human being."

In the words of the good Doctor Seuss: "There is no one alive who is you-er than you!"

MAURICE SENDAK:
KING OF ALL
THE WILD THINGS

PHOTOGRAPH © 1982 BY THOMAS VICTOR

This is the way the fairy tale begins: "Brother took his little sister by the hand and said, 'Since our mother died we have not had one happy hour. Stepmother beats us every day and when we want to come to her she kicks us away with her foot. Come, we will go out into the wide world together.' All day they walked over meadows, fields, and stony paths and when it rained sister said, 'God and our hearts are weeping together.' In the evening they came into a great forest and were so tired from misery, hunger, and the long journey that they sat down in a hollow tree and went to sleep." Bewitched by the evil stepmother, Little Brother is transformed into a deer, but Little Sister promises never to leave him. Untying her garter, she ties it around his neck and leads him deeper into the forest. "And when they had gone a long, long way, they came to a hut and the girl looked in and thought, here we can stay and spend our lives. And so she collected leaves and moss to make a soft bed for the deer, and every morning she went out and found roots and berries and nuts for herself, and for the deer she brought tender grasses which it ate out of her hand and it was happy and gamboled all around her. At night, when sister was tired and had said her prayers, she laid her head on the fawn's back and that was her pillow on which she fell gently asleep. And if only Brother had his human form, it would have been a lovely life."

"Perhaps it is only in childhood," Graham Greene has said, "that books have any deep influence on our lives." But it is important to realize that it is exactly in those books that children have adopted as their own that our deepest wishes and fantasies are most simply expressed.

One of the most haunting of these fantasies concerns the Two Forsaken Children who, as these archetypal siblings are beautifully described by the poet H. D. in her meditative *Tribute to Freud,* form a "little group, a design, an image at the crossroads." One child, H. D. tells us, is sometimes the shadow of the other, as in Greek tragedies. Often one is lost and seeks the other, as in the ancient fairy tale of the twin brother and sister of the Nile Valley. Sometimes they are both boys, like Castor and Pollux, finding their corresponding shape in the stars. In the nineteenth century we discover them in the story written by Edmond Goncourt about two acrobats (actually foils for himself and his beloved brother Jules) who "joined their nervous systems to master an impossible trick," as well as in the unsurpassed visionary tales of George MacDonald. But they are most deeply imprinted in our minds in the Grimms' "Little Brother, Little Sister."

When Maurice Sendak was six years old, he and his eleven-year-old brother Jack collaborated on a story called *They Were Inseparable*, about a brother and sister who, Maurice says, "had a hankering for each other—it was a very naïve and funny book. We both idolized our sister, she was the eldest and by far the prettiest, and we thought she was the crown jewel of the family. So because we idolized her, we made the book about a brother and a sister. And at the very end of the story, as I recall, an accident occurs: The brother's in the hospital, they don't think he's going to recover, the sister comes rushing in, and they just grab each other—like at the conclusion of *Tosca*—and exclaim: *We are inseparable!* Everybody rushes in to separate them as they jump out the hospital window. . . . Yes, you see, we *did* know dimly that there was something wrong, we were punishing them unconsciously.

"I imagine that all siblings have such feelings," Maurice continues. "The learning process makes children become aware that there's a taboo with regard to these feelings, but before you learn that, you do what comes naturally. My parents weren't well-to-do, and we had only two beds—my brother and I slept in one, my sister Natalie in the other, and often we'd all sleep in the same bed. My parents would come in—sometimes with my uncle and aunt—and they'd say: 'Look, see how much they like each other.' I loved my brother, and I didn't know that that could be this, and this that . . . kids find that out later."

Nine years ago [1973], Sendak illustrated "Little Brother, Little Sister" in *The Juniper Tree*, a collection of twenty-seven tales by the Brothers Grimm—with accompanying Dürer-like drawings by Sendak—in the brilliant, unadorned translations of Lore Segal and Randall Jarrell. "A story like 'Little Brother, Little Sister' says everything in metaphor," Maurice comments, "so that it isn't upsetting to anybody. It's something we've always known about fairy tales—they talk about incest, the Oedipus complex, about psychotic mothers, like those of Snow White and Hansel and Gretel, who throw their children out. They tell things about life which children know instinctively, and the pleasure and relief lie in finding these things expressed in language that children can live with. You can't eradicate these feelings—they exist and they're a great source of creative inspiration."

This is, of course, what the child psychologist and writer Bruno Bettelheim has pointed out in his acclaimed *The Uses of Enchantment*, a strong, humanistic/psychological defense against the always-continuing attempts to bowdlerize and palliate fairy tales. But Bettelheim has certainly made an about-face since the time he admonished parents not to buy Sendak's immensely popular *Where the Wild Things Are,* warning them that little Max's dreamlike foray into the world of befanged and beclawed monsters would scare children, and that Max's rebellion against adult authority was psychologically harmful.

Sendak himself has answered these and other criticisms (my favorite comes from the *Journal of Nursery Education*'s review of *Wild Things*: "We should not like to have it left about where a sensitive child might find it to pore over in the twilight") in the acceptance speech he gave upon receiving the 1964 Caldecott Medal:

"[There are] games children must conjure up to combat an awful fact of childhood: the fact of their vulnerability to fear, anger, hate, frustration—all the emotions that are an ordinary part of their lives and that they can perceive only as ungovernable and dangerous forces. To master these forces, children turn to fantasy: that imagined world where disturbing emotional situations are solved to their satisfaction. Through fantasy, Max, the hero of my book, discharges his anger against his mother, and returns to the real world sleepy, hungry, and at peace with himself.

"Certainly we want to protect our children from new and painful experiences that are beyond their emotional comprehension and that intensify anxiety; and to a point we can prevent premature exposure to such experiences. That is obvious. But what is just as obvious —and what is too often overlooked—is the fact that from their earliest years children live on familiar terms with disrupting emotions, that fear and anxiety are an intrinsic part of their everyday lives, that they continually cope with frustration as best they can. And it is through fantasy that children achieve catharsis. It is the best means they have for taming Wild Things.

"It is my involvement with this inescapable fact of childhood— the awful vulnerability of children and their struggle to make themselves King of All Wild Things—that gives my work whatever truth and passion it may have."

Here are the inescapable facts of Maurice Sendak's childhood. Born in Brooklyn in 1928, he was the youngest of three children of Philip and Sarah Sendak, both of whom came to America before World War I from Jewish *shtetls* outside Warsaw.

One of Maurice's earliest memories dates from the age of three or four. "I was convalescing after a long, serious illness. I was sitting on my grandmother's lap, and I remember the feeling of pleasant drowsiness. It was winter. We sat in front of a window, and my grandmother pulled the shade up and down to amuse me. Every time the shade went up, I was thrilled by the sudden reappearance of the backyard, the falling snow, and my brother and sister busy constructing a sooty snowman. Down came the shade—I waited. Up went the shade—the children had moved, the snowman had grown eyes. I don't remember a single sound."

Perhaps Sendak's later interest in animated toys and transformation books begins here. His love of wonder tales certainly derives from the stories his father told him as a child. Philip Sendak was apparently an inspiring improviser of stories, and would embroider and extend a tale over a period of nights. Maurice recalls one of the more memorable of these in an illuminating *New Yorker* profile written in 1966 by Nat Hentoff:

"It was about a child taking a walk with his father and mother. He becomes separated from them. Snow begins to fall, and the child shivers in the cold. He huddles under a tree, sobbing in terror. An enormous figure hovers over him and says, as he draws the boy up, 'I'm Abraham, your father.' His fear gone, the child looks up and also sees Sarah. He is no longer lost. When his parents find him, the child is dead. Those stories had something of the character of William Blake's poems. The myths in them didn't seem at all factitious. And they fused Jewish lore with my father's particular way of shaping memory and desire. That one, for instance, was based on the power of Abraham in Jewish tradition as the father who was always there—a reassuring father even when he was Death. But the story was also about how tremendously my father missed his parents. Not all his tales were somber though. My father could be very witty, even if the humor was always on the darker side of irony."

Maurice's sister Natalie gave him his first book, *The Prince and the Pauper.* "A ritual began with that book," Sendak once told Virginia Haviland, "which I recall very clearly. The first thing was to set it up on the table and stare at it for a long time. Not because I was impressed with Mark Twain; it was just such a beautiful object. Then came the smelling of it . . . it was printed on particularly fine paper, unlike the Disney books I had gotten previous to that. *The Prince and the Paper—Pauper*—smelled good and it also had a shiny laminated cover. I flipped over that. I remember trying to bite into it, which I don't imagine is what my sister intended when she bought the book for me. But the last thing I did with the book was to read it. It was all right. But I think it started then, my passion for books and bookmaking. There's so much more to a book than just the reading. I've seen children touch books, fondle books, smell books, and it's all the reason in the world why books should be beautifully produced."

Following his brother Jack's example, Maurice first began writing his own stories when he was about nine, hand-lettering and illustrating them on uniform pages, then binding them with tape and decorated covers. He combined cutout newspaper photographs and comic strips with sketches of the Sendak family. And he began to draw.

"I was miserable as a kid," Sendak recalls. "I couldn't make friends, I couldn't play stoopball terrific, I couldn't skate great. I stayed home and drew pictures. You *know* what they all thought of me: sissy Maurice Sendak. When I wanted to go out and do something, my father would say: 'You'll catch a cold.' And I did . . . I did whatever he told me.

"People imagine that I was aware of Palmer and Blake and English graphics and German fairy tales when I was a kid. That came later. All I had then were popular influences—comic books, junk books, Gold Diggers movies, monster films, *King Kong, Fantasia.* I remember a Mickey Mouse mask that came on a big box of cornflakes. What a fantastic mask! Such a big, bright, vivid, gorgeous hunk of face! And that's what a kid in Brooklyn knew at the time."

In the Night Kitchen, one of Sendak's greatest works, shows little Mickey falling naked through the night into the Oliver Hardy bakers' dough, kneading and pounding it into a Hap Harrigan plane, flying over the city, diving into a giant milk bottle, then sliding back into his bed to sleep. It is a work that pays extraordinary homage to Sendak's early aesthetic influences—especially to Winsor McCay—to the cheap, full-color children's books of the period, as well as to the feelings about New York City he had as a little boy.

"When I was a child," he told Virginia Haviland, "there was an advertisement which I remember very clearly. It was for the Sunshine bakers, and it read: 'We Bake While You Sleep!' It seemed to me the most sadistic thing in the world, because all I wanted to do was stay up and watch . . . it seemed so absurdly cruel and arbitrary for them to do it while I slept. And also for them to think I would think that that was terrific stuff on their part, and would eat their product on top of that. It bothered me a good deal, and I remember I used to save the coupons showing the three fat little Sunshine bakers going off to this magic place at night, wherever it was, to have their fun, while I had to go to bed. This book was a sort of vendetta book to get back at them and to say that I am now old enough to stay up at night and know what's happening in the Night Kitchen!

"Another thing is: I lived in Brooklyn, and to travel to Manhattan was a big deal, even though it was so close. I couldn't go by myself, and I counted a good deal on my elder sister. She took my brother and me to Radio City Music Hall, or the Roxy, or some such place. Now, the point of going to New York was that you *ate* in New York. Somehow to me New York represented eating. And eating in a very fashionable, elegant, superlatively mysterious place like Longchamps. You got dressed up, you went uptown—it was night when you got there and there were lots of windows blinking—and you went straight to a place to eat. It was one of the most exciting things of my childhood. Cross the bridge and see the city approaching, get there and have your dinner, then go to a movie and come home. So, again, *In the Night Kitchen* is a kind of homage to New York City, the city I loved so much and still love."

At fifteen, Sendak worked after school drawing backgrounds for All-American Comics, adapting Mutt and Jeff comic strips, fitting them into a page, filling in backgrounds (puffs of dust under running heels), and extending the story line when necessary.

"I began illustrating my own books during this period," Maurice recalls. "My first book was Oscar Wilde's *The Happy Prince*, which is a story I don't admire any more, but as a young person I felt was extraordinary. And I illustrated Bret Harte's *The Luck of Roaring Camp*. It was my favorite story, and what is it about? A baby that is adopted by a lot of rough men, lumberjacks—an illegitimate child abandoned after the death of its mother. I'm writing a book now [*Outside over There*] about a baby—most of my books are about babies—and it seems as if I've been doing the same thing since I was six years old. I'm a few inches taller and I have a graying beard, but otherwise there's not much difference.

"People used to comment continually on the fact that the children in my books looked homely—Eastern European Jewish as opposed to the flat, oilcloth look considered normal in children's books. They were just Brooklyn kids, old-looking before their time. But a baby *does* look a hundred years old.

"I love babies' faces and I draw them all the time. They're uncanny. When my father was dying, he'd dwindled—he had the body shape of a boy—and as I held him, I noticed that his head had become bigger than the rest of him and was rolling back like an infant's. Death at that moment was like going to sleep: 'Shhh, it will be all right.' It's what you'd say to a feverish baby, except that he was dead.

"Infants' heads are wonderful to draw because they're so big and ungainly. You know how they fall back? Babies cry when they're held badly, they always know when they think they're going to be dropped, and when some klutz holds them, they cry. They're enormous kvetches with those mean little faces—'Give me this!'—and at the same time there's a look that they get that makes them so vulnerable, poignant, and lovable."

Shortly after graduating high school, Sendak began to work full time at Timely Service, a window-display house in lower Manhattan, where he assisted in the construction of store-window models of figures such as Snow White and the Seven Dwarfs made out of chicken wire, papier-mâché, spun glass, plaster, and paint. With his brother, he began to make animated wooden toys that performed scenes from *Little Miss Muffet* and *Old Mother Hubbard*, which led to his being hired as a window-display assistant at F.A.O. Schwarz toy store. His only formal art study took place at this time—two years of evening classes at the Art Students League. Unbeknownst to him, Frances Chrystie, the children's book buyer at Schwarz, and Richard Nell, the store's display director, arranged for Ursula Nordstrom of Harper & Row to see his work, and she immediately asked him to illustrate Marcel Aymé's *The Wonderful Farm*, which was published in 1951. "It made me an official person," Maurice says.

Since then, as a writer, illustrator, and both, Sendak has published more than seventy books here and abroad, and he has been the recipient of scores of prizes and awards. He thinks of *A Hole Is to Dig* (1952)—with his exiguous and playful illustrations accompanying the poet Ruth Krauss's assemblage of children's definitions like "A face is so you can make faces"—as "the first book that came together for me." And he is still half pleased with *Kenny's Window* (1956)—the story of a little boy who, upon waking from a dream, remembers meeting a rooster who gave him seven questions to answer ("Can you fix a broken promise?" Kenny's reply: "Yes, if it only looks broken, but really isn't"). "It's the first thing I wrote," Maurice explains. "The pictures are ghastly—I really wasn't up to illustrating my own texts then—and the story itself, to be honest, is nice but overwritten: 'Singing chimes in the city lights and the songs of the city.' Today that kind of stuff sounds like Delius combined with Bruckner!"

After the introverted Kenny, Sendak introduced us to the fussy and sulking Martin in *Very Far Away* (1957). But it was in 1960 that Sendak's most indomitable character appeared on the scene: Rosie of *The Sign on Rosie's Door*. Based on a ten-year-old girl he spotted on the streets of Brooklyn in 1948, she is the prototype of all Sendak's plucky children, and he lovingly describes her genesis and transformations in his essay-portrait, "Rosie."

Sendak's *Nutshell Library* (1962)—four tiny books, each of which can be held in the palm of one's hand—is intimately tied to *The Sign on Rosie's Door*: Alligator, Pierre, Johnny, and the nameless hero of *Chicken Soup with Rice* are modeled on the "men" in Rosie's life. In 1975, Sendak drew all these characters into a marvelous half-hour animated film entitled *Really Rosie Starring the Nutshell Kids*— a film which Sendak both wrote and directed and which features the music and singing of Carole King. (The film soundtrack, *Carole King —Really Rosie*, is available on Ode Records.)

From Kenny and Martin to Pierre, Max, and Mickey, Sendak's characters have their origins in those Brooklyn street kids he used to observe and sketch while leaning out of his parents' second-story window—all of them enlivened and connected by that amazingly animated anima-figure who could, in Sendak's words, "imagine herself into being anything she wanted to be, anywhere in or out of the world." As her discoverer and creator remarks: "A mere change of sex cannot disguise the essential Rosieness of my heroes."

Although Sendak has an apartment in New York City, he works and spends most of his time in the country just outside Ridgefield, a small Connecticut town which, ironically, is the birthplace of Samuel Griswold Goodrich (1793–1860)—perhaps the best-known and most influential figure in nineteenth-century American children's literature. Goodrich's Peter Parley books (about 116 of them) sold 7 million copies—not including the thousands of imitations and pirate copies printed and sold in the United States and England. Illustrated with wood engravings, they were generally nationalistic but occasionally tolerant utilitarian schoolbooks written in the compendious and moronic style that has served as the model for generations of first-grade primers: "Here I am! My name is Peter Parley! I am an old man. I am very gray and lame. But I have seen a great many things, and had a great many adventures, and I love to talk about them. . . . And do you know that the very place where Boston stands was once covered with woods, and that in those woods lived many Indians? Did you ever see an Indian? Here is a picture of some Indians."

Aside from the fact that—a century apart—they resided just a few miles down the road from each other, two creators of children's literature more dissimilar than Goodrich and Sendak would be hard to imagine.

At the age of twelve, Goodrich read *Moral Repository* by Hannah More (1745–1833), an evangelical English educator and writer, and was instantly bowled over. (To counter what she considered "vulgar and indecent penny books" popular among young people at the time, More produced amiable-sounding works such as *The Execution of Wild Henry*. It is frightening to remind ourselves that 2 million of her Cheap Repository Tracts—sobering and moralistic tales largely designed to keep the poor in their place—were sold in their first year of publication, and this at a time when the population of England numbered fewer than 11 million.) So, when Goodrich visited More in Bristol (he was thirty and she was seventy-eight), he was thrown into a state of ecstasy. As he recalled this meeting in his *Recollections of a Lifetime*: "It was in conversation with that amiable and gifted person that I first formed the conception of the Parley Tales—the general idea of which was to make nursery books reasonable and truthful, and thus to feed the young mind upon things wholesome and pure, instead of things monstrous, false, and pestilent."

Goodrich particularly objected to the moral obliquity of *Puss in Boots* and *Jack the Giant Killer* ("tales of horror, commonly put into the hands of youth, as if for the express purpose of reconciling them to vice and crime"), and he detested nursery rhymes, declaring that even a child could make them up. To prove his point, he produced the following nonsense on the spot: "Higglety, pigglety, pop!/The dog has eaten the mop;/The pig's in a hurry,/The cat's in a flurry,/Higglety, pigglety, pop!"

Irony upon irony. A century later, Maurice Sendak wrote and illustrated perhaps his most mysterious and extraordinary work, *Higglety, Pigglety Pop! or There Must Be More to Life* (1967), a modern fairy tale about Jennie the Sealyham terrier—modeled after one of Sendak's own dogs—who packs her bag, goes out into the world to look for something more than everything, and winds up as the leading lady of a theatrical production (costarring Miss Rhoda, Pig, Cat, and a lion) of the "Higglety, Pigglety, Pop!" nursery rhyme itself. "Hello," Jennie begins the letter to her old master that concludes the book: "As you probably noticed, I went away forever. I am very experienced now and very famous. I am even a star. Every day I eat a mop, twice on Saturday. It is made of salami and that is my favorite, I get plenty to drink too, so don't worry. I can't tell you how to get to the Castle Yonder because I don't know where it is. But if you ever come this way, look for me. Jennie."

The morning I was supposed to take the train up to visit Sendak in Connecticut, I received a call from him. Visit postponed, I thought.

"My dogs aren't well," Maurice said sadly. "But I think it will cheer me up to have company. . . . It's my birthday today."

"What would you like as a present?" I asked.

"Well, if it's no trouble, some sandwiches from a deli. Any kind. Anything. It's hopeless around here."

"What about hot pastrami with coleslaw and mustard on rye?"

"Fantastic."

"And pickles?"

"Fantastic. And perhaps a really gooey chocolate layer cake for dessert?"

When Maurice picked me up at the station, he apologized for being late. "There are hundreds of children parading through town," he said incredulously. And as we began to drive slowly back to his house, I saw hordes of kids marching silently along the roads, as if they were following an invisible and inaudible Pied Piper. "What's going on?" I wondered aloud.

"I live here," Maurice grimly replied.

Sendak's house is hardly grim, surrounded as it is by beautiful ash, sugar maple, dogwood, and locust trees, and with irises, lilies, phlox, and roses growing near a little wood hut, the whole scene reminding me of a German landscape.

"Mahler went into the woods to write his symphonies in *his* little *Waldhütte*," Maurice says as he shows me his cottage. "And in the first movement of his Third Symphony, you can almost hear him in those woods, with those menacing trees and ferns that turn into fingers—like the trees that catch Snow White. You get a sense of that forest in the first movement—very ambivalent to the artist: is it going to give him something or frighten him to death? [See Sendak's cover illustration for RCA's recording of Mahler's Third, which depicts a silhouetted Mahler in his *Waldhütte* receiving the gift of inspiration from an angel.] And Mozart, too. When he was alone in Vienna writing *The Magic Flute*, he was invited to live in a tiny summer cottage outside the theater grounds to continue his work. . . . The only way to find something is to lose oneself: that's what George Mac-Donald teaches us in his stories. And that's what this little hut, where one can be alone, means to me."

Sendak takes me back to the main house, which is filled with the most wondrous, imaginative, and variegated things. On the walls are posters by Penfield, Will Bradley, Lautrec, and Bonnard; a glorious Winsor McCay triptych showing Little Nemo and a princess walking down a resplendent garden path surrounded by daffodils with smiling faces; children's toys, a pillow in the shape of the *Night Kitchen's* Mickey and his bottle of milk, and a bunch of stuffed Wild Things; and in almost every room, books by James, Melville, Dickens, Stifter, MacDonald, Blake, Beatrix Potter, Palmer's illustrated Milton . . . as well as art books (Dürer, Grünewald) and books on music (Mahler, Wolf, Wagner, Beethoven, and Mozart).

Birthday presents from friends are lying on the dining-room table: a Mickey Mouse mirror and Mickey Mouse music box, an eighteenth-century tin coach from Germany, miniature bottles of Dry Sack, a floral bouquet, a T-shirt inscribed "Some Swell Pup"—the title of his recently published cartoon book—and three little scissors for cutting cloth, paper, and letters. I add the sandwiches, and we begin lunch.

"Maurice, this is as good a time as any to ask you about the idea of incorporation in your work."

"While I'm eating the sandwich?"

"In *Pierre* the lion eats Pierre. In *As I Went over the Water* a sea monster ingests a boat. In *Higglety Pigglety Pop!* Jennie eats a mop. Things and people get swallowed, and out they come again.

And in one of your best fantasy sketches, you show a baby eating its mother. This happens a lot in Grimms' tales and especially in Winsor McCay's early animation films about dinosaurs. What's this all about?"

"Well," Maurice says, "I'm certainly not going to disgorge this sandwich—it's delicious, and I feel better already. You know, I used to love *biting* into my first books when I was a child, so maybe it's a hangup from that time . . . but a pleasant one: things being eaten and then given out again—it's an image that constantly appeals to me, and to most children, too. It's such a primary fantasy of childhood—the pleasure of putting things in the mouth, of chewing, of swallowing, of shitting, and pissing. Before children are told it's not a nice thing— the whole toilet-training process—there's nothing nicer."

"Sometimes, though, it can be scary," I add, remembering how Maurice once described his feelings as a child when grown-ups would endearingly lean over him and say, "Oh, I could eat you up!" "I was very nervous," Maurice had then recalled, "because I really believed they probably could if they had a mind to. They had great big teeth, immense nostrils and very sweaty foreheads. I often remember that vision and how it frightened me. There was one particular relative who did this to me, and it was really quite terrifying. I immortalized him in *Wild Things*.

"In the fantasy sketch that shows the child devouring his mother," Maurice now adds, ". . . of course that's what children must feel: that great big luminous breast hanging over its head is sent there by God. Obviously it's there for you, why not? Until you're told differently, how are you going to know? There's something both monstrous and poignant about it: the poignancy comes from the fact that a child's going to realize soon enough that it's not so, that he's mortal, that he'll have to compete for it, but that for the second's worth that it's there it's a glorious pleasure. And all I'm saying is, what's wrong with the pleasure? Why must we assume that the know- ing is the correct thing and that the pleasure is the bad thing, which is what most people do feel.

"People who objected to Mickey bathing in milk and floating naked—every part of his body having a sensuous experience . . . as if that's naughty. Why? Why are we all so screwed up, including me? But at least creatively I try to convey the memory of a time in life when it was a pleasure.

"I don't understand the destructive aspect. In my little cartoon, the baby eats the mother—on the surface, what could be more de- structive? But in fact the child doesn't think of it as a destructive act,

Fantasy Sketch by Maurice Sendak. Copyright © Maurice Sendak

it's the most natural thing to him: If you have that much of the mother, have more!"

"Well," I interject, "someone could look at it another way: mother destroys child/child destroys mother."

"That's just mental maneuvering to me," Maurice replies. "I take from the image as much as it's necessary for me to use creatively. I'm not going to analyze it. Now, I'm not against psychology or analysis on principle. I'm sure that the things I draw—little boys flying and falling—reveal something. In one sense it seems very obviously Freudian, as if coming out of my own analysis. People fear that analysis will castrate and dry up artists, but it's just the contrary, in my opinion: it gives wonderful clues and cues as to what you're doing. I don't think of what I'm creating in strict Freudian terms, but surely it's a result of the fact that a large part of my twenties was spent on the analyst's couch. And it enriched and deepened me and gave me confidence to express much that I might not have without it.

"Coming back to the fantasy sketch: The bird is in there because birds were my father's favorite fairy tale symbol. He used to tell stories of birds taking children away. And I think that they enter into a lot of my things because it's an image of his that has always appealed to my heart.

"Incidentally, I did another and earlier version of this sketch in the fifties, and in that version the baby comes out of the fish, the mother is there—furious that the baby's been lost—turns the baby over on her knee, and spanks him. And he, in his rage, this tiny baby in his little diaper, pulls away from her, pulls out a gun and shoots her dead.

"*That* sketch, shall we say, was *unsynthesized*. Whatever it was, it certainly was blatant, and I think that this later one is much better. The earlier version was done while my mother was living, and this one after she died. So, obviously, I've thought and rethought a lot about her during that interval."

"I was reading," I say, "that certain librarians were covering up Mickey's little penis in copies of *Night Kitchen* and that others had suggested that you draw in a little diaper on Mickey in later editions of the book. But take a look at these illustrations I brought up to show you from Jacques Stella's seventeenth-century *Games and Pastimes of Childhood*—all of them depicting naked little putti capering and frolicking."

"It's an amazing coincidence," Maurice exclaims. "I was given this book again recently because my new work is in part concerned with babies doing odd things, and I've been looking at the book for weeks. The illustrations are beautiful . . . and strange. There's a hallucinatory quality about them: they're just children playing games, but why are they all naked? Yet we often make a mistake of reading heavy, tedious, psychological overtones into things that in the seventeenth and eighteenth centuries weren't considered that way at all. I couldn't do that book today, I'd be thrown out of the country. But *that* book is a classic. Adults will take their kids to museums to see a lot of peckers in a row on Roman statues and say: That's art, dearie, and then come home and burn *In the Night Kitchen*. Where's the

From *Fly by Night* by Randall Jarrell, illustrated by Maurice Sendak

logic in that? Art in people's minds is desexualized, and that would make the great artists sick.

"In the illustrations I did for Randall Jarrell's *Fly by Night*—the last book he wrote for children before he died—I have an eight-year-old boy flying naked in a dream. I tried to draw the boy first with pajamas—he looked too much like Wee Willie Winkie. Then I tried him in underwear, and it looked like an ad for Fruit of the Loom. I tried him wrapped in sheets and blankets, but it looked too baroque. He had to be naked. But I know they're going to say it's typically me, arbitrarily making somebody nude. I had a picture showing a girl with her vagina in full view in *The Light Princess*, and nobody made a fuss about that, which makes me think the whole world is male chauvinist—vaginas don't count."

"What's *Fly by Night* about?" I asked Maurice.

"It's a dream: the boy David dreams. Every night he dreams he floats. During the daytime he tries to remember that he can float at night, but he can't. When he wakes up he can't remember. And the entire story is about what happens to him in this one dream. He floats out of his house, over certain animals, and each of the animals has a little poem written by Jarrell—they're delicious poems—and yet they're much deeper, with a kind of funny, starved feeling in them.

"David meets the owl, floats into her nest, and she sings David

Illustration from *Higglety, Pigglety, Pop! or There Must Be More to Life.*
Copyright © 1967 by Maurice Sendak. Reprinted by permission of Harper
& Row, Publishers, Inc.

and her baby a song about getting a little sister and being taken care
of by a mother. For me, that's what the whole book is about—it may
or may not have been for Randall. It's about being starved for a
mother or for safety or protection or for some place where you can
nest or land or be.

"It has a happy ending. David comes home, floats back into his
bed, and when he wakes up, there's his mother who's made breakfast
for him. He looks at her, she looks familiar—someone looks just like
her. Of course it's the owl, he's losing all memory of his dream.

"I drew myself as a baby in it—you can see me in my mother's
arms in the book's only double-spread picture. And I may have taken
a very lopsided and fanciful view of the story, but what I read into it
was a great hunger pain—that longing I once felt in Jarrell's *The
Animal Family*—and I interpreted it as a looking-for-Mama pain. . . .
Maybe it's my pain.

"Come back next week," Maurice says to me, "and I'll tell you
the rest."

Maurice has three dogs: Agamemnon, a male shepherd; Erda, a female
shepherd; and Io, a female retriever. "Zeus had a fling with Io,"
Maurice says, "and jealous Hera transformed her into a bull calf who

From *Some Swell Pup*

was bitten by a gadfly throughout eternity. The minute I saw Io, she looked like a victim—blond and beautiful."

Aggie and Erda are immortalized in the dream sequence of Sendak's cartoon book, *Some Swell Pup, or Are You Sure you Want a Dog?* Written in collaboration with Matthew Margolis, director of the National Institute of Dog Training, the book is an *echt*-Sendak burlesque, telling a cautionary tale of two kids and how they learn to train and love their rambunctious new puppy—which ironically takes on the role of the stereotypical unruly child—with the guidance of a caftanned canine saint.

"I love this book," I say to Maurice the following week, having read *Some Swell Pup* in the interval. "How did it come about?"

"Matthew suggested the ideas about puppy rearing, and I found a group of scenes for them and refashioned his language. The rules had to be simplified and humorized because we wanted kids to enjoy it.

"I was looking for real crazy kids who could act out these little scenes, and so I chose the two I had first used some years back in a sequence of drawings for *Family Circle* magazine and who later appeared as the players of *King Grisly-Beard*. Matthew and I realized that these two would be perfect. She's an aggressive and hysterical yenta, and he's a passive and selfish kid. Their secret names, by the way, are Vernon and Shirley. She's really a Shirley, and he's a real *vaserdiker gornisht* type."

"It's certainly the wittiest tale about how to get gently and humanely socialized that I've ever read," I say. "Just compare it to the typical late-Georgian English stories for children whose 'message,' as the critic Gillian Avery once put it, was 'Be punctual and diligent, obedient and dutiful, do not lie or thieve or blow up your sister, beware of mad dogs and gaming, and you will live to be a successful sugar planter and give your rivals a handsome funeral.' But *Some Swell Pup* is all about true human nature and relationship and patience and acceptance and love and light and . . .'"

". . . and orifices," Maurice adds.

"It's probably your most complete work."

"Jesus, I hope not," Maurice replies. "In terms of orifices it is. One reviewer said: 'There's all this fuss about whether the puppy is a girl or a boy, but we don't even see the anatomical truth.' The reviewer thought I'd gotten coy. But, I mean, how do you show a puppy's sex organ? You'd have to have a microscope to see it at that stage."

"I just saw another review, Maurice, in which the writer spends most of her time commenting on puppy poop."

"Naturally. What does she say?"

I read: " 'Sendak is up front about dog droppings, liberally sprinkling in piles and puddles and deliberately risking a flap similar to the one over frontal nudity in *Night Kitchen*.'"

"Here we go again," he sighs with resigned good humor.

Maurice invites me to drive with him to the veterinarian's to pick up Aggie. To cheer him up, I quote what I think is an appropriate little vignette that appears in Gustav Janouch's *Conversations with Kafka*. Janouch writes:

"Out of a house in the Jakobsgasse, where we had arrived in the course of our discussion, ran a small dog looking like a ball of wool, which crossed our path and disappeared round the corner of the Tempelgasse.

" 'A pretty little dog,' I said.

" 'A dog?' asked Kafka suspiciously, and slowly began to move again.

" 'A small, young dog. Didn't you see it?'

" 'I saw. But was it a dog?'

" 'It was a little poodle.'

" 'A poodle? It could be a dog, but it could also be a sign. We Jews often make tragic mistakes.' "

Maurice laughs so hard he almost has to stop driving. "*It could be a dog but it could also be a sign.* What book *is* that?"

"Janouch was a teenager when he met Kafka. Kafka befriended him, and Janouch later wrote down and published their conversations, which are filled with wonderful statements such as: 'Art like prayer is a hand outstretched in the darkness, seeking for some touch of grace which will transform it into a hand that bestows gifts. Prayer means casting oneself into the miraculous rainbow that stretches between becoming and dying, to be utterly consumed in it, in order to bring its infinite radiance to bed in the frail little cradle of one's own existence. . . . Life is as infinitely great and profound as the immensity of the stars above us. One can only look at it through the narrow keyhole of one's own personal existence. But through it one perceives more than one can see. So above all one must keep the keyhole clean.' "

"That's too much," Maurice says. "It's so wonderful it's like getting drunk. Whistle clean keyholes . . . every metaphor describes his own work. You didn't know this, but one of my fantasy projects has always been to illustrate Kafka. For years I've been thinking about it, wondering whether I was old enough to do it—just as I waited until I thought I was old enough to do *The Juniper Tree.* He's one of the few writers who could express the act of creating so beautifully. I feel so close to him. The only difference is that he's a genius."

"I've noticed," I mention to Maurice, "that a lot of the theatrical performances that take place in your books—*Higglety Pigglety Pop!* and *King Grisly-Beard* especially—share certain characteristics with the Nature Theater of Oklahoma as Kafka describes it in *Amerika.*"

"To put it mildly," Maurice responds. "Where do you think I got it from? From there and from Richard Strauss's *Ariadne auf Naxos*—characters and an impresario looking for a performance. I love opera, theater, pantomime, ballet, and I've tried to express this love and appreciation in my books."

At the vet's, Aggie seems to be feeling better, and when we

arrive back at Maurice's, he happily greets Erda and Io, and off they go running around the grounds. Maurice keeps a watchful eye on them as we sit under the trees, and I ask him about the picture book he's just started.

"This will be the last part of my trilogy that began with *Wild Things* and *Night Kitchen*. And of the three, this one will be the strangest. *Wild Things* now seems to me to be a very simple book—its simplicity is probably what made it successful, but I could never be that simple again. *Night Kitchen* I much prefer—it reverberates on double levels. But this third book will reverberate on triple levels. It's so dense already . . . I don't know what it means and I can't get beyond the first seven lines.

"But I'll get there, I feel it in me—like a woman having a baby, all that life churning on inside me. I feel it every day: it moves, stretches, yawns . . . it's getting ready to get born. It knows exactly what it is, only I don't know with my conscious mind, but every day I get a little clue: Listen, dumdum, here's a word for you, see what you can make of it. So it throws it out and I catch it: oh, a word, fantastic! And then I do without for three days, and the unconscious says, This man's too much to believe, he walks, he thinks, sits, he doesn't do anything, he's a bore, throw him another word, otherwise he'll sit there forever and have a coronary. . . . And one by one it throws me words.

"Is it the right time for a book? It's like getting pregnant when you've just gone crazy and you've found out your house has burned down. Externally I'm in turmoil, I didn't want to get pregnant now. When I write the book, it may be an abortion, but let's hope not. I'm definitely with life, as they say, sitting like a mother on a stump, thinking, Thank you, God, thank you."

"D. H. Lawrence," I interject, "used to describe the pregnant mother as feeling at one with the world."

"The *maven* on how women felt!" Maurice replies. "What does that mean? It sounds like being glued to something. I don't feel at one with the world, I never have. The only thing that's miraculous is the creative act, and I call it miraculous because I don't understand it. I don't understand, for example, how Mozart could write semitrivial but deliciously funny letters to Daddy at the very moment he was composing his sublime works. And when Daddy says: 'Look, Wolfgang, I don't want you messing around in Munich, you're there to get a job, I don't like your going out dancing every night—your mother's written to me all about it. Pull yourself together. You're not the type to do this kind of thing. Your loving father.' 'But Daddy, Daddy,' Mozart writes back, 'I just went out with Fraülein so-and-so, she's a nice girl, I had two dances, came home at eleven o'clock, I've been good, haven't been drinking wine, and on top of that I just wrote the horn concerto, two violin concertos, and the famous *Sinfonia Concertante*. Isn't that enough for this week, Daddy? I'll try and be better.'

"Now, of course I made that up, but that's the sound of it, and Mozart wrote those pieces that same week he was thinking those nothing thoughts and trying to get his boring father off his back. And while he was doing this, he was creating something that was completely beyond his father, beyond anyone's father, and beyond any of us two hundred years later. *That's* the miracle.

"I've always loved Mozart. I read Alfred Einstein's wonderful book on him, and I've read a dozen books since then, although not one of them is up to that. But best of all is Mozart's letters. I'm only up to age twenty-two, but it doesn't matter. Every letter is beautiful, no matter how trivial it is. And they're very scatological—not only Wolfgang's but sober Frau Mozart's as well: 'When you go to bed, shit well till it busts,' she writes to her husband. Now, you *know* she's not a maniac. And Wolfgang writes something like: 'My darling, my quintessential sister, I kiss you, stuff your arse in your mouth tonight and bite with all your heart. Then shit and let it bust good.' It's so strange! What does it mean? Very conceivably one might think that Mozart was an anal retentive, that he never got past the toilet-training stage. . . . But it was the eighteenth century. And there's also that very Germanic quality of every day being based on the quality of the bowel movement."

"I seem to remember," I add, "that in one of his letters he writes: 'Do we live to shit, or shit to live?' That's very advanced existential humor."

"It's that combination of gravity and grace that I love so much in Mozart," Maurice says. "He's the ideal, and God knows I'm not like him. I'm not good-humored and I don't juggle the problems of life well.

"Recently I've been reading about Beethoven and his relationship with his nephew, Karl. When Karl said he wanted to go out, Beethoven suffered terribly: the child didn't want him all the time, unlike the music that was so compliant. Beethoven could be who he was, do what he did, and then try to apply the same grandiose, creative rules of art to everyday life. The dummy just couldn't accept the fact that it wasn't possible to force a little boy to love him the way he could force the *Hammerklavier* to appear on paper. Beethoven's special kind of love—'I-hypnotize-you-into-total-love'—overlooked what did come from the child: affection, pleasure in having an extraordinary man named Beethoven as his uncle. But it wasn't enough for him.

"And yes, I do identify with Beethoven—it's like the Achilles' heel of the artist who lives on a grandiose plane, conjuring his art up, but failing in real life because his inflated ego can't be satisfied. I don't like Beethoven the man, but I have tremendous sympathy for him.

"I hope," Maurice says suddenly, "that you don't think of me as some kind of *shlump*."

"As you've been talking," I say to him, "I've been thinking of that early nineteenth-century Mother Goose illustration you praised so highly in one of your essays. It's an illustration that juxtaposes the curmudgeonly Man in the South slopping porridge over his head and the mysterious, ambiguous and graceful Man in the Moon floating through the mist and clouds. This seems to be the Beethoven-Mozart split in your being, this one image suggesting the unity of personality. You've been talking about two composers, but you really seem to be talking about reality and imagination, heaviness and lightness."

"Music," Maurice replies, "is a metaphor for everything."

It is possible to see Sendak's books as falling into either the major or the minor *key*—in the musical sense. The major works consist of the color picture and cartoon books like *Night Kitchen, Hector Protector*, or *Some Swell Pup*, which feature simple, broad, outlined drawings, often done with a Magic Marker. The minor works—his haunting illustrations for *The Juniper Tree, Higglety Pigglety Pop!, Fly by Night*, MacDonald's *The Golden Key*, and *The Light Princess* —are distinguished by their elaborate pen-and-ink crosshatched style.

Sendak continually talks about the illustrator's task in musical terms. "To conceive musically for me means to quicken the life of the illustrated book," he wrote in his essay "The Shape of Music." And he speaks of his favorite illustrators as if they were musicians.

The pictures of the Victorian artist Randolph Caldecott, Sendak writes, "abound in musical imagery; his characters are forever dancing and singing and playing instruments. More to the point is his refinement of a graphic counterpart to the musical form of theme and variations, his delightful compounding of a simple visual theme into a fantastically various interplay of images. In one of his greatest and most beautiful pictures—'And the Dish ran away with the Spoon' from *Hey Diddle Diddle*—you see a cat playing his violin for objects in the kitchen (a flask, dishes, bowls) and, in the foreground, the dish running away with the spoon. You can almost hear the music coming from the back room as you observe the couple fleeing, obviously in love."

From *Mother Goose's Melodies* (the Munro and Francis "copyright 1833" edition)

About the illustrations for La Fontaine's fable "The Wolf and the Lamb" by the late-nineteenth century artist M. Boutet de Monvel, Sendak writes: "The lamb performs, before meeting an unjust fate, a sequence of linear arabesques, a superb dance of death that painfully conveys and dramatically enlarges the fable's grim meaning. The eye follows from picture to picture the swift development of the story—the fatalistic 'folding up,' the quiet inevitability of the lamb's movements, ending in a dying-swan gesture of hopeless resignation. And then the limp, no longer living form hanging from the raging wolf's mouth. I think of these fine, softly colored, and economically conceived drawings as a musical accompaniment to the La Fontaine fable, harmonic inventions that color and give fresh meaning in much the same way that a Hugo Wolf setting illuminates a Goethe poem."

Sendak admires the "tremendous vitality" of Wilhelm Busch ("Mickey in *Night Kitchen* gets baked, just like Max and Moritz"), the clarity and simplicity of the French artists Felix Valloton (especially his illustrations for *Poil de Carotte*) and Bonnard ("their simple lines, strokes, washes of color—it's that Mozart quality I don't have, my things are so heavy . . . like latkes and mashed potatoes"), and, most of all, the "terse, blocked images" of the English artist Arthur Hughes—"so graphically precise and unearthly. Hughes is one of the most important influences in my life, especially his illustrations for the fairy tales of George MacDonald.

"I love immaculate, rigid, antiquated forms where every bit of fat is cut off, so tight and perfect you couldn't stick a pin in it, but within which you can be as free as you want. And I'm not an innovator—that's not my talent. I've just taken what's there and tried to show what else you could do with it. Like the picture-book form, which requires an extraordinary condensation of feeling and words. It should last just a few minutes for the child, since most children have very short spans of interest. But I personally love the art of condensation, squeezing something big into its pure essence.

"I'm an artist who does books that are apparently more appropriate for children than for anyone else, for some odd reason. I never set *out* to do books for children—I *do* books for children, but I don't know why. And, to me, the greatest writers—like the greatest illustrators—for children are those who draw upon their child sources, their dream sources—they don't forget them. There's William Blake, George MacDonald, Dickens . . . that peculiar charm of being in a room in a Dickens novel, where the furniture is alive, the fire is alive, where saucepans are alive, where chairs move, where every inanimate object has a personality.

"There's Henry James, whom I would call a children's book writer, why not? He would have dropped dead if you had said that to him, but his all-absorbing interest in children and their relationships to adults creates some of his greatest stories. Just the way he allows children to stay up and see what the grown-ups are really doing. In *What Maisie Knew*, children are constantly mixing in the most deranged adult society, and they're permitted to view and morally judge their elders. It's like a fantasy come true. It's like Mickey not wanting to go to sleep in order to see what goes on in the Night Kitchen. James's children stay up at night, too. Maisie hardly says anything, but we all know what she knows, and we see her know it.

"Finally, there's Herman Melville. I wanted to write something that had the same title as a book by Melville, but I couldn't call it *Moby Dick* or *The Confidence Man* or *Typee*. It had to be something a little vaguer. Finally I hit on *Pierre*. I needed a rhyme for the name, and that's how I came up with Pierre's favorite line: 'I don't care.'

"It's the two levels of writing—one visible, one invisible—that fascinate me most about Melville. As far down as the whale goes in the water is as deep as Herman writes—even in his early works like *Redburn*, which is one of my favorite books. The young man coming to England for the first time . . . I swear, I'll never forget that walk he takes in the English countryside. There's a mystery there, a clue, a nut, a bolt, and if I put it together, I find me."

"There's a theme that appears in much of your work," I say to Maurice on my last visit to Connecticut, "and I can only hint at it because it's difficult to formulate or describe. It has something to do with the lines: 'As I went over the water/the water went over me' [from *As I Went over the Water*] or 'I'm in the milk and the milk's in me' [from *Night Kitchen*]."

"Obviously I have one theme, and it's even in the book I'm working on right now. It's not that I have such original ideas, just that I'm good at doing variations on the same idea over and over again. You can't imagine how relieved I was to find out that Henry James admitted he had only a couple of themes and that all of his books were based on them. That's all we need as artists—one power-driven fantasy or obsession, then to be clever enough to do variations . . . like a series of variations by Mozart. They're so good that you forget they're based on one theme. The same things draw me, the same images. . . ."

"What is this one obsession?"

"I'm not about to tell you—not because it's a secret, but because I can't verbalize it."

"There's a line by Bob Dylan in 'Just like a Woman' which talks about being 'inside the rain.' "

"Inside the rain?"

"When it's raining outside," I explain, "I often feel inside myself, as if I were inside the rain . . . as if the rain were my *self*. That's the sense I get from Dylan's image and from your books as well."

"It's strange you say that," Maurice answers, "because rain has become one of the most potent images of my new book. It sort of scares me that you mentioned that line. Maybe that's what rain means.

It's such an important ingredient in this new work, and I've never understood what it meant. There was a thing about me and rain when I was a child: if I could summon it up in one sentence, I'd be happy to. It's such connected tissue. . . ."

The connecting tissue in the work of Maurice Sendak is the continually experienced awareness of the deepest child-self. "I don't believe, in a way, that the kid I was grew up into me," he once told Nat Hentoff. "He still exists somewhere, in the most graphic, plastic, physical way. . . . I communicate with him—or try to—all the time. One of my worst fears is losing contact with him. I don't want this to sound coy or schizophrenic, but at least once a day I feel I have to make contact. The pleasures I get as an adult are heightened by the fact that I experience them as a child at the same time. Like, when autumn comes, as an adult I welcome the departure of the heat, and simultaneously, as a child would, I start anticipating the snow and the first day it will be possible to use a sled. This dual apperception does break down occasionally. That usually happens when my work is going badly. I get a sour feeling about books in general and my own in particular. The next stage is annoyance at my dependence on this dual apperception, and I reject it. Then I become depressed. When excitement about what I'm working on returns, so does the child. We're on happy terms again."

A little boy once wrote Maurice a letter that read: "How much does it cost to get to where the wild things are? If it is not too expensive my sister and I want to spend the summer there. Please answer soon."

The "wild things" are, of course, the feelings within us, and if we lose contact with them and with our childhood being we become defenders of the Social Lie and the forces of death, as we mouth platitudes about "reverence for life." But life demands us to defend not denatured human beings but rather transformed and transforming boys and girls, men and women. The psychoanalyst Wilhelm Reich knew this when he wrote his great visionary oration in *Cosmic Superimposition*:

"Outside on the meadow, two children in deep embrace would not astonish or shock anyone. Inside on the stage, it would immediately invoke police action. Outside, a child is a child, an infant is an infant, and a mother is a mother, no matter whether in the form of a deer, or a bear, or a human being. Inside, an infant is *not* an infant if its mother cannot show a marriage certificate. Outside, to know the stars is to know God, and to meditate about God is to meditate about the heavens. Inside, somehow, if you believe in God, you do not understand or you refuse to understand the stars. Outside, if you search in the heavens, you refuse, and rightly so, to believe in the sinfulness of the natural embrace. Outside, you feel your blood surging and you do not doubt that something is moving in you, a thing you call your emotion, with its location undoubtedly in the middle of your body and close to your heart."

"I feel it in me—like a woman having a baby," Maurice had said in 1976, describing the early pains of conceiving *Outside over There*, the third in the trilogy of picture books that began with *Where the Wild Things Are* and continued with *In the Night Kitchen*. At the time that this latest book was gestating, Maurice had not wanted to speak directly of its plot, theme, or idea. As the Jungian analyst Marie-Louise von Franz has wisely put it:

> Everyone who has done creative work knows that *in statu nascendi* the creative idea should not be talked about. A writer should not show or discuss what he is writing with too many people. He usually knows when the work is in the delicate state of growth. Someone may say, "yes . . . very good," but just that little hesitation after the "yes" can rob you of your courage to go on—it is as delicate as that before it is finished. A hesitation in the response or a silly question may lame you. One may even criticize it oneself once the child has been born, and there is a certain distance; but when it is half formed, you cannot talk about it.

Now, five years later, the long-awaited delivery of the child was in sight. And on April 6, 1981—exactly one month before the book's official publication date—Maurice agreed to meet me at my apartment to discuss *Outside over There*—over a dinner of deli sandwiches (some things never change).

During this five-year period of delayed parturition, Maurice had suffered and gradually overcome a long-standing depression, intensified, in part, as he nurtured his newest creation—as Baudelaire said he nurtured his hysteria—with "joy and terror." But at the same time he also managed to oversee the production of the beautiful "picture biography" *The Art of Maurice Sendak*, with a text by Selma G. Lanes; contributed sets, costumes, and a libretto for the English composer Oliver Knussen's operatic score for a Brussels Opera production of *Where the Wild Things Are*; provided the book and sets for an expanded off-Broadway musical version of his 1975 half-hour animated television special *Really Rosie*; and, when I met Maurice for dinner, was just about to complete work on his costumes and sets for a New York City Opera production of Janáček's *The Cunning Little Vixen*, directed by Frank Corsaro.

It was, in fact, Corsaro—a longtime Sendak admirer—who, shortly after Maurice had painfully started work on *Outside over There*, had asked the artist to do sets and costumes for a production of Mozart's *The Magic Flute* that Corsaro was going to direct at the Houston Opera in the fall of 1980. (This production was brought to the Kennedy Center in Washington D. C. a year later.) The timing could not have been more perfect. For *The Magic Flute*—Maurice's favorite opera—combines many radically different elements: opera buffa, opera seria, singspiel, popular song, bravura aria, ritual chorus, and chorale. And in the way Mozart synthesizes and reconciles the sacred and the profane, the serious and the comic, and the elevated and the popular suggest, *mutatis mutandis*, Sendak's own all-embracing powers to use and transform the most disparate kind of materials from creators as diverse as Caldecott and Walt Disney, Dürer and Winsor McCay, Mozart and Carole King.

And like *The Magic Flute, Outside over There* is a fairy tale, telling of a little girl named Ida who turns briefly away from her infant sister, whom she is tending, in order to play her Magic Horn. But on turning around she discovers that goblins—seen first as disembodied, faceless wraiths in cloaks and later as five naked babies—have substituted a changeling for the real baby and have hidden her away. Ida flies backward out of the house in a yellow rain slicker, then switches directions and finds her sister in a cave where, in a trial by water—like that undergone by Tamino and Pamina in *The Magic Flute*—she makes the goblin babies dissolve into a "dancing stream," rescues her sister, and takes her home. And as Ida returns through a wood, we notice a little cottage in which we see the seated, silhouetted figure of Mozart, whose presence betokens his role as the muse of the book. For *Outside over There* is, in fact, a homage to Mozart ("My book is my *imagining* of Mozart's life," Sendak says), as well as to the literature (the Brothers Grimm, Kleist) and the art of late eighteenth- and early nineteenth-century Germany.

Unlike *Wild Things* and *Night Kitchen*—which drew their inspiration from *King Kong*, Laurel and Hardy movies, and the cartoons of Winsor McCay—*Outside over There* presents a series of extraordinarily intense, luminous, almost frozen-in-time illustrations that reveal the influence of the visionary painters Kaspar David Friedrich and, especially, Philipp Otto Runge, whose work, in the words of art historian Robert Rosenblum, combines "the closest scrutiny of nature and an awareness of a divine immanence within nature's surface manifestations" and "encompasses simultaneously the visionary and the empirical." And in *Outside over There*, the simultaneous presentation of different moods, characters, and actions—we see the goblins planning and performing their kidnapping while Ida is obliviously taking care of her baby sister—testifies to Sendak's compositional brilliance: The double-page illustration, for another example, showing Ida, in search of her sister, flying backward seemingly over and through inner and outer worlds, is one of Sendak's greatest achievements . . . while the muted but radiant colors of grass, trees, sunflowers, moons, and skies are the means by which the story's emotions are expressed.

But in pointing to these influences, we should not overlook the fact that *Outside over There* is also, of course, *echt*-Sendak. With her pluckiness and indomitability, Ida might well be an incarnation of Rosie in *Really Rosie*; Ida and her sister remind us of the dog Jennie and Baby in *Higglety Pigglety Pop*; Ida flying resembles David flying in *Fly by Night*; and Ida's rescue mission parallels Max's and Mickey's night journeys in *Wild Things* and *Night Kitchen* respectively. But it is interesting that in *Outside over There* Sendak has given us the first female protagonist of his trilogy (in fact, as Sendak says in the following discussion, the goblin babies, too—and everyone else in the book except Mozart—are female), as if their creator had contacted the realm of his anima. One can make such a speculation because *Outside over There*, like most great fairy tales, has the simplicity of an elemental story and at the same time the mysteriousness, the depth, the multiplicity of meanings, and the condensation and intensification of a dream . . . as we, like Ida, enter the underworld of the goblins' cave, where what is outer becomes inner, and where what is lost is found.

Outside over There is the first of Sendak's works to be published and distributed as both a children's and an adult book. This is as it should be, for Sendak has always had the uncanny ability of making us, as adults, reexperience the way a child experiences his or her earliest emotions, reawakening in us our own childhoods. As Runge once said: "We must become children again if we wish to achieve the best." And in *Outside over There* Maurice Sendak has achieved the best.

You once said: "My stories come in bits and pieces of memories that don't seem related for a very long time. But something in me determines they will be related." So I wanted to ask you about certain of the elements that influenced you and which you transformed in Outside over There.

First, there was a children's book that I looked at when I was very young with a friend, a girl named Selma who lived next door. It was a book, which I haven't seen since, about a little girl in a rainstorm. Selma read better than I did, and as we went through the book together, I was riveted by the pictures, which were thirties-type illustrations. And I remember a very wet street and a little girl in a yellow slicker that was way too big for her, and her reflection was upside down in the rain (I recall that vividly)—you could see two of her. And she was very big and the wind blew up and it billowed her out and her umbrella went inside out and the sky was gray. . . . It either frightened me or excited me, but I've never lost the image of that child—that was the original Ida, whoever she is and whatever book that was. So it was almost an obsession, really, to recover that original child in that original book and do my own book about her. I didn't know why I had to do that, I just knew I had to.

Then there's the tiny Grimms' tale called "The Goblins" that you illustrated in The Juniper Tree—*it's less than two hundred words, and since it seems to be the "seed," so to speak for* Outside over There, *I'll quote it here in the translation by Lore Segal:*

> Once there was a mother and the goblins had stolen her child out of the cradle. In its place they laid a changeling with thick head and staring eyes who did nothing but eat and drink. In her misery, the woman went to ask her neighbor for advice. The neighbor told her to take the changeling into the kitchen, set him on the hearth, light a fire, and boil water in two eggshells. This would make the changeling laugh, and when a changeling laughs, that's the end of him.
>
> The woman did just what the neighbor told her, and as she was putting the eggshells full of water on the fire, the blockhead said:

"Now am I as old/As the western woods/But never heard it told that people cook water in eggshells," and he began to laugh and as he laughed there suddenly came a lot of little goblins who brought the right child and set it on the hearth and took their friends away with them.

It *is* the seed. The effect the story had on me was enormous, but I don't know why. And the illustration in *The Juniper Tree* for that story—the giant baby being *heaved* by those little goblins surrounding that great mound of flesh and that baby face staring out . . . somebody once wrote and said, I love the picture, but which baby is this—the normal baby or the changeling? And that was funny because you couldn't really tell—all babies are slightly idiotic and drooly-looking at the corner of the mouth—it might have been the changeling baby.

Sendak's illustration for "The Goblins" from *The Juniper Tree and Other Tales from Grimm*

And the reason the eggshells appear in *Outside over There* is mostly in homage to the original source: You know that you have a changeling after boiling water in an eggshell.

The folklorist Katharine Briggs says that eggshells are one of the main ingredients in almost all stories about changelings.

And the other is music. If you play an instrument and the baby begins to dance to it, you know it can't be your baby. And that's why Ida plays an instrument. The two ingredients that you check a changeling out with—music and eggshells—are both incorporated into my story. So I used all the inner material of the original source, the ur-text; *Outside over There* is my version of "The Goblins," that's all. But what we're missing here—and I can't give it to you because that's where Freud drew the curtain—is *why*: What were these things, what did they mean, that they had to be so obsessively pursued and riveted into a book?

What about Wilhelm Busch's Ice Peter, *in which the boy Peter falls into a frozen lake and turns to ice; and when he's thawing out, instead of becoming himself again, he dissolves into water—somewhat like the changeling and goblins in your work?*

I wasn't conscious of that. But I *was* conscious of the influence of one of my favorite childhood books, *Little Black Sambo*, in which the tigers, by running around the tree, melt into butter. I loved that. And here the children dissolve into the ether by dancing frantically—that's the only possible association. Well, maybe there's one with the witch in *The Wizard of Oz*, who, when they pour water on her, just melts and dissolves—I remember that scene as a child, her shrieking and going "Ahhhhhhahhhhh . . .". But those are the only two associations I can point to.

You've mentioned that the fact that there are five baby goblins in your book might have something to do with your recollection of the Dionne quintuplets.

Yes, but again, that's an unconscious thing. It was my sister who pointed out, when she looked at the page showing all five baby goblins, that it was just like the newspaper photographs showing all the quintuplets lolling around—you saw them every day in sort of

unwittingly sexy poses. And I guess that influenced part of the composition of the five babies, but then again there are five Wild Things
and there are five Sendaks—two parents and three children. I think
that if there are five members in your family, and you're a child, then
the number becomes important.

There are certain paintings and drawings that seem to have influenced
Outside over There. *One of them is, obviously,* The Hülsenbeck
Children *by Philipp Otto Runge, in which two older children, loom-
ing surrealistically above a picket fence, hold onto the handle of a
wheelbarrow in which is sitting an intensely staring baby clutching
onto a gigantic sunflower plant.*

My book jacket pays tribute to Runge's painting. Look at the fence,
look at the baby staring out and clutching part of the flower just the
way Runge's baby does. There's no question about that.

Writing about this painting, Robert Rosenblum, in his book Modern
Painting and the Northern Romantic Tradition: Friedrich to Rothko,
*speaks of the "red-cheeked faces of children looked at neither as little
adults nor as adorable pets, but as containers of natural mysteries."*

And that, too, I read after *Outside over There* was started, so it was
a great impetus—I felt I really had honed into Runge, and it was
being confirmed by what Rosenblum was saying.

I sense that William Blake, too, was an important model for you.

Before I started working on the paintings for *Outside over There,* I'd
done pencil drawings that were so finished and powerful that I wasn't
sure how to reconceive them in terms of color. And I really wasn't involved so much with Runge at that point. So I needed a clue—a color
clue. I found the first in the film version of *The Marquise of O.,*
which was perfect in terms of time and setting . . . all the greens and
mauves excited me. And the second was a visit to the Morgan Library,
where I sat and looked through a magnifying glass at Blake's illustrations for Milton's "L'Allegro" and "Il Penseroso," a suite of illustrations
that I've always loved. At that period in Blake's life he was using an
extremely controlled amount of colored stippling . . . like Seurat,
though it only seems that way under magnification. And I simply
grabbed hold of what Blake was doing technically, and decided that

I'd take a brush and, with a very fine infinitude of points of color, I'd stipple faces, clothing, everything. And that was a way of getting myself going.

So the first illustrations I did are very stippled, and only after I'd gotten two or three pictures done did I start to relax, and I began to look at Runge, among others. The style of *Outside over There* changes almost from page to page—it becomes much more secure and much more purely mine. But the early illustrations are very strongly influenced by the stylistic effects of those particular William Blake pictures.

The drawing of Ida playing her magic horn reminded me immediately of Mahler's song cycle The Youth's Magic Horn.

Absolutely. That piece is based on songs collected during the same period in which the Grimms were collecting their tales, and for a similar reason: to get them all down before they disappeared. And it's my favorite period—the time of the Grimms, Brentano, a little bit of Novalis, and Kleist . . . though Kleist is slightly later. And I love the title *Das Knaben Wunderhorn*, and I love the songs—they are my favorite works by Mahler—so uninflated and unpretentious. . . . And, of course, in that list I forgot to mention Mozart!

I was just going to say that the overriding and underlying influence on Outside over There *is Mozart—the presiding muse of the book— whose silhouetted figure we see near the end, sitting in his little wooded cottage.*

In some way, *Outside over There* is my attempt to make concrete my love of Mozart, and to do it as authentically and honestly in regard to his time as I could conceive it, so that every color, every shape is like part of his portrait. The book is a portrait of Mozart, only it has this form—commonly called the picture book. This was the closest I could get to what he looked like to me. It's my *imagining* of Mozart's life.

I believe in this book as though it were a factual thing that happened. I'm talking about a fantasy, of course, but I believe in it the way some people believe in spiritual things. When I was dreaming this book, what I was imagining was the most real thing I've ever felt. It seemed as if nothing that would occur after this book would be as real or as intensely wonderful. That's why when I had done the sets and costumes for *The Magic Flute*—my other Mozart project—I cried during the performance because I couldn't believe that I had been in the position of working on this opera, it was almost too much. But everything concerning Mozart is almost too much.

I know that your set for The Magic Flute *featured a cave; and in* Outside over There *we find a cave, too.*

The whole production of the opera begins in the Queen of the Night's cave—it's like the bowels of the earth. Tamino is lying down and looking up at the sky. But then everything really occurs at the bottom of the world. My view of *The Magic Flute* is that when Tamino and Papageno depart on their journey, they may leave in a balloon, but it's not because they're traveling a great distance, they're just going two seconds away, as in a dream. In fact, everything happens where everyone is, in the Queen of the Night's cave—it's just that the scene changes. Things keep on unfolding, but you haven't moved, you're always in the same place, you're in your head. But it *is* an immense journey that they're taking . . . of another nature.

The philosopher Heraclitus said: "The way up and way down are one and the same." I imagine he was talking about psychic space—and this seems to be the space of Outside over There, *where up and down, high and low, and inside and outside appear to exchange identities.*

I may be pushing it too far, but in a way the book is like a mirror reflection: it's called *Outside over There,* but if you hold the title up to the mirror, so to speak, it says *Inside in Here.* You're right. And the whole construction of the writing, which is what I'm so proud of, gives the sense of being written backwards. Some people will be disturbed by the construction of the sentences—they may be anxious to put commas in places like "Ida mad"—but the words are going their own strange route, and it's critical to the book. I don't want to give away what I know it's all about (because in a sense I do know what it's all about), but one of the clues is to reverse everything that happens. I mean, Ida has to reverse things: Only when her father tells her what to do in his song ["If Ida backwards in the rain/would only turn around again/and catch those goblins with a tune/she'd spoil their kidnap honeymoon!"] does she turn right side round and begin to solve the dilemma. Until then she's done everything wrong side round.

Selma G. Lanes tells of your discovering one day that the letters ida, *when reversed, form part of the name* Sadie, *the name of your mother.*

Yes. And that fact both chilled and delighted me, and verified forever the devious machinations of the unconscious.

So, halfway through the book, Ida, instead of flying up, goes in the opposite direction.

Yes. By going backwards she made a serious mistake. She went backwards out the window into outside over there.

But how else, if you want to go back in time, can you go unless you go backwards?

Well, you've got to puzzle that one out. Nothing is as easy as it looks. Backwards has its price, even though that seems to be the right direction.

I suppose I felt that she was trying to get back in time *as well as trying to get to some* place.

That could be. But one has to be careful that in one's eagerness to pursue the meaning of a dream one doesn't tread the dream to nothing. . . . You see, my point in this book is that nothing is as simple as it seems—what else have I learned from therapy and from all these difficult years? When you say that something is happening in the book, that may be true, but something else is occurring at that moment, too. And the book is full of choices—is *that* why that happened? Or is *that* why that happened? Or, in fact, is it *all* of those reasons why that happened?

There seem to be several actions occurring at the same time—for instance, while Ida is doing something, the goblins are planning their kidnapping. Things happen contrapuntally.

Yes, there are two stories going on—Ida's story and the baby's story. Anyone who thinks the baby is a passive, inert creature doesn't appreciate or acknowledge what infants are capable of feeling. There are two separate books here. So when you know that, you know that anything that's happening is not happening just to one person but to two people, and it complicates things.

Couldn't one imagine that Ida and the baby are two parts of the same person?

In this case I would say that there are two stories and two people and not simply the psyche of one person. There really are two distinct cases and two defined histories and experiences being explored here . . . and they both conclude in a different way, even though the book concludes in a single way.

But at the end you get a feeling of stability, of being back home.

Yes, that is what was specifically intended; however, there's another way of interpreting the end, too. A friend of mine who read the book said: "I can't stand it, I mean, are you trying to tell me that this is a happy ending when the father's away somewhere and he's writing this letter that just dumps everything on Ida? I mean, what kind of happy ending is that?" "But who said it was a happy ending?" I replied. I'm not saying my friend is right, I'm not admitting anything, but in fact it's interesting that my friend was offended by the father's letter. There's a certain irony there. The father's really assuming that a nine-year-old can take care of the baby and the mama. Is he suggesting that the mama can't?

I felt that, throughout the book, the mother wasn't really there and that Ida took on the mother's role.

Because her husband has left, the mother is lost in thought—maybe a bit melancholic—so she's of no help to Ida. But appearances aside, we are really looking at only a minute's worth of life. And if the mother is distracted for that minute, can we draw the conclusion that she's indifferent or comatose? Or isn't it just that she's unwittingly distracted, like any normal mother who, at any given moment of the day, gets distracted . . . and during that moment something happens to the child—bad luck, bad timing?
    My intention was to leave room for a break to occur: In every child's life it happens that at a critical moment the mother—unbeknownst to her that this *is* a critical moment—is inattentive to the

child. And the child is then given his or her opportunity to make out for him- or herself, because there's no mama there . . . and there's also the impulse in the child to *be* the mama anyway, to use this opportunity to see if he or she can do without her. So yes, at that moment Ida takes over for the mother, but that doesn't mean that that's a permanent state of being.

It's also interesting that Outside over There *is your first picture book in which you have a female as a protagonist—actually, two female protagonists.*

Everybody in the book is female. The father isn't there; and the mother, Ida, her sister, and all the goblins are girls. Look carefully: They're all female. It's a female world. And I don't know why that's so, but I just know it's as right as rain.

I should say that I don't know how you could avoid dealing with the things you've been talking to me about. I mean, you can't talk about this book in terms of its plot—like, isn't it interesting that Ida goes out a window? *Outside over There* isn't about a plot—anybody who comes to it with any degree of seriousness knows that the book is a metaphor for something else. It's not a terrific story, it's, not a "good read": There's something else happening here, and the story is the mere flesh that covers the bone; it's the bone that's interesting.

You once pointed out that the German word Reise *signified both a physical and emotional "journey." And I wanted to compare and contrast the three "journeys" that take place in and make up your three most important picture books. In* Where the Wild Things Are, *Max contacts his feelings of anger and loneliness as he travels to the land of the Wild Things. In* In the Night Kitchen, *Mickey explores the feelings of his unrepressed body as he journeys in the world of the Night Kitchen. And now in* Outside over There, *Ida and the baby experience feelings of loss—the loss of identity and of dissolution—only to recover both themselves and each other.*

My association with *Outside over There* is just the opposite of yours. To me, the dissolution is the eradication and *conquest* of fear and depression, of hallucination, of obsession, of neurosis—breaking through and making it literally disappear by one's own act; and by one's own perseverance and attempt one destroys an obsession. But that's only *my* interpretation—my "journey," so to speak.

This is Ida's story you're referring to.

Exactly. That's her story. The baby's story has nothing to do with the dissolution of anything. The baby has another story in this book . . . maybe it's not there, but I think it is.

Which you're not going to talk about.

Illustration from *Outside over There* by Maurice Sendak. Copyright © 1981 by Maurice Sendak. Reprinted by permission of Harper & Row, Publishers, Inc.

Right [laughing]. . . . But coming back to Ida—that picture of her by the water. She's so big she almost bursts out of the frame. I think of her as Judith with the head of Holofernes; she's a gigantic Amazon, she's Penthesilea. Ida has an enormous victory then—at that moment something extraordinary happens to her, not to the baby. Something else happens to the baby.

In a letter you once wrote about In the Night Kitchen, *you said: "It comes from the direct middle of me, and it hurt like hell extracting it. Yes, indeed, very birth-delivery type pains, and it's as regressed as I imagine I can go." But in* Outside over There *you seem to have gone back even further.*

Absolutely. It reminds me of that awkward scene in *Altered States*—which could have been an interesting movie—where at the end the hero's determination is to go back and go back and go back to the very origins of man. And he does, he almost succeeds, he turns into . . . I don't know *what* that psychedelic imagery on the screen was supposed to be, but he looks as if he's a fetus, a cell, a sperm . . . he's going and going, and his girl friend sees this happening and she puts her hand into the void and pulls him back. And then, in the end, he accepts the fact that you'd best not look, because if you look that far into it you can never come back. (Kleist, for example, couldn't disconnect himself from looking; once he looked, he got sucked right into the black hole!) And that was like a cartoon version of what I think I went through in this book.

It sounds as if you allowed Ida and the baby to go very far back.

Yes. Meaning me, too. And the way Pamina in *The Magic Flute* says to Tamino just before the trial scene (and remember, she's been such a frightened girl, not knowing whether she's going to live or die, not knowing why Tamino hasn't talked to her, not knowing whether or not he loves her anymore): Put your hand on my shoulder, even roses have thorns, my love will guide us through.

And why am I bringing this up? Well, she's almost lost her life, I mean she's nearly committed suicide. And who brings her back from the edge of the grave? Three genie . . . three children, three babies, three infants. But more important to this discussion than the fact that they're like the goblins or that they have infant bodies is the fact that it is almost as if Pamina's infant self or some part of her had remembered something crucial to living. But when she comes back after having been near death—having been revivified by three genie, three infant spirits—she is more poised than she has ever been before in the whole opera, and she says: I will lead you through the thorny roses. I mean, she has that absolute assurance. And why? Because she has been somewhere, somewhere that was appalling. She's looked at something that's nearly cost her her life, and she's come back, barely; but from having looked and just come back she has turned into the great woman she is at the end of that opera. So you can come to a kind of reductive assumption that to be that kind of person you have to go back, you have to look, and you probably nearly have to die. You have to take the risk of dying.

In a famous letter that Mozart wrote to his father in 1787, he says: "As Death, properly understood, is the true goal of our life, I have made myself so familiar these past years with this truest and best friend of mankind, that his face not only frightens me no more, but is of the greatest comfort and consolation to me! And I thank God for having bestowed on me the opportunity (you know what I mean) of learning to know it as the key to our happiness." And it's been suggested that that parenthetical phrase "you know what I mean" refers to a Freemasonic initiation ritual—a mimed death and resurrection—that Mozart underwent.

Yes: "You know what I mean" because if he said what he meant, Maria Theresa [the Austrian empress who abhorred Masonic ideas] would have come and torn it out of the letter. He couldn't have put it in words . . . And—I know this letter very well!—Mozart goes on in it to say (and I'm paraphrasing): If you think I'm fearful of knowing about your illness and your possible death (Mozart's father had been ill, had not written, and did, in fact, die a month later), don't spare me, because I understand these things. And he continues: There is not a night that I do not go to sleep and think I might not wake in the morning. And yet there is no one who will say that your son is a morbid person—I am the most cheerful person in the world—but knowing this makes me cheerful.

I know that you understand what he's saying very well.

Of course. If I had died of a heart attack in 1967, my career would have ended with *Higgelty Piggelty Pop!*—a book that's all about death. And even in a comic work like *Really Rosie*, all that the characters talk about is death—the whole thing is a theme and variations on how many ways you can die.

In Kleist, I've noticed, when people are confronted with an overwhelming situation they faint or swoon (think of "The Marquise of O" or "The Earthquake in Chile"). And, in a sense, this blacking out is a form of dying. Something happens which is so terrible—it's like a Gorgon's head—that when you look at it, it kills you. But you wake up as if into another life, refreshed—you wake up better for having died.

Now, look at the first scene of *The Magic Flute*: Tamino is struggling with the monster—he's choking with horror and fear—and he faints. But then he's rescued, he wakes up in this new world where there's new adventure, where he's now a sexual male, in a sense—he's able to fall in love with a portrait—suddenly everything is galvanized because of this. And in the very first scene of the next act, Pamina is being dragged in by Monostatos, she's screaming, and as he approaches to molest her, she faints. And she wakes up to the knowledge that there's a prince who loves her, rejoicing at the sound of the word "love." Suddenly she's very savvy about something she didn't know minutes before.

So you have these two pendent scenes showing the hero and the heroine confronted with very sexual images—the serpent and Monostatos. . . . Of course, anyone who doesn't like Freud will take a hammer to you for saying things like this, because it *is* reductive, but there's some truth in it, too. The point is, however, that you have to die in a metaphoric sense.

"And whosoever will lose his life for my sake shall find it."

I'd forgotten about that. And I know I'm not saying anything new. Yes, in a sense, that's the beautiful point of it all.

You once said: "I live inside the picture book; it's where I fight all my battles, and where, hopefully, I win my wars." And you really seem to have fought your battle in Outside over There—*just as Tamino and Pamina fought theirs.*

I don't believe in miracles—I'm a pretty cynical person, and I have no religious faith at all—but the fact that I did *The Magic Flute* right after *Outside over There* is a miracle. It's like some kind of present to me for having been brave, it's my medal of honor. Because the two go together—it sounds so vainglorious to suggest that this book is even anything like *The Magic Flute* . . . God knows, that's not what I'm saying. But thematically and in terms of what the opera means to me—just to me—is what *Outside over There* is.

They're both rites, in a way.

I've taken many things from the opera for my book: the test of air—Ida floats; the test of fire—Ida underground; the test of water—when the goblins dissolve: These are all of my variants on *The Magic Flute*. *Outside over There*, of course, goes back to the 1930s, when I was sitting on a stoop with a little girl named Selma, so that everything else that has grown like Topsy over the years has been added to the project. But that I started to conceive of the book and that I would associate it with my favorite work of art and then, by luck, became a designer for a production of that particular work of art . . . it is incredible that it's all just a coincidence.

We always end up with music, Maurice. And recently I came across a passage from one of Kleist's letters that I wanted to read to you, since it points to something that I think connects all of your work. "I regard [music]," Kleist writes, "as the root or rather—to put it more scientifically—as the algebraic formula of all the other arts; and just as we already have a writer [Goethe?] . . . who has based all his ideas about art on colors, so I, from early youth, have based all my general ideas about the art of literature on tones. I believe that the figured bass holds implications of the utmost importance and relevance to the art of literature." And, I would add, to your art as well.

That's an extraordinary statement. I don't know for sure what Kleist really meant, but I personally think of music as a kind of preverbal state of being—it brings you back to a primeval time of life. It's just

Sendak's curtain for Mozart's *Magic Flute*. Photograph by Gregory Heisler

that where he says "figured bass," I'd say "preverbal." For music is a kind of mystic babble that we all understand now because we all understood it once. Most of us have more trouble with poetry, because poetry is language that is trying to re-create the babble, whereas music just does so by its very nature. So you employ music because it is bone close to you, it's your primal state of being. It's a language you once understood thoroughly . . . as a child, as a baby.

WILLIAM STEIG
AND HIS PATH

© PHOTOGRAPH BY JOAN C. BARKER

When he was a little boy, William Steig's oldest brother, Irwin, taught him how to draw a smile and a frown:

"I heard a child, a little under four years old," wrote Charles Darwin in 1872, "when asked what was meant by being in good spirits, answer, 'It is laughing, talking, and kissing.' It would be difficult to give a truer and more practical definition. A man in this state holds his

"Weeping" and "laughing" photographs from Charles Darwin's *The Expression of the Emotions in Men and Animals,* 1872

body erect, his head upright, and his eyes open. There is no drooping of the features, and no contraction of the eyebrows. . . . The whole expression of a man in good spirits is exactly the opposite of that of one suffering from sorrow."

"I draw those same emotions that Darwin studied in *The Expression of the Emotions in Man and Animals*," William Steig says. "We're reading each other's faces all the time—it's a natural interest. We're constantly looking at another person to see what he or she is feeling or pretending to feel." And by attending to the expressions of the emotions ("Attention—perhaps the most wonderful of all the wondrous powers of the mind," wrote Darwin), Steig, with his smile and frown as starting points, has shaped a career as one of the finest cartoonists and creators of children's books of our time.

Mama, Mama!   it's me again.

From *The Rejected Lovers*. © William Steig

Now seventy-five [1983], Steig didn't turn to children's literature until he was sixty years old. Throughout the preceding four decades —and continuing to the present—he was contributing regularly to *The New Yorker* (he celebrated the fiftieth anniversary of his association with the magazine in 1979) and was working on ten of his twelve collections of cartoons. The most remarkable of these—*About People* (1939), *The Lonely Ones* (1942, reissued 1970), *All Embarrassed* (1944), and *The Rejected Lovers* (1951, reissued 1973)— present faces with sardonic grins, helpless grimaces, and embittered smiles, as if smile and frown had intermixed and had become inextricably locked together in oxymoronic perplexity. In this world of characterological distress, each of Steig's figures seems to be an almost allegorical representation of an unhappy body and consciousness—the actual implication of these drawings being that a happy consciousness is a function of a happy body and incapable of existing independently of a fulfilled sense of life. As Steig later wrote in the preface to *Dreams of Glory* (1953): "I believe that people are basically good and beautiful, and that neurosis is the biggest obstacle to peace and happiness. In my symbolical drawings I try to make neurotic behavior more manifest."

At first glance, however, many observers assumed that famous cartoons such as "I Mind My Own Business," "People Are No Damn Good," and "I Do Not Forget To Be Angry"—included in *The Lonely Ones* and widely reproduced for many years on paper napkins, coasters, and ashtrays—were simply scornful tauntings of neurotic behavior. Many people, moreover, expected and wanted sickness to be made fun of. And because Steig embodied, rather than exploited, this sickness, his work was often thought of as being cruel. In fact, the intense and expressive lines of his "symbolical drawings" allowed Steig instinctively to discover and render the frozen movements of suffering humanity; what people often took to be negative statements about existence were actually brilliantly acute revelations and mirrorings of armored consciousness.

Unbeknownst to Steig, the psychiatrist Wilhelm Reich had also, in the twenties and thirties, been observing and analyzing the distorted expression of the emotions in human beings. And in *Character Analysis*, as if to comment on Steig's cartoon figures, Reich wrote:

> When, for example, the armoring of the oral zone has been sufficiently loosened to release a suppressed impulse to cry, while the neck and chest armorings are still untouched, we observe how the lower musculature of the face takes on the expression of wanting to cry but not being able to. The expression of being on the verge of tears is transformed into a hateful grin of the mouth-chin zone. It is an expression of desperation, of extreme frustration. All this can be summarized in the following formula: AS SOON AS THE MOVEMENT EXPRESSING SURRENDER IS OBSTRUCTED BY AN ARMOR BLOCK, THE IMPULSE TO SURRENDER IS TRANSFORMED INTO DESTRUCTIVE RAGE.

In Steig's first published collection, *Man About Town* (1932), for example—a series of his earliest social realist-looking cartoons—we see a doctor looking smugly at a V.D. patient, a bum ordering around a humiliated waiter, a father with six kids in a room telling one of them: "Don't bother me! I don't know nothing about sex!" and scores of litigious husbands and wives, masters and servants. Simply, *Man About Town* is, among other things, an American rendering of the powerful critique of compulsive marriage, the authoritarian family, and the pandemic sense of social powerlessness and sexual misery that Reich had observed in Vienna during the twenties, and about which he wrote in *The Sexual Revolution*. It was not until 1946, however, that the artist first met the psychiatrist, becoming his patient and, later, his collaborator and friend. Rarely has a deeper affinity between a psychologist and an artist existed than between Wilhelm Reich and William Steig. ("Real scientific activity," Steig wrote in 1952, "is of the same order as real artistic activity. It arrives at its truths—its *creations*—by reenacting the movements of nature.") For, working independently, and unknown to each other, both Reich and Steig seemed to be connected by the same concerns, the same focus of attention.

Persecuted and slandered during his life and forced into exile several times (he settled in the United States in 1939), Wilhelm Reich was eventually attacked by the American Psychiatric Association and the American Medical Association for his cancer research and treatments. In 1956 he was prosecuted by the Food and Drug Administration, which ordered the destruction of his orgone accumulators (devices made of alternating nonmetallic—e.g., Cellotex, wood—and metallic—e.g., fine steel wool, galvanized sheet iron—materials that, according to Reich, accumulate orgone energy—a universal energy which, Reich asserted, was demonstrable both in the living organism and in the atmosphere). Outrageously, his books were ordered to be burnt. He died of a heart attack in Lewisburg Penitentiary, Pennsylvania, in 1957.

Throughout his career, Reich made a number of far-reaching, still-uncorroborated claims in the fields of physiology, sexology, biology, chemistry, meteorology, ecology, physics, and astronomy. Although they were often only grudgingly acknowledged, he also made many contributions in the same areas. For those who are unfamiliar with the scope of Reich's activities and concerns, it may be useful to quote from David Boadella's fair-minded, comprehensive *Wilhelm Reich: The Evolution of His Work*, at the conclusion of which the author clearly sums up Reich's development and accomplishments:

> Reich had studied his energy first as the libido and had characterized the condition in which one was able to surrender to the flow of energy in pleasurable, outgoing, contactful feelings in his

term "orgastic potency." When the flow was blocked a stasis set in that was the energy source of the neurosis. In his character-analytic theory he had followed the antithesis between the primary drives of the self-regulated person and the destructive secondary drives that were pent-up behind the rigid armoring of the character-neurotic. He had followed the social implication of expressing productive energies in creative work with his concept of "work-democracy," and had diagnosed the social havoc that arises when productivity is thwarted in his analysis of Fascism and the exploration of the cultural pathology that he called the "emotional plague."

In his biological work he had pursued the life-energy functions as they worked through the expansive, parasympathetic processes, and had observed the connection between contractive, sympathetic processes and illness. As a therapist he had witnessed for thirty years how skillful work on the tense constrictions of the muscular armor will set free the involuntary vegetative currents that he measured on his oscillograph and believed were electrical. The pursuit of these currents took him to the realm of the microscopic. The blood picture revealed the same antitheses: healthy tissue disintegrated into vigorous, luminating vesicles, unhealthy tissue broke up into shrunken microscopic forms that he termed "T-bacilli." His work encompassed equally the pleasurable energetic contact between mother and infant that he recognized as the foundation of all later emotional health; and the biopathic illnesses in which energy pulsation in the body was deeply disturbed, withdrawn, dammed up, and immobilized.

In the atmosphere he discovered a pulsating energy form that was life-enhancing and promoted hydration in body tissues. In the presence of noxious pollutants of various kinds, the atmospheric energy became stagnant and a source of illness. He followed the process of "atmospheric self-regulation" that was responsible for the natural rhythms of weather and studied the atmospheric "armor"— the immobilized Dor layers—that he held contributory to desert formation and decay.

At the end of his life he experienced in his own person the battle between creative and destructive processes. He fought back with great courage against physical illness and a worsening heart condition, aggravated by relentless belittling of his achievements. He retained his rationality and his sanity and pursued the truths of his research for decades after rumor had it that he was crazy, was in a mental hospital, and so forth. In the end paranoia did begin to eat into him with the insidiousness of a mental cancer. His grandiose feelings in the last few years were an inflammatory defence against the crippling cold of the world's rejection and an example of the very energy processes he studied.

Perhaps, because of Reich, men will find it easier to make that basic choice that governs every act, in every area of human conduct: creation or destruction?

Inspired by Reich's fortitude and ideas, William Steig irreversibly chose the path of creation. (With the nuclear clock of the *Bulletin of the Atomic Scientists* standing at a few minutes before midnight, the choice for everyone is even more importunate today.) As he wrote in "Some Notes on Art Inspired by Reich" (published in the *Orgone Energy Bulletin* in January, 1952):

> Life is CREATION—the ceaseless movement of cosmic *creative* orgone energy weaving the universe. We, being nothing but vessels of cosmic orgone energy, continually, inevitably create—or we die. We create pies, gestures, chairs, houses, thoughts, songs, pictures, ourselves, our societies—and when we create without impediment, we feel the wonder that always accompanies flowing creation.

"I remember how I felt when I wrote those 'Notes,' " William Steig told me when I first visited him and his wife, Jeanne, in their Kent, Connecticut, home in early 1979. "I was in Maine, it was the summer of 1951, Reich was very inspiring, and I felt very good.

"I first met Reich in 1946. I had been going to see various doctors (one guy recommended cream mixed with beer!) because I'd gotten very sick with meningitis. Then one day I ran into a woman I knew who looked marvelous, and she told me she was in therapy with Doctor Wolfe, a disciple of Dr. Reich. I thought it must be good because I'd never seen her look that well, so I went out and bought *The Function of the Orgasm*, stayed up all night reading it, and the next day I got in touch with Reich. And when I saw him, he told me he couldn't treat me because I was too run down. So he got me an accumulator, and I sat in it over a period of a week before anything happened—I started tingling all over and became beet red— and then began therapy with him that lasted for about a year.

"The beginning of my treatment with Reich consisted mostly of conversation. He didn't do much physical manipulation with me, though he prodded me in a couple of places; he mostly concentrated on breathing. He had a sense of humor, too. At one point he had a little pile of pennies on his table, and he said he'd give me a penny for every breath I'd take.

"Reich could tell what was wrong just by looking at you. One day I sat at home doodling—I was doodling clowns—and when I went to see Reich later that afternoon, the first thing he said was, 'You're a clown today.' Instantly. And I remember his telling me that he thought I'd become a cartoonist because of my horror of what I saw on faces. That's what he thought.

"My last several sessions with him were all laughing sessions. He kept making me laugh, and the laugh went further and further down. He referred to me as a melancholic and said that if I didn't go through with this I'd end up in the booby hatch—he felt I needed to laugh a lot. I was a real depressive. I was so depressed sometimes that I didn't even know where I was, stumbling down the street.

"At one point in therapy, he said, 'Steig, I just can't do anything with you, you're hopeless.' So I got up and started to dress—he was testing me, rejecting me. And when I was half-dressed he said that we'd give it another whirl. I went back to the couch, and all sorts of things began to happen: my hands became paralyzed, I felt shrunken, and he asked me, 'Where are you?' And I said, 'I'm in the garbage,' and then I went into convulsions. It was a big breakthrough.

"I was in my forties when I went into therapy, and at one moment I was crying in the voice of an infant—I couldn't believe it. Reich could make you relive early experiences, like suckling. I didn't do it, it just happened itself, involuntarily. And that reliving of ancient experiences is strange: You know you're a forty-year-old man and you're doing one-year-old things. It's all locked in there.

"Reich was helping people and giving all this important knowledge to the world and had one accusation after another thrown at him, so he may have sometimes gotten irrationally angry. There were a lot of people spying on him. But, as someone has pointed out, it's not paranoia if you wind up in jail. If Reich had defended himself in a sneaky way, if he had used tricky legal devices, he could have stayed out of jail. I collected money for him when he was in trouble—from ex-patients and people like that. And I delivered some mathematical formulas to the C.I.A. for him, but I never knew what happened to them. He trusted me.

"At the end of his life he speculated as to whether his true father might have been a spaceman. I was bothered about how people would understand that. I think that he was saying that since he was so different from everybody else, he didn't feel he belonged on this planet. People said he was crazy before he ever said anything like that. People always called him crazy, but at different points down the road,

I DO NOT FORGET TO BE ANGRY   PEOPLE ARE NO DAMN GOOD   I MIND MY OWN BUSINESS

From *The Lonely Ones.* © William Steig

depending on how far they could follow him. Reich was immensely sane, and fought a tremendous battle almost single-handedly, managing somehow to keep a clear head in spite of unbelievable harassment.

"He was a remarkable person. You knew he was a great man as soon as you were in his presence. It was his whole bearing. He'd enter a room from the back, and everyone would turn around because something was happening there. I'm sure that the things I learned from Reich appear in what I do—I didn't speak of 'energy,' for instance, before I knew him. But mostly I think these things happen because you observe what goes on around you.

"After I became acquainted with his work, I realized I had seen a few truths in my own work. And I was flattered that one of my books, *The Lonely Ones*, was on Reich's table when I first went to see him. I had seen a little bit of the truth that Reich exposed for all to see."

Shortly after Steig finished his therapy with Reich, the latter asked him if he would do the drawings for his recently completed *Listen, Little Man!* ("It was sort of a present from him to me—that's the way I felt about it," Steig comments.) Published in 1948, this acerbic manifesto at once excoriates, often with ferocious ill-temper, the pathologically resigned, pathic, self-enslaved common man ("I've said it before and I say it again: you feel wretched and small, and stinking and mentally mutilated; you feel impotent, tense, rigid, lifeless, and empty. . . . You don't know the meaning of love") and at the same time promulgates, with almost Dostoyevskian fervor, Reich's frustrated hopes for and belief in the continually thwarted possibilities of humanity ("It is said that culture requires slaves. I say that no cultured society can be built with slaves. This terrible twentieth century has made all cultural theories from Plato down seem ridiculous. *Little man, there has never been a human culture*").

Steig's accompanying cartoons, drawn in the style of *About Peo-*

ple and *The Lonely Ones*, are perfectly attuned to the deep anger and love of Reich's polemic. As in the greatest weddings of picture and text, in which writer and artist seem to share the same perceptual apparatus and nervous system, Steig serves the words faithfully as he illuminates them in his idiosyncratic style—the crossing of these two creators' paths revealing an unusual harmony of purpose, sympathy, and understanding.

"Living is creating," Steig wrote in "Some Notes." "We move about in relation to an environment; and we must sense and feel—and being 'conscious' animals we must 'know'—if we are to remain fluid and mobile. An alive man is a proving-ground for all that goes on about him; he is in a constant creative activity of 'sizing things up,' re-creating them in his own body. He 'imitates' and he rehearses, as he moves. He imitates the path he is about to take, the branch he is about to bend under, the person he is dealing with, the cloud his truth-loving wonder turns upon."

As a cartoonist Steig has always confronted the various manifestations of armored human life, depicting those epiphanic moments and situations that reflect the ways in which people stunt the growth of both themselves and their children: "Your first gifts are fetters," Rousseau wrote in *Emile* (a work that foreshadows many of Reich's own ideas), "your first treatment, torture. . . . One would think they were afraid the child should look as if it were alive." And in *The Agony in the Kindergarten* (1950), Steig illustrated the words of parental guards ("He's not very B-R-I-G-H-T"; "Whatever I ask him to do he does just the opposite") with the corresponding gestures and grimaces of their prisoner offspring—one of the most powerful of the drawings showing the face of an enraged, screaming mother with a scared little child in her open mouth. (As the Old Testament tells us: "The fathers have eaten sour grapes, and the children's teeth are set on edge.")

In *Small Fry* (1951) and *Dreams of Glory* (1953), however, Steig created and gave a group of mostly rambunctious young boys—looking a bit like Palmer Cox's Brownies—their head, drawing them at their games, their scrapes, their adventures, their fantasies. He was imitating the path he was about to take. But it wasn't until he started making children's books in the late sixties that we saw Steig (the name means "path" in German) truly heading down the path of "truth-loving wonder." And if, in his earlier work, Steig embodied

Illustration from *Dominic*

the characterological attributes of unhappy individuals, in his children's books he created and tested the possibilities of an unarmored life. For it is axiomatic that one has to be in touch with one's unarmored feelings to create lasting, meaningful, and enjoyable books for children.

"The expression of the armored organism," Reich stated in *Character Analysis*, "is one of 'holding back.' . . . Literally defined, the word 'emotion' means 'moving outwards' or 'pushing out'." It is interesting that one of Steig's cartoons for *Listen, Little Man!* simply contrasts these two antithetical character attitudes in the figures of a walled-in human and a lively, unbounded dog. And it is this dog that seems to have jumped out of the cartoon into Steig's *Dominic* (1972), one of the most inspired and inspiring children's books of recent times.

"Dominic was a lively one, always up to something" is the way the text begins. After picking up his piccolo, bandanna, and an assortment of hats, we see the hound hero taking off on his life journey. Meeting a witch-alligator at the crossroads, she advises him:

> "That road there on the right goes nowhere. There's not a bit of magic up that road, no adventure, no surprise, nothing to discover or wonder at. Even the scenery is humdrum. You'd soon grow much too introspective. You'd take to daydreaming and tail-twiddling, get

absent-minded and lazy, forget where you are and what you're about, sleep more than one should, and be wretchedly bored. Furthermore, after a while, you'd reach a dead end and you'd have to come all that dreary way back to right here where we're standing now, only it wouldn't be now, it would be some woefully wasted time later."

Needless to say, Dominic chooses the path of adventure and wonder.

At the beginning of his travels, he meets a dying one hundred-year-old pig named Bartholomew Badger ("As Mr. Badger paused to rest, Dominic tried to visualize him as a baby, but he could only imagine a tiny pig looking old and wrinkled") who bequeaths to the dog a fortune in precious jewels, as well as a special golden piccolo. After burying Mr. Badger ("His turn was over. Dominic's turn was still at the beginning," he meditates), Dominic "had to get moving."

With the help of a wasp, he wards off the first of many attacks by the dreaded, rapacious Doomsday Gang (consisting of weasels, rats, ferrets, and foxes—some of whom look surprisingly like the woman investigator in *Listen, Little Man!* and various other mean-spirited Steig cartoon figures). After his victory he goes swimming in a beautiful pool under a waterfall, "enjoying the fluid feeling of union with the cool liquid," and then meets a jackass named Elijah Hogg, who agrees to carry Dominic's heavy chest of jewels. But after a short haul, Elijah decides to return to his grazing: "He intended to live near that field of alfalfa for as many days as it took him to eat it, not rushing to finish, and indulging in all the daydreaming and star-gazing that such work required."

Next, Dominic encounters a turtle named Lemuel Wallaby, who describes his encounters with the Doomsday Gang:

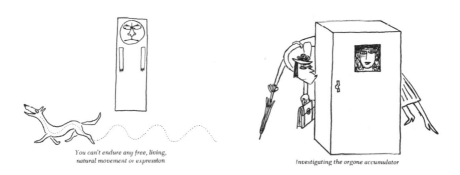

You can't endure any free, living, natural movement or expression

Investigating the orgone accumulator

Illustrations by Steig for Wilhelm Reich's *Listen, Little Man!*

"I know *them*," said the turtle. "Everybody hereabouts knows them. But they're no problem for me. They turn up, I go into my shell. They can rap on it all they want, I don't pay attention. Flip me over, I just lie on my back. After a while they get fed up with nothing happening and leave. Sooner or later help comes along and I get straightened out and go on about my business. Too bad you don't have a shell like me."

Dominic didn't understand the turtle's point of view. If he had a shell, he wouldn't hide in it. Whenever there was trouble, his philosophy was to go right out and meet it at least halfway. And he was surprised that anyone should react otherwise.

Lemuel agrees to carry Dominic and his treasure ("How far?" asked Lemuel. "Reasonably far," said Dominic. "And if you like my company, you can continue after that"). But the dog gets fed up with the turtle's slow pace, and again takes off on his own.

Dominic and the Doomsday Gang, from *Dominic*

Soon, he meets Barney Swain, a love-stricken boar ("Oh, she's wonderful! Such bristles. Such snow-white teeth. Such warm brown eyes") whose wedding plans have been aborted by the Doomsday Gang's pilfering of all his money. Dominic, of course, gives Barney some of his jewels, then goes down the road to save a goose named Matilda Fox, hanging upside down in a Doomsday trap. She invites him to visit her home, where, after wonderful meals, he lies dreaming in the hammock or sitting by the pond talking to Mrs. Fox and her children. When he asks her which she likes to do best, walk, swim, or fly, she answers: "Walking is good for thinking. And different kinds of walking are good for different kinds of thinking. . . . Swimming is not as good for thinking as walking is, but swimming is wonderful for woolgathering. I love to float with the current of the stream. . . . It's like being back in the egg, floating without a care in benign albumen. . . . Flying is pure delight unless you are being chased by birds of prey. There's a rhythm to flying and it's the rhythm of the universe." (It is interesting that the Hindu word for wild gander, *hamsa*—*ham*=I, *sa*=that—refers to the spirit that animates the universe—"the ultimate, transcendent yet imminent ground of all being" —and is therefore perfectly applicable to a creature that can live on three levels: water, earth, and air.) And when he decides to continue

on his path, Dominic gives Mrs. Fox the remainder of his fortune, saying: "I really have no use for wealth. I'm young, I'm free, and I have a God-given nose to guide me through life."

Continuing on his way, Dominic meets up with a colony of rabbits who beseech him to become their protector: "But the rabbits' fearfulness made him uncomfortable. In a way, he respected the members of the Doomsday Gang more than he respected the rabbits. The Doomsday Gang were sometimes cowards too, but they also had plenty of brass." After trapping several members of the Gang with the help of the artist-mouse Manfred Lyon's *trompe l'oeil* paintings, the rabbits try to "rehabilitate" their tormentors and to teach them "the unwisdom of evil and gradually to inculcate into them sentiments of pity, mercy, charity, and love." But the Gang members think that "such decency was based only on fear," and make their escape.

Next, Steig sets a moonlit scene—a true midsummer night's dream:

> All moonlight is magical and puts us under a spell, but some moonlight nights move our tides more than others and even make us a little bit daffy. This was such a night. It was out of the question for Dominic to go to sleep, though it was his usual hour for retiring. He wasn't tired. The night and everything under its influence was alive, awake, and spellbound. Fireflies flickered high and low. It was not clear where the fireflies ended and the stars began.
>
> Dominic wandered into a field where he saw what appeared to be miniature Japanese lanterns. They *were* miniature Japanese lanterns. Mice were having a moonlight revel in a clearing surrounded by tall grass and they had strung their prismatic lanterns between stalks of timothy. Dominic, enchanted, watched the proceedings from the top of a rock. There was delicate, stately mouse music produced by tiny zithers, lutes, and tambourines. Dominic took out his piccolo and played, softly, ever so softly. The mice heard but didn't question where the piccolo notes were coming from. They too were bewitched.

The revelry grows more ecstatic, the music strives "nearer and nearer to the elemental truth of being"; and Dominic, his soul overflowing, raises "his head and, straining toward infinity, howled out the burden of his love and longing in sounds more meaningful than words."

In the grass he discovers a doll, "a long-eared puppy with shoe-button eyes, one of them hanging by a thread from its socket," whose smell intrigues him and which inspires more longing in him. Tucking it away in his bandanna, he looks up to the heavens and declares: "Oh, Life, I am yours. Whatever it is you want of me, I am ready to give"; and again, he howls "without restraint, embarrassment, or self-consciousness. The howls had been gathering in him for a long time and it was wonderful release to vent them in their fullness."

He comes upon a sleepwalking goat named Phineas Matterhorn (looking much like the sleepwalker in the cartoon on the first page of Steig's *Male/Female*), dressed in a nightcap and nightshirt:

> So he walked quietly alongside the goat and they moved into grass over Dominic's ears, disturbing two hedgehogs who had been trysting in the moonlight and who made outcries of indignation; and then they went up a small hill and over a knoll and into a wood—the goat all the while holding his own dreamy counsel—and through some underbrush and out again into an open field and then down a slope and then ankle deep into a cool rill and then over some rocks, and finally Dominic had had enough of traipsing alongside a somnambulist. He guided the goat into a tree that proved to be unyielding.
>
> "Where am I?" said the goat, with the tree in his embrace. "What am I doing here?"
>
> "You are on the planet Earth, embracing a tree in a field under the full moon," answered Dominic, "and it's as lovely a night as ever there was since time began."

Phineas informs Dominic of the forthcoming wedding of Barney Swain, and they decide to attend. On their way, they meet a pygmy elephant named Mwana Bhomba who has forgotten the magic word that, upon saying it, will return him in a jiffy to Africa and will make all wishes come true; and they observe a dervish-type ritual performed by a woodchuck, beaver, raccoon, and porcupine who salaam to the moon then to one another; walk slowly in a circle; bow north, east, south, and west; and sprinkle coconut oil and sesame seeds on one another. ("It was very impressive and mysterious, and Dominic, Phineas, and Mwana never found out what it all meant. . . . [The other animals] knew what they were doing, just as you and I know what we're doing when we do the things we do, and that's all that matters.")

After arriving in town, Dominic "was now so impatient for the forthcoming event that he just had to keep moving. He hastened about the town once more, sniffing here and there, increasing his store of olfactory information." Now he remembers the soiled little doll, unwraps it, and holds it in his arms:

> What was there about this lost plaything that he cared for so intensely? Why did it make him dream of things to come? Sitting with the doll in the rosy light of the setting sun, he knew he would be pleased with his future. He fell into a reverie and was no longer

conscious of his surroundings or of passing time. Images of tender April flowers on soft hillsides, of limpid minty pools in sweet, purling brooks, of hushed, fern-filled, aromatic forests, of benign, embracing breezes and affectionate skies, of a peaceable world of happy creatures passed before his mind's eye.

The Doomsday Gang sets fire to the wedding party, and when Dominic pleads with the elephant to remember the magic word in order to save them ("Try. Don't get excited. Relax and, presto, you'll have it"), Mwana screams out that "presto" is indeed the word. The fire stops, Mwana wishes himself back home, and the other guests at the wedding go out to attack the Gang; but during the ensuing fracas, Dominic gets wounded: "The villains had concentrated their fury on Dominic, since they hated him the most."

After being brought back to health by his friends, he takes off again, as he thinks to himself: "Fighting the bad ones in the world was a necessary and gratifying experience. Being happy among the good ones was, of course, even more gratifying. But one could not be happy among the good ones unless one fought the bad ones. He felt he was serving some important and useful purpose."

Asleep in the aromatic, moonlit woods, he is surrounded by the remnants of the Gang: "They hated Dominic with all their hearts, and their hearts were capable of drastic hatred. Now they intended to subtract him from the sum of existing things." But the trees love Dominic, and they are moved to "speak out, to break their lifelong silence. . . . They had become impatient with standing around in silent tableau, doing nothing but looking grand and storing up resentment, indignation, and grief while all the evil-doing, the doom-delivering, of the Doomsday Gang went on." The trees cry out "For shame!" and the Gang members, scared out of their wits, flee forever: "The terror of this experience, the condemnation from the lords of the hitherto silent vegetable kingdom, had penetrated to their souls. Convinced that Nature itself could no longer abide their destructive, criminal ways, they each slunk about separately, making efforts to reform and get into Nature's good graces again, as every wanton one of them had been in his original childhood."

Later that night, Dominic finds himself in a garden, watched over by a resplendent peacock (whose tail, it is interesting to note, is in certain traditions considered to be the symbol of perfectly expressed psychic fulfillment). Admiring the peacock's tail, and standing by a marble fountain, Dominic looks at the spectacle of flowers:

"What are those flowers?" asked Dominic, pointing at a row of very large blossoms of deep crimson and royal violet speckled with white.

"Touch one," said the peacock. Dominic did and there was a delicate ringing of bells.

"Touch another." He did. And now there was music, a lovely, light melody as if breezes were playing on a wind instrument. He touched other flowers and there was orchestration—strings, soft brasses, reeds, light percussion. Dominic felt called upon to join in. Under the golden moon he played his golden piccolo, and he and the flowers understood one another and rose to greater and greater heights of loveliness.

At the back of the garden is a miniature palace. Upon entering it, Dominic again smells the scent of his beloved doll, and then, in a room lit by candles and the moon, he realizes that "the most beautiful dog he had ever seen lay sleeping. She was black and shimmered in patterns of luminous purple, yellow, green, blue, and carmine from the windows. She looked unreal." Shyly, he touches her. "Are you the one?" she asks, waking:

> "I think I am," said Dominic.
> "Do you have the doll?"
> "Yes, I do," said Dominic.
> "You're the one," she said.

Then she tells him:

> "One day, when I'd grown up and decided I was no longer a child, I threw it away. I remember I was standing in a field thinking about life and about myself and about growing up. I became eager for the future and I felt the doll chained me to the past. So I got rid of it. But even while I was walking away from that field, I began to have doubts. I had been happy in my puppy days. Would I be a happy grownup? I wandered about in a sort of trance, until I found myself standing in front of an alligator-witch. . . . She brought me here. 'You are going to sleep,' she said, 'maybe for a long time. Someone will find your doll, and whoever finds it will also find you, you can be sure of that.'"

Dominic gives her the doll:

> "Let's leave right away," she said. "I've been here so long, I want to be out in the world again."

Dominic realized he was at the beginning of a great new adventure.

"Let's go," he said.

Together they left the little palace.

This is the way the book ends, as we understand that to find some-one's "doll" is to rediscover that person's childhood self, and also, in the process, one's own childhood; and that to be truly like a child is not to regress, like Peter Pan, but to "be out in the world again" and on that road which, as St. Augustine knew, was a path not from place to place, but of the affections.

"Originally," Steig explains, "I had the idea of doing a book in which a dog, going to visit his cousin or some other relative, comes to a fork where there are three roads. And I was going to try to have included in the book some kind of spinning toy that would determine which road the dog would take. Each road was going to have a different set of adventures, and each was to have been represented by a separate strip of color on the same page, so that the dog would have followed the red, blue, or green path. And at the end, the roads came together and ended up in the same place.

"I quickly wrote down a list of characters the dog would meet: a witch-alligator, a rich pig, a goose, a boar, an elephant that loses its memory. And when I decided to do *Dominic* a couple of years later, I just used every animal I had originally written down, as if they be-longed together because they had all come to me at the same moment."

"Why talking animals?" someone once asked Steig, who re-sponded: "I think using animals emphasizes the fact that the story is symbolic—about human behavior. And kids get the idea right away that this is not just a story, but that it's saying something about life on earth" . . . adding, "When you write about a dog, you're really writing about a child, because a dog's mature when it's only a year old."

"The terrible cuteness and triteness of most children's books," writes Roger Sale in *Fairy Tales and After*, "sometimes seems little more than the result of ignorance or incomprehension or carelessness about the materials being used, most of which concern animals in one way or another." As with the greatest creators of animal tales, Steig's carefulness about the materials being used can be seen in the way he respects the doglike nature of Dominic, that passionate lover of liberty who leaves the path to sniff and explore, always to return to it—

howling and yodeling (the original primal screamer!) in sorrow and joy.

But, standing erect on his hind legs, Dominic is obviously, as Steig says, a symbolical human being. "We who stand," writes the psychologist Stanley Keleman, "are the only animals capable of loving. Other animals have contact, have connection. But the development of richer, more tender relationships as a consistent possibility in one's existence depends upon standing and exposing the tender side of the body. . . . To stand up is to open up, open out."

In many ways, of course, Dominic is a prototypical picaresque hero who shares the Odyssean qualities of agility, courage, persistence, and inventiveness; the Whitmanesque celebration of "health, defiance, gayety, self-esteem, curiosity" (Dominic certainly embodies Whitman's journeyer in "Song of the Open Road"—"Afoot and light-hearted . . . healthy, free, the world before me"); the Emersonian sense of self-reliance and nonconformity; and the Tolstoyan notions of loving-kindness and openheartedness. ("I'd read *Anna Karenina* before starting on *Dominic*," Steig told me, and Jeanne's daughter, not knowing that, said to me one day after reading *Dominic*: 'You've been reading Tolstoy, haven't you?' Now that's very strange!")

Dominic is also a classic children's literature protagonist, like Kipling's Kim or Dorothy in *The Wizard of Oz*, about whom Sale has beautifully written: "To be able to go, without meaning to, into a strange and magical land, and to be able to accept each moment there as it comes and for what it brings—it is like having it always be morning, to be always setting out, and that is one of the most enchanting and elusive of life's possibilities. In Thoreau's terms, Dorothy is fully awake. She does not worry or fret or plan, and so everything can be fully itself." And with his Sleeping Beauty princess, Dominic also takes on the role of a classic fairy-tale hero, about whom Max Lüthi, in *Once Upon a Time*, says: "The fairy tale sees man as one who is essentially isolated but who, for just this reason—because he is not rigidly committed, not tied down—can establish relationships with anything in the world. And the world of the fairy tale includes not just the earth, but the entire cosmos."

It would, of course, be egregiously reductive and slighting of Steig's remarkable literary and pictorial style—which combines the rough-hewn, the gentle, the comic, and the noble—to see *Dominic* simply as some kind of mouthpiece for Wilhelm Reich's social and ethical ideas. As Steig once told James E. Higgins: "When I wrote *Dominic* I didn't mean it to be about anything. . . . I have a position—

a point of view. But I don't have to think about it to express it. I can write about anything and my point of view will come out. So when I am at work my conscious intention is to tell a story to the reader. All this other stuff takes place automatically." But it is fascinating to realize that the character of Dominic perfectly exemplifies what Reich at various times, and often interchangeably, called the "self-governing," "genital," or "unarmored" character, which he saw and valued as the pinnacle of health and the optimum of human functioning.

In *The Murder of Christ*, Reich interprets and portrays Jesus— and in a sense Dominic himself—as exactly this type of character, "knowing and yet naïve . . . streaming with love and kindness, and yet able to hit hard; gentle and yet strong, just as the child of the future is. . . . The more he gives off in strength and love, the more new strength he gains from the universe, the greater and closer is his own contact with nature around him, the sharper his awareness of God, Nature, the air, the birds, the flowers, the animals, to all of whom he is close. . . . Christ did not like to remain sitting in the home with his brothers and sisters and his mother, though he loved them dearly. He liked to wander about the beautiful countryside, to greet the sun when it rose over the horizon in glaring pink."

"Aglow with energy" and opposed to all forms of acedia, Dominic, Steig tells us, is "master of himself and in accord with the world. . . . He never debated these impulses, hemming and hawing over what he should do. Thought and action were not separate with Dominic; the moment he thought to do something, he was already doing it."

As mentioned before, Dominic even respects the Doomsday Gang more than he does the rabbits because the former "had plenty of brass." The Gang, of course, is an apt embodiment of what Reich called the "emotional plague"—a term he first used to describe the kind of group irrationalism and group sadism that manifested itself in, for example, the Inquisition, the Salem witch trials, and the Third Reich. Like Blake (who wrote: "Nought can deform the Human Race/Like to the Armour's Iron brace"), Reich respected all forms of energy, and as he writes in *Character Analysis*:

> In the course of almost thirty years of biopsychiatric work, I have come to realize that a predisposition to the emotional plague is indicative of very high quantities of biological energy. Indeed, *the high tension of the individual's biological energy* makes him sick with the emotional plague if, because of a rigid character and muscular armor, he cannot realize himself in a natural way. . . . He differs from

the genital character inasmuch as his *rebellion is not socially oriented* and is therefore incapable of effecting any rational changes for the better. He differs from the neurotic character inasmuch as he *does not become resigned.*

But as Dominic knows, "one could not be happy among the good ones unless one fought the bad ones." And Reich naturally and forcefully aligned himself with the forces of creation. As he wrote in *The Murder of Christ*: "*Learn, finally, to fight for Life as heretofore you have only fought for emperors and dukes and fuehrers and ideas and honors and wealth and ephemeral fatherlands and motherlands. Finally, start fighting for Life!*"

Believing that "everything that lives is functionally identical," Reich affirmed: "*We comprehend the expressive movements and the emotional expression of another living organism on the basis of the identity between our own emotions and those of all living beings*" (*Character Analysis*). And it is interesting to discover what animal Reich felt closest to:

> A general may or may not be a person of "high esteem." We want neither to glorify nor to deprecate him. Yet we will not have ourselves deprived of the right to look upon him as an animal having a special kind of armor. It would not bother me if another scientist wanted to reduce my thirst for knowledge to the biological function of a puppy who goes around sniffing at everything. Indeed, it would make me happy to be compared biologically to a lively and lovable puppy. I have no desire to distinguish myself from the animal. (*Character Analysis*)

"A couple of years ago at about eleven o'clock one night," Arthur Steig (William's youngest brother) told me, "I was rolling around on the sofa trying to lose my sense of time—trying to feel the way a dog feels, having *no* feeling of time—and suddenly I saw my brother Bill reclining on a big white pillow, and I was sure it was so. The next time I wrote him, I mentioned it to him, and he told me that he had had the flu and was lying all day and night on a big white pillow.

"Heidegger talks about 'forgetfulness of being,'" Arthur Steig continued. "My idea is that we were once beasts, like all the other beasts, and some of them, like chimpanzees, used twigs to do various tasks. But at a certain point, early man conceived of a stone with a handle—a clumsy hammer or arrowhead—and he had to sit down and make it (it might have taken hours to do), and while he was doing that he was no longer functioning as an animal. All the things that previously would have been done spontaneously or instinctively had to be held in check. And the reason he gave up his present desire was for the future, since it would make him more secure. But eventually people began to think so much about security that they lost their animality, and that's where it all began to get messed up. But if I really try, I can lose that sense of time we've had for a million years and know how a dog feels when it walks around. . . . Incidentally, the reason why I saw Bill and not someone else that night when I succeeded in losing my sense of time is that we've always been very close."

Arthur Steig lives with his wife Aurora, a potter, and two beautiful dogs—Lizzie, a short-haired mutt that looks like a foxhound, and Ruby, a long-haired mutt that looks like a small collie—in New Jersey. The youngest of four brothers (two others in addition to the four had died in infancy), he is the founder of Steig Products, which manufactures inks and watercolors. In addition, he is a poet, an artist specializing in spontaneous line drawings in ink, and an unusually percipient untaught graphologist.

"I was walking with a friend one day," he told me when I visited him in April 1979, "and the subject of graphology came up. My friend said he couldn't see how you could tell something about a person just by looking at his handwriting. And I said, everything you do is you and I bet that I could do it. He took out a letter from his pocket and I told him a great deal about that person. Later, I spoke to a very fine graphologist and Rorschach analyst, Ernest Schachtel, and he showed me a facsimile of Kafka's handwriting. I'd read a bit of Kafka but knew absolutely nothing about him, and I wound up telling Schachtel a lot about Kafka's personal life. So he advised me not to study graphology because he felt I'd lose what I had."

Having seen one of William Steig's letters, I mentioned to Arthur how similar I thought William's handwriting seemed to the lines of his drawings.

"I never connected the handwriting and the drawing," Arthur remarked. "But they're not in two different spheres; it's a good observation, and you're right: Bill is himself all the time. Even if I didn't know him, his handwriting would seem special because there's no separation in it between psyche and hand. And what comes through it is very beautiful because *he's* very beautiful."

When talking to Arthur, you discover that he is also a kind of autodidact with a special interest in psychology (his article "The Dynamics of Minority Hatred" was published in *Dissent* in 1959), music ("Jazz, Clock and Song of Our Anxiety" was published in *Politics* in 1945), and wit.

"When I was eighteen or nineteen," Arthur says, "I worked out a theory of wit—I just had a bunch of notes, I never wrote it up formally—but I still think it's valid. The family had gone away for the summer, and I read Freud's *Wit and Its Relation to the Unconscious* and Ludovici's *The Secret of Laughter*, which was an elaboration of one sentence in Hobbes ('The passion of laughter is nothing else but sudden glory arising from some conception of some eminency in ourselves'), and Ludovici made it radiate in all directions, coining the term 'superior adaptation' as a substitute for Hobbes's 'sudden glory.'

"Among the many examples Ludovici gave to support Hobbes's original insight was that even nonsense could make you feel that 'sudden glory'—the world suddenly becomes unrigid, and you're free from the burden of having constantly to keep your head, make a living, etc. If you meet a friend and are happy to see him, you smile because you were alone and now feel better. If a Chinese coolie, who's suffered terribly all his life, sees someone fall on a banana peel, he'll die laughing: The smile and the belly laugh are related psychologically.

"One of the things that Ludovici made me think about was the phenomenon of the self-destructive comic—the comic who makes a living ridiculing himself, which is destructive of himself and of other people who identify with him and learn not to take themselves seriously, putting themselves down. What they're doing, then, is presenting themselves for the sudden glory of others."

In 1939, William asked Arthur to write a foreword to *About People*—some of William's most imaginative depictions of the repressed and the resigned, the sclerotic and the spiteful. In two prefatory pages, Arthur related his ideas about humor to his brother's drawings, which he called the "most acute kind of social commentary: the responses of a man's total character to the world in which he lives. . . . All honest humor," he asserted, "is *constructive* in that it manipulates the victory of basic human values over social values that are wholly or partially fraudulent. In asserting these primary values it may be necessary to destroy those who represent their distortion or denial ["I didn't mean that literally," Arthur explained to me]. The only humor that is truly destructive is the humor that people employ to assert their helplessness."

Five years later, he contributed a foreword to his brother's *All Embarrassed*, writing: "The man of the fifth decade of the twentieth century is the Embarrassed Man. He is the technically omnipotent, helpless man—inadequate at every turn of the day, from the snide morning alarum of the electric clock to the leering, cosmic fall of midnight. . . . Our world, in making embarrassment our constant lot, deadens our feeling for it. This book serves the purpose of renewing our recognition of embarrassment. It is important that we recognize it because, arising from equivocations in our relations with one another, it produces new and more complex equivocations. . . . The well of the embarrassment illustrated in this book is the interior chaos born in a world of facades. The artist illustrates it with the eye of a poet, satirist, and the eclectic (embarrassed) eye of a contemporary."

Just as William Steig and Wilhelm Reich were, as Arthur Steig says, "human beings both seeing the truth in parallel ways," so Arthur, with his words, and William, with his drawings, reveal, *pari passu*, a collaborative symbiosis based more on shared feelings and ideas than on mere fraternal identification. (As Arthur says, "Bill perhaps over-appreciated me and gave me things like those forewords to do; he never knew what I was going to write.")

And in *Male/Female* (1971)—a collection of some of William's most passionate drawings of men and women in various guises, either squabbling or making love—the artist chose as his preface one of Arthur's most joyous poems in praise of sunlight, creation, the life-force, and the mothers of the world's often raging sons (and brothers):

Poem for My Brother's Book
How lucky we are
that our planet is not bald like the Moon

that its skin nourishes mushrooms and orchids
and enchambers waters and coals

that serpents find damp joys here
that bulls are made rapturous by cows
and Earth's gown of air carries their bellows

that when at 5 AM the Sun squints
his wild vermilion eye over the rim of the world
the light is gathered by forests of flittering pennons

that no matter the rages of some Ages and some sons
our mothers are born and born again

· · ·

"If Dominic reminds me of anyone," William Steig said to me, "it's my father. He was always sniffing into things, always poking around, coming into my room and examining my brushes."

Joseph Steig was born and grew up in Lwow in the Carpathian Mountains—a then-Polish, now-Russian part of the Austro-Hungarian Empire and a region where, it is interesting to note, both Martin Buber and Wilhelm Reich were also born. Joseph was brought up in a Hasidic family, and as a child was known as Joseph the Hasid's. At eleven, he became an apprentice to a housepainter. "He told great stories," Arthur Steig recalls, "about working in the master's household, whose shop was attached to the house. In those days, you had to buy pigment, which often came in the form of a solid mass that had to be ground and mixed with oil. . . . Anyway, my father told us about the master's daughter. One day, the master noticed that she had a little blue paint on her ankle; he got curious about it, lifted up her skirt, and found out that the paint went all the way up. So he found the kid who was grinding blue that day and gave him the business. . . . It wasn't my father [smiling], though it could have been."

When he was just a teenager, Joseph became an atheist and joined the Socialist party. He organized union strikes and went to jail a couple of times, where his wife-to-be, Laura (who came from an Orthodox Jewish family), used to visit him and bring him chicken soup. Drafted into the Austrian army, he won a couple of medals—though he often found himself in trouble with the authorities—then pursued his profession as a housepainter, married Laura, had his first son Irwin, and, when the child was a year old, emigrated with his family to the United States.

"As a tradesman," Arthur says, "my father had lived fairly well in Europe, but in New York he and the family were very poor, living for many years with twenty-six other families in a Bronx tenement. Painters worked for one month and were out of work the rest of the year. Also my father's competition wouldn't tell him what calcimine was (it has a calcium carbonate and gum arabic base and is used for painting ceilings), so he lost a lot of work, and at the height of his glory he just barely got by. He was a very strong man physically and he stood up for what he believed in. And he was a good Socialist, like my mother, who herself was free of envy and ambition and had a contempt for money."

Joseph spent a lot of time at the Second Assembly District Meeting House, and his wife felt he was flirting with the women there.

As Arthur says: "There had been six children (two died in infancy) and three abortions; he was in a continual state of rage, and she was in a state of rage from being too often pregnant. If Margaret Sanger had come along a generation before, I think that their life would have been different." William Steig's many cartoons of men and women fighting—in the early *Man about Town,* the later "Punch and Judy" section from *Continuous Performance* (1963), and *Male/Female*— derive, the artist confesses, "from my parents—they squabbled like hell. They were always either quarreling or making love."

The words of a quarrel are usually a mask for the emotions underlying them. And as Reich wrote in *The Function of the Orgasm:* "Words can lie. The mode of expression never lies." In *Character Analysis* he asserted that human language often functioned as a defence. "In many cases," he stated, "the function of speech has deteriorated to such a degree that the words express nothing whatever and merely represent a continuous, hollow activity on the part of the musculature of the neck and the organs of speech" (*Continuous Performance,* as William Steig titled one of his collections). And Steig himself succinctly and quietly communicates and links up his sense of expressivity and language in his "Notes": "When the creative flow is blocked in an activity, the sense of wonder turns to bewilderment and we feel an imminence of death. In conversation, for example, anxiety sets in if nothing is being formed—a friendship, or a truth, or just a new sentence."

Reich himself was, of course, almost always an extraordinarily clear, expressive, and truthful writer; but because he felt that "the beginnings of living functioning lie much *deeper* than and *beyond* language" (think of Dominic howling out the burden of his love and longing "in sounds more meaningful than words"), he seemed to place greater importance on the activities of painting and music, affirming that "the artist himself speaks to us in the form of wordless expressions of movement from the depth of the life function, but he would be just as incapable as we of putting into words what he expresses in his music or in his painting. Indeed, he strongly objects to any attempt to translate the language of expression of art into human word language. He attaches great importance to the purity of his language of expression." (And it is interesting to note that in most of his children's books, Steig's characters, if they do have any professional gifts at all, are almost always flute players or painters.)

Reich would have agreed with St. Augustine's notion that bodily movements are "the natural words of all peoples." And he would also have supported Wittgenstein's attempt to reconnect language to its roots in the field of *movement* from which it originally sprang. Because unless nature was able, as Reich always hoped, to guide the flourishings of culture, nature would be blocked and culture would become unnurturing, distorted, and destructive.

William Steig is a direct, relaxed, communicative human being, but he has little time or inclination for garrulous theorizing, small talk, or fustian chatter. During his two years at City College (which he entered at sixteen), he spent most of his time on the swimming and water polo teams. Later, at the National Academy of Design, he especially remembers playing football in the backyard. "I wasn't interested in any form of culture at that time," Steig recalls. "In fact, I started out with the idea of going to sea—I wanted to go around and see the world. But I couldn't, because my father lost all his savings in the Wall Street crash. My two older brothers were married, and I had to take care of the family. But I vaguely had the idea of becoming a writer, when I thought of doing anything. I love the physical act of writing, by the way. I used to keep a journal—not because I had anything to say but because I liked moving the pen. I always wondered what this signified. But, anyway, I found it pleasurable.

"So in order to support my family, I started doing cartoons. In my family it was understood that the only thing to do was to be an artist. Henry talked of being a dentist, and everyone just laughed. My old man thought that going into business was vulgar, and so we were sort of driven into the arts. Later, I did a lot of advertising, which I always felt bad about—I felt that I was never really being true to myself."

Irwin Steig, who was six years older than William, made his living as an advertising manager, but he was also a ranking chess player and a bridge champion of Connecticut. He wrote a number of stories and took up portrait painting at the end of his life. Henry Steig, who wound up being a jeweler, was a writer, painter, cartoonist, and a musician who had a recorder group and who made shepherd's pipes. "Henry introduced me to jazz and the blues—Bessie Smith and Robert Johnson," William states. Henry's son, Michael, played banjo in The Red Onion Jazz Band, and William's son, Jeremy Steig, is one of the finest contemporary jazz flutists, as well as a visionary painter.

Entering William Steig's country house on a hillside near Kent,

Connecticut, is like visiting a little museum, filled as it is with innumerable artistic manifestations of the Steig family's exuberant creativity. Surrounded by birches, maples, and apple trees, the house looks out on a pond filled with ducks and geese, peopled in and around with live creatures that could have crawled, swum, and flown out of William's children's books—redwing blackbirds, redheaded woodpeckers, cowbirds, starlings, fat robins, crows, peppers, and bullfrogs.

As you enter the house, you walk past one of Jeanne Steig's fantastic, large soft-sculpture figures—her "grandmother," she tells me—made of kidskin and stuffed with kapok. A beautiful dog named Kasha (a mutt that acts like a terrier) greets you affectionately, while a black cat named Maybelline sizes you up nearby. As you walk around the house, you notice drawings and paintings on the walls done not only by Steig himself, but by Jeanne's daughter Terry, William's daughter Lucy (his other daughter, Maggie, is a metalsmith), and his son Jeremy. Most fascinating of all are the works by William's mother Laura—radiant "primitive" paintings of flowers, fruit, and suns that she began to create in her sixties—and by her husband Joseph—intense but delicate Dufyesque paintings of groups and crowds. "He'd spend Sunday mornings painting and listening to old seventy-eight opera recordings," Arthur recalls. "Then he'd take a postcard and copy it in oil paint on a little panel. One day in the thirties, we told him that was a waste of time, and showed him reproductions of great paintings, and all of a sudden he became a good painter."

Each member of the Steig family has a distinct style and personality, yet there are strong connections, aesthetically as well as familialy, and they would be interesting to study. What seems most obvious, however, is the deep bond between William and Arthur—as we have seen—and between William and Jeremy. Rarely have I observed relationships as loving, respectful, and devoted as those between these two brothers and this father and his son.

Jeremy Steig—who was thirty-nine when I visited him in May 1979—is both a musician and a painter ("I played the recorder at six, the flute at eleven, and was painting when I was seventeen"). As a child, he listened to his father's blues and jazz record collection—which, along with Thelonius Monk albums he heard later, inspired him to become a professional musician—and he learned to draw by watching over his father's shoulders as he drew his smiles and frowns. ("There's something I'd like to learn from Jeremy," William says. "When I draw, I always start with the face, but he can start anywhere and work up from the torso or whatever.")

"My father only uses what he needs to use," Jeremy comments, sitting in his Greenwich Village apartment living room. Near him an assortment of different sized flutes are laid out on a table; above and around him, covering the four walls, is a glorious oil-pastel mural showing satyrs, chimeras, mermaids, maidens—all romping and frolicking in a teeming Garden of Eden presided over by a dervish snake-charmer flutist (Krishna with his Shakti?), the head seducer of the forest.

"My father only uses what he needs," Jeremy continues in this room of riotous colors. "I'm the opposite. I put in everything I *don't* need—lots of different stories, some of which mean something and some of which don't. My father's things are full of meaning. There are lots of paths, and his is only one, but it's a wonderful one. He has a lot of insight into people's expressions; he's like Charlie Parker, and the rest of the music out there is just disco."

"But he has more fun," William comments. "A lot of the meaning of my stuff is there only because I have to sell it. Otherwise I'd just draw. I don't have the natural impulse to put meaning into it."

"He gets better every time," Jeremy says, putting on one of his own most recent, and best, recordings entitled *Outlaws*—on which he plays with bassist Eddie Gomez—and with the enthusiasm of a child tells me: "My favorite children's book of my father's is *The Bad Island* [1969, now out of print, and originally titled *The Rotten Island* but changed because the publisher found the word "rotten" too extreme]. Kids could never get their hands on that book; the librarians didn't like it because there's no hero in it—it deals with monsters and ugliness. There's this island with all these monsters. All their thoughts are ugly, they hiss at one another and fight, and at night the place freezes; they're all locked in the frozen motion of fighting. And when it thaws out the next day, they start fighting again. What happens is that a flower starts growing on the island, and it freaks them all out, and they start playing games, trying to push each other into the flowers. Some more flowers come up, and they provoke this more hysterical fight. There are incredible battle scenes and amazing drawings of gigantic insects. At the end they all die, the whole island burns up, and there's no more ugliness. The volcanoes look like vases with flowers coming out of them, and a bunch of ducks are flying overhead."

Here is how the author describes the monsters:

> They loved the life they lived. They loved hating and hissing at one another, spitting fire, making clouds of smoke, tearing and breaking things, screaming, grunting, roaring, caterwauling, and giving vent to any kind of jarring noise that expressed their hideous feelings. They were very happy at being unhappy, and were very pleased to be mean and cruel, to terrify and give each other bad dreams, to smell bad and be disgusting. To them, this rotten island was Paradise.

When the first flower appears, it makes the monsters "afraid at first, and then insanely angry. They panted fire and made terribly threatening sounds, but somehow they did not dare to touch this large, gentle flower. None of the plants on this rotten island grew flowers and they had never before seen anything beautiful. But to them the flower was ugly."

As Jeremy comments: "There are people in the world who are upset by beauty, and that's why a lot of beauty never gets to be made —music and art. People reject something because it's different. . . . People who like only disco have a disco mentality, and that's their beauty," he adds. "I started off with rock and roll—Elvis, Bo Didley, Chuck Berry, Fats Domino. But I got to a point where I felt there weren't enough chords in it, so I went out for jazz. It's like in school— each year you learn something a little bit harder, and, one hopes, more interesting. That's the way it should be in music, too. You wouldn't want to eat the same thing everyday. If someone accepts only a disco beat, they'll just let that beat into their heads for the rest of their lives, and never know what kind of enrichment they could have if they checked other things out."

"Soon everyone heard about the flower and came to see it," *The Bad Island* continues. "And everyone was angry. . . . The creatures grew more and more suspicious of one another. They slunk around disturbed, depressed or delirious, and they began blaming one another for trying to upset the natural order of things on their rotten island paradise. . . . Eventually things really got out of hand, or out of claw and talon. From blaming and cursing and insulting, and threatening and shoving and hitting, they went on to serious fighting. And all their deepest demons of hate broke loose."

It is interesting, though it was probably unknown to Steig when he wrote *The Bad Island,* that the first flowers appeared during the Cretaceous Period when the dinosaurs were becoming extinct. (It is interesting in this context to recall Italo Calvino's brilliant story "The Dinosaurs" in *Cosmicomics,* which tells of the love affair between the Ugly One—the sole survivor of the dinosaur species—and Fern-Flower—one of the New Ones.) Now, the monsters of the rotten island are, of course, like the Doomsday Gang, champions and carriers of the emotional plague. And it is also tempting to see in the rage of these creatures, as they are affected by the appearance of the flower, a brilliant metaphor for the way in which the bound-up and repressed energy of the character armor is liberated. As Reich states in *Ether, God and Devil:*

> *Armored life encounters unarmored life with anxiety and hatred.* . . . Close examination of the process shows that the armored organism either cannot fully establish contact or cannot maintain it. Sooner or later the warm, loving impulse is blocked by the armor. This is followed by the tormenting feeling of frustration. *The armored organism does not know that its love impulses have been blocked, and behaves as if the unarmored organism had denied it love.* In its desperate attempt to break through and express its love, the love impulse turns into hatred and destructiveness.

How does one become armored? Through self-awareness or the need for self-protection? For whatever reason, the process by which one becomes bound up is hauntingly described by Emily Dickinson:

> After great pain, a formal feeling comes—
> The Nerves sit ceremonious, like Tombs—
> The stiff Heart questions was it He, that bore,
> And Yesterday, or Centuries before?
>
> The Feet, mechanical, go round—
> Of Ground, or Air, or Ought—
> A Wooden way
> Regardless grown,
> A Quartz contentment, like a stone—
>
> This is the Hour of Lead—
> Remembered, if outlived,
> As Freezing persons, recollect the Snow—
> First—Chill—then Stupor—then the letting go

The image of the mechanical Feet reminds us of Steig's cartoon "I Mind My Own Business" in *The Lonely Ones*. And there is a strong connection between the "Freezing" that the poet sees as the aftermath of pain and the "frozen history" that Reich saw as the role of the character armor—congruent with his notion of structure as frozen energy: instead of the upturned smile we see someone "down in the mouth"; instead of holding one's head high, pulling it in; instead of expansion, contraction; instead of walking down the path of wonder, withdrawal and retreat.

Illustration from *Sylvester and the Magic Pebble*

In his most popular children's book, *Sylvester and the Magic Pebble* (1969)—which appeared shortly after *The Bad Island* and which won the 1970 Caldecott Medal—Steig presents in picture-book form the story of a donkey named Sylvester Duncan who lives with his parents in Oatsdale. One rainy day, the hero, who collects unusual and beautifully colored pebbles, comes across a special one— "flaming red, shiny, and perfectly round, like a marble." Shivering from excitement he wishes it would stop raining . . . and the rain ceases. He rushes home to show his parents his magic pebble; but, coming across a lion, he feels afraid:

If he hadn't been so frightened, he could have made the lion disappear, or he could have wished himself safe at home with his father and mother.

He could have wished the lion would turn into a butterfly or a daisy or a gnat. He could have wished many things, but he panicked and couldn't think carefully.

"I wish I were a rock," he said, and he became a rock.

Having armored himself—"a Quartz contentment, like a stone"—he wishes he were *himself* again, but nothing happens because he can't touch the pebble—which is lying by his side—to make the magic work. He is alone and feeling hopeless. ("I made a connection," Steig says, "with the fact that I'd read *Pinocchio* in my youth, and that it's a similar case of a real boy being locked up in a piece of wood, inside himself, misunderstood, and armored.")

Back home in Oatsdale, Mr. and Mrs. Duncan worry and look all over for their son, talking to everyone—puppies, kitten, colts, and piglets; they even go to the police—charming-looking pigs in fresh blue uniforms.

It must be mentioned here that in December 1970, the Illinois Police Association sent out to all law-enforcement officers a letter which read, in part:

This book contains a full color picture depicting the law enforcement officer as a pig, and the public as "jack asses." It is written for our youngsters in their formative years, ages 5–8. The picture shows two "jack asses" requesting assistance from the police and has the police officers as pigs dressed in police uniforms. This most certainly must mold the minds of our youngsters to think of police as pigs, rather than as their good friends. . . .

Please check your grade school libraries and public library to see if this book is there. If it is, ask them to remove it, and if they do not, please go to your local press. I am sure they are in favor of proper recognition of the police officer.

Liberty and Democracy without controls is chaos. You represent this Liberty, this Democracy and supply the controls.

Victor J. Witt
Secretary-Treasurer

With the encouragement of the International Conference of Police Associations, the Illinois Police Association instigated the removal of copies of *Sylvester* from a number of local Illinois library shelves. Grade school library officials denied reports that the book was subversive (it had been suggested that *Sylvester* might be part of a Communist-Yippie plot to indoctrinate young people), and tried to explain that "children's books frequently characterize people as animals." The book, however, was removed from libraries in Lincoln, Nebraska; Palo Alto, California; and Toledo, Ohio, among other places. The American Library Association was appalled, and strongly resisted this attempt at censorship. And Steig himself, both amazed and amused at the scandal, wrote an essay for *The New York Times Book Review* (May 4, 1969) in which he reflected on his interest in pigs:

> Factually, from the point of view of actual, personal contact and living experience, I know very little about live, fully functioning pigs—but one doesn't think of the pig as being very aggressive, resourceful, independent, creative, self-esteeming, duly indignant when necessary, and so forth.
>
> One thinks of a pig lying in mud with half-closed eyes, perfectly contented with the surroundings, uncomplaining because there is no urge to complain, uncritical of himself and his fellow pigs, swallowing, indeed wallowing in, all sorts of garbage, as if that were a perfectly natural, perfectly acceptable way of life. And perhaps here we have a clue as to why the pig occupies so large a place in the literature of today. Isn't the situation of the passive pig (at least as we imagine it) the situation of modern man—a creature surrounded with filth and danger, a victim of circumstances created by himself, unwilling and unable to do anything about his condition—and even, perhaps, in a way enjoying it?
>
> But this passive acceptance of an inferior lot is surely not all there is to pigs. One must consider that their quiet, speechless dignity might really turn out to be an eloquent silence—if we but knew what they were being silent about. The stars, after all, hang over pigs as they do above all the rest of creation, and who knows what deep dreams a pig may be dreaming? I think we can accept the possibility that a pig too has a fitting sense of wonder about things, and identify with him accordingly.

Back in Oatsdale, the Duncans are miserable. "Life had no meaning for them any more." In a series of three beautiful double-page spreads, we see the stone in autumn, leaves blowing over and around it ("Night followed day and day followed night over and over again.

Sylvester on the hill woke up less and less often. When he was awake, he was only hopeless and unhappy. He felt he would be a rock forever and he tried to get used to it. He went into an endless sleep"); then the stone in winter, covered with snow and with a wolf sitting on top of him and howling in hunger; and then in spring, under blue skies and blossoming flowers. As Steig says: "I think kids are interested in the weather, day and night, winter and summer. I feel it's important. Moonlight and snow and wind."

In spring things come alive, and the Duncans decide to take a picnic. Naturally, they sit down on the rock: "The warmth of his own mother sitting on him woke Sylvester up from his deep winter sleep." Mr. Duncan notices the lovely magic pebble near the rock, goes to pick it up, and as he and his wife sit down to eat, she wishes that Sylvester were with them. "And in less than an instant, he was!" In blazing sunlight Sylvester is unlocked and released and embraces his parents with tears of happiness, as they return home and hide the pebble forever.

To me," says Jeremy Steig in his living room, "the book is about love. When the family gets back together, they put the pebble away because what was important was their being together." And later that evening, Jeremy invited me to sit in his orgone accumulator. Like Dominic on his golden piccolo ("softly, ever so softly"), he played a melody on one of his flutes outside; inside, after several minutes, I began to feel my fingers tingle and throb, sensing for myself the reality of the connection Reich had made between orgone energy and love—the love that dissolves armor and rocks, unites what is separated, and makes the world go round. As Kenneth Rexroth wrote in his poem "On Flower Wreath Hill":

> . . . The world
> Is alive tonight. I am
> Immersed in living protoplasm,
> That stretches away over
> Continents and seas. I float
> Like a child in the womb. Each
> Cell of my body is
> Penetrated by a
> Strange electric life. I glow
> In the dark with the moon drenched
> Leaves, myself a globe
> Of St. Elmo's fire.

. . .

Having for many years made most of his living from advertising, and having grown to dislike intensely drawing to order for banks and insurance companies, Steig decided in 1968 to do his first children's book, *C D B!* (standing for See the Bee)—a kind of code book with witty and goofy drawings accompanying entries like L-C S-N X-T-C (Elsie Is in Ecstasy).

As a child, Steig himself remembers liking adventure books— Howard Pyle's *Robin Hood*, the King Arthur stories ("My friends and I used to go to the park and beat each other with cudgels and speak Arthurian language"), and especially the works of Joseph Altsheler. "He was a lousy writer," Steig says; "I found a copy of one of his books recently and can't imagine why I liked him, but all the kids were crazy about his stuff. We used to go to libraries in big gangs, kind of kicking each other on the way, and would always try to get hold of one of his books—books about woodsmen, guys who could walk through the forest without cracking a twig so that the Indians couldn't hear them. My brother Irwin, who had a phenomenal memory, could name every character and remember every story."

But Steig, then or later, must have also absorbed fairy tales and fables—as well as works like *Robinson Crusoe* and *The Golden Ass*— for his children's books take off from these basic plots and situations, although in remarkably inventive ways. His second and first "real" children's book, for example—*Roland the Minstrel Pig* (also published in 1968)—tells the traditional tale of a lute-playing pig (musicians, unlike policemen, never seem especially concerned about being depicted as pigs!) who "sang so sweetly that his friends never had enough of listening to him. He was a natural musician—from his hoofs to his snout." Under starlit skies, he would play at outdoor parties for his friends, many of whom—the donkey, the elephant, the bear, and, of course, the dog—would appear in Steig's later books.

Having decided to travel in order to find wealth and fame, Roland comes across the proverbial friendly-but-deceiving fox who offers to take him to see the king, all the while devising ways to kill him. The fox finally tricks him into hanging from a tree ("I always had the idea that this image," Steig says, "must have been connected with my being dragged feet first out of the womb. I always connected that with the idea of doctors turning the baby upside down and slapping it on the buttocks. Dangling . . . like Roland"), as he sets a roaring fire beneath him and as the minstrel sings his farewell song:

Farewell, dear world, dear hill, dear shore,
Dear butterflies, dear birds, dear bees,
Dear night, dear day, dear seasons four,
Dear flowering fields, dear fruited trees,
Dear warming sun, dear gentle breeze.
My heart's so sore
I'll be no more.
I feel an aching in my knees.

Just then the king (a stately lion) appears; he has been traveling through the forest and been dazzled by Roland's song, so he saves his life, punishes the villain, and rewards the hero who, now rich and famous, graces his benefactor with a song: "Hail the heavens up above,/Hail to honor, courage, love./Let these halls with music ring!/ All hail His Majesty the King!"

Roland the Minstrel Pig, a charming but hardly major work, was Steig's testing ground as a children's book creator. "I thought that anybody could write for kids when I first started doing the books," he says, "but it's not always that simple. And it's a nice feeling to discover that you can do something new—like Roland's farewell song. . . . I thought, Hey, I can write verse!" And he learned that he could illustrate, much as he says he dislikes to. "I don't like illustrating," he told me, "because it's very unspontaneous. When I'm illustrating, I know that a character has to walk in a certain way, and I have a hard time doing it. I'm incapable of making the drawing conform to the requirements of telling a story, making the pig look like the pig on the previous page." But despite himself, his gouache illustrations for *Roland* are ardent and witty—especially his double-page spread showing the masked dancers under magic lanterns and the stars; and also his drawings of Roland leaning on a rock, lute nearby, contemplating the possibilities of fame and wealth; and of Roland, purple beret on his head, singing a lonesome plaint in the moonlight.

Steig's next major work, after the audacious *The Bad Island* and the now-classic *Sylvester and the Magic Pebble* (both published in 1969), was another picture book, *Amos and Boris* (1971)—a brilliant variation on the fable about the lion and the mouse. Amos, a mouse who lives by the ocean and who, like William Steig when he was young, has the desire to go to sea, builds a boat and takes off. And like Dominic—about whom Steig would write in his next book—Amos is "full of wonder, full of enterprise, and full of love for life." Lying on his open deck like Melville's Ishmael, under the immense starry sky, rocking on a phosphorescent sea (which might be Reich's "primal orgone ocean"), he marvels at the sight of whales spouting luminous water. And we see Amos in a beautiful two-page painting—blue-gray washes of sea and sky, glimmering whales and stars—"a little speck of living thing in the vast living universe" who feels "thoroughly akin to it all." (We are of such stuff as stars are made on. And as Reich wrote in *Ether, God and Devil*: "The same energy that guides the movements of animals and the growth of all living substance indeed also guides the stars.")

But "overwhelmed by the beauty and mystery of everything," Amos rolls over right off the deck into the sea. Trapped, and feeling small, cold, wet, and worried, he decides just to keep afloat, but his strength starts to give out: "He began to wonder what it would be like to drown. Would it take very long? Would it feel just awful? Would his soul go to heaven? Would there be other mice there?"

Suddenly, Boris the whale appears. "What sort of fish are you?" he asks Amos, who replies: "I'm a mouse, which is a mammal, the highest form of life. I live on land." "Holy clam and cuttlefish!" says the whale. "I'm a mammal myself, though I live in the sea. Call me Boris." So Amos climbs aboard the whale's back, and Boris heads for shore. On their way to Amos's home, the two mammals get to know each other and become close friends. "They developed a deep admiration for one another. Boris admired the delicacy, the quivering daintiness, the light touch, the small voice, the gemlike radiance of the mouse. Amos admired the bulk, the grandeur, the power, the purpose, the rich voice, and the abounding friendliness of the whale." But, approaching land, they must say goodbye. "We *will* be friends forever," says Boris, "but we can't be together. You must live on land and I must live at sea. I'll never forget you, though." But years later Boris is washed up on the beach, and Amos, with the help of two friendly elephants, saves his friend's life. And as they say goodbye to each other, "they knew they might never meet again. They knew they would never forget each other." Not since Edward Lear's Owl and Pussy-Cat or Kipling's Mowgli and Baloo have the love of characters so different from each other been so totally accepted and perfectly portrayed in children's literature.

With *Dominic* (1972), Steig presented his first work for older children, a short novel that featured some of his greatest line drawings, and showed him developing a prose style combining grace and muscularity, lyricism and drama, one that moved from scene to scene like an inspired jazz improvisation. He must have been delighted by his newly realized powers, for a year later he published another long story, *The Real Thief*, which revealed the author in complete possession of a spare, unadorned style that was the appropriate match for its dark theme of injustice and betrayal. An unfairly underrated work, *The Real Thief* is, in fact, the only one of Steig's books that started out with what he calls a "deliberate idea." As he told James E. Higgins: "I was thinking of the way kids sometimes are treated unjustly, and how they feel about it. So I decided to do a story in which someone was treated unjustly, and then I would have the father figure express repentance."

Gawain the goose is Chief Guard of the Royal Treasury and totally devoted to King Basil the bear: "His heart warmed in the King's presence. He admired his strength. He loved the smell of honey on him, on his fur, on his robes, on his breath. He wanted to please him, to stay forever in his gruff, good graces." Only Basil and Gawain have the keys to the treasury, so when rubies, gold ducats, silver ornaments, and then the prized Kalikak diamond disappear, Gawain is accused of the thefts. He stands trial, and is attacked with mechanistic logic and uncorroborated evidence; excoriated by the king himself, he is found guilty and is about to be imprisoned.

One of Steig's greatest talents is the way he enters into and conveys the experience of his characters' sensations and feelings (think of Sylvester "shivering with excitement" as he studies his pebble for the first time). And now upon hearing the sentence of imprisonment, Gawain, Steig tells us, "stared at the ground and saw his own yellow feet. They, at least seemed real. He could feel no compassion from anyone around him. He felt leaden, benumbed." So, seeing the wide blue sky outside the courtroom, he honks loudly and escapes through the open window.

In the second part of the book, we learn the story of the real thief, Derek the mouse. An aesthete and gourmet who enjoys truffles and champagne, he loves the light and sparkle of jewels: "The bright red rubies made a brilliant sort of rug on the dun-colored earth. Later he sat cross-legged on his burlap bed, playing on his tiny zither, enjoying the new décor."

Then one night he decides that "all the color in his little mansion was on the warm side—red rubies, gold ducats, brown earth, tan burlap, wood—all yellowed by candlelight. He needed some offsetting coolness in the color scheme." So he steals the diamond that, in his room, "not only reflected the yellow light but shot heavenly blue arrows everywhere, and the lights, the reflections, and the interreflections created a marvelous atmosphere that completely turned Derek's small head."

Hearing about Gawain's plight, he comes to realize what it means to be a thief. "He looked in his mirror many times. He didn't look like a criminal. He looked as he always had, only sadder, more worried. . . . Why had he wanted to be rich, or to feel rich? Was he an unhappy mouse before? Didn't he see the King himself often looking sad? Was anyone completely happy?" So he decides to vindicate Gawain by continuing to steal from the treasury and then, later, returning the treasure. Realizing that he had accused the goose unjustly, Basil is devastated. Everyone is devastated. "Gawain's name had been cleared—but [Derek] knew that Gawain was miserable. He knew that King Basil was miserable, that everyone in his realm is miserable, and that he, Derek, was the sole cause of it. Tears blurred his eyes. The pall of gloom that hung over the whole kingdom hung thickest over him."

The third part of the book returns us to Gawain in exile. Having "soon used up the energy provided by his anger," the goose hides in a cave in the countryside: "How he yearned for friendship. How he longed to be in a community with other loving souls again. . . . Lake and forest, the whole shimmering world was painfully beautiful. He loved this world, but he was too hurt to enjoy it."

One day he is discovered by Derek, who has been searching for him everywhere. "He felt so many emotions—joy at having been vindicated and at being with Derek, anger at what had happened, misery that such things *could* happen, pity for Derek, bitterness toward his faithless friends and toward the King he had loved, longing for a good life, sweetness at thinking how beautiful it could be, and sorrow that it wasn't so. It was all too much for him." And as Reich wrote in *Listen, Little Man!*, as if to comment on Gawain's—and of course, his own—situation:

> You've got to realize that you have raised up your little men to be oppressors, and made martyrs of your truly great men; that you have crucified and stoned them, or let them starve; that you have never given a moment's thought to them or to what they have done for you; that you haven't the faintest idea who brought you the true benefits of your life. . . .
>
> By making him into a pariah, you sow the terrible seed of loneliness in him. Not the seed that engenders great actions but the seed of fear, the fear of being misunderstood and abused by you.

And filled with bitterness, Gawain gradually comes to forgive Derek and his former friends, and he returns home in honor. "He was able to love them again," Steig writes, "but he loved them now in a wiser way, knowing their weakness."

In 1974, Steig left this bittersweet kingdom and brought out *Farmer Palmer's Wagon Ride*—a Buster Keatonesque tale about Palmer the pig and his hired hand, Ebenezer the donkey (looking a lot like Sylvester), who load their wagon with vegetables, then drive to market and return with provisions (camera, bicycle, harmonica) for Palmer's family—driving on a joyous spring day through the perfect New England countryside (pictured in another of Steig's gorgeous two-page drawings). In the woods, they get caught in a storm, trees crash onto the wagon, and they lose a wheel and most of their gifts. Eventually, Farmer Palmer has to pull the wagon himself until it totally collapses; and we see pig and donkey bicycling back home together, greeted happily by the Palmer wife and children.

This divertissement was followed by Steig's most ambitious work, *Abel's Island* (1976). And nowhere else are Steig's verbal and illustrative gifts so beautifully matched as in this novel that takes its inspiration from *The Odyssey* and *Robinson Crusoe*, and which tells how Abel the mouse, picnicking with his new wife Amanda, gets caught in a violent thunderstorm. While attempting to retrieve his wife's scarf, Abel gets carried off in a torrential stream and winds up on an island, from which he tries unsuccessfully to escape by means of boats, makeshift bridges, and catapults. Filled with loneliness and self-pity, he is befriended by his personal star, which tells him, "You will do what you will do."

The rest of this novel narrates the ways in which Abel makes himself a home inside a hollow log and learns, like Robinson Crusoe, to accept his solitary existence and to turn the chance of isolation into an occasion of spiritual realization. As Jeremy Steig comments: "When Abel's finally in touch with himself for the first time in his life, he realizes he can learn to do everything. That's my father—having Abel do what he'd see himself doing in that situation."

Meditating on rain, dreaming of Amanda and sharing psychic thoughts with her, Abel turns into a true self-governing creature who decides to become a sculptor—participating, like nature, in the "designing and arranging of things"—and who, at the first signs of a false spring, exclaims: "What a lovely day! It's February, isn't it? I need to be moving."

After a while, however, he begins in the cold to feel resentment toward Amanda: "How could he go on having warm, alive feelings for merely remembered beings? Living was more than remembering, imagining. He wanted the real Amanda at his side, and he tried to reach out to her. His messages, it seemed, could not travel through the icy air. . . . As far as he really knew, he himself was the only, lonely, living thing that existed, and in his coma of coldness [think of Emily Dickinson's poem], he was not so sure of that."

Real spring arrives, and Abel goes mad on flowers and wine. He also meets up with one of Steig's most fantastic creatures, Gower the frog, who played "country music, had great-grandchildren by the dozen, all of whom were musical, and was happy with his old wife, though they often quarreled and spent whole days sitting around in a huff, trying to remember what they were angry about." The spaced-out Gower has a habit of forgetting and of going into trances: "He was in one of his reptilian torpors again. There he crouched with heavy-lidded, unseeing eyes, not asleep, not awake, not dead, not alive, still as a stone, gyrating with the world."

One day Gower leaves, and Abel feels lonesome again. But looking at the sculpture he has made of the frog, Abel "had new insight into the mystical expression on his face. He realized that if Gower was not drilled into remembering the everyday world, it became a dream that faded from mind as he dwelled on the ultimate reality beyond it. If he remembered his family, that was because a family is the one thing nobody can ever forget. Abel built fires to make smoke signals again and sent messages down the river. . . ."

Remembering the "dreaminess and vivacity" of his wife, Abel aches to be with her. In late summer he finally is able to cross the river, and, touching the other shore, experiences "a burst of astonishing joy. . . . He was imagining ahead to Amanda, and beyond her to his family, his friends, and a renewed life in society that would include productive work, his art; but he was also remembering his year on the island, a unique and separate segment of his life that he was now glad he had gone through, though he was also glad it was over."

After a final menacing encounter with a cat, he arrives at his home town, spies his wife in the park, but decides that "their reunion should be theirs alone." And in a series of four drawings—Abel lying on the couch, Amanda returning to her home and noticing the scarf Abel has left by the door, then running ecstatically to the couch, and finally embracing her husband—Steig wordlessly concludes his book.

· · ·

Since 1976, William Steig has published five additional picture books. *The Amazing Bone* (1976), like *Roland*, is about a pig, but for the first time in Steig's children's books he presents us with a heroine ("I guess it's easier for a boy to write about a boy than about a girl," Steig says, smiling). Pearl, walking home from school, dawdles in the woods to enjoy the odors of spring flowers (shown in a radiant, Bonnardesque double-page drawing), whereupon she comes across a magic bone that can make any sound in the world. The bone scares off a pack of robbers, but has less luck with a dapper fox, who takes Pearl to his den of iniquity to eat her for supper. Luckily, at the last moment, the bone remembers certain magical spells that transform the fox into the size of a mouse. Pearl returns home, and "anyone who happened to be alone in the house always had the bone to converse with. And they all had music whenever they wanted it, and sometimes even when they didn't."

Caleb and Kate (1977) is a more complex transformation tale and the first of Steig's children's books in which he talks about and draws adult human beings. And one is reminded that children's books—certainly picture books—are usually read by adults to and with children, and that the best of these books must therefore be meant for and significant to adults as well as to their supposed audience. What makes *Caleb and Kate* so interesting is the way in which it undoubtedly speaks to parents who may find themselves at odds with each other, and to children who may be upset by their parents' arguments. As with all the best children's books, there are thus "two" versions of *Caleb and Kate*—one for adults, one for children—both read simultaneously.

"Caleb the carpenter and Kate the weaver loved each other," the book begins, "but not every single minute. Once in a while they'd differ about this or that and wind up in such a fierce quarrel you'd never believe they were husband and wife." After one especially crazy quarrel, Caleb walks out of the house and into the nearby woods, where, like Gower the frog, he immediately forgets what the fight was about. "He could only remember that he loved her. He could only remember her dimples and her sweet ways, and what fragrant noodle pudding she made."

Instead of returning home immediately, however, he takes a nap, during which time Yedida the witch discovers Caleb and decides to test out her latest spell. When Caleb wakes up he realizes he has been transformed not, like Sylvester, into a rock but into a dog. And with this *donnée*, Steig turns the table on the positive notions of animal faith and animal happiness that he had promulgated in *Dominic*. For Caleb, returning home as a dog, is no longer able to communicate with his wife. Unlike Dominic, he is not a "symbolical human being"—he walks on all fours like the "dog" (despicable fellow) he has been to his wife and has now turned into. "Poor lost animal!" Kate calls him. "Stand aside, silly dog," she scolds him. "This is no time for games. I must find my dear husband. He may be in serious trouble."

Trailing Kate, Caleb the dog follows her into the gray, lifeless woods (another characteristically powerful double-page illustration), past a group of rocks that remind us of Sylvester's fate. "There was no finding Caleb because there he was behind his wife, with the shape and the shadow of a dog." In a sense, then, we might see in this hopeless search the loss of intimacy and understanding that must have provoked Caleb's and Kate's original quarrel:

> When Kate went to bed that night, Caleb got into his rightful place beside her, snuggled against her dear body, kissed her sweet neck as he'd always done, and sighed out his sorrows. She welcomed the dog's warmth. With him there, she felt less bereft.
> She fell asleep with her arm around him, but he was awake all night, wide-eyed, wondering. How could he manage to make himself known to his wife? If he could only tell her somehow that the dog in her arms was her husband? If he could only return to his natural state. Or if Kate could perhaps become a dog. Then they could be dogs together.

But Kate grows to love her dog. She trains him and shows him off to her and his old friends ("He enjoyed these gatherings, the human conversation, but he didn't like to have his head patted by his old cronies"). And then, in an extraordinary scene, we see Caleb reveling in the green smell of the grass, as some other dogs turn up and entice him into romping with them. "Caleb loved it, but soon quit and retired into the house, where the others dared not follow. He had discovered that being a dog among dogs could be a joyous sport, but he didn't want to forget who he was." Neither dog nor man, he returns sorrowfully to the woods, hoping to find "in that luckless spot some clue to the secret of his transformation. . . . He watched Kate move through the house, hopeless now about ever being able to reveal his true self."

At this static point, something has to change. (As Reich wrote in *Ether, God and Devil*: "The immobility that strikes us as the hallmark of all human errors—the static, the absolute, the immovable, the eternal—might very well be an expression of human armoring." And as Blake put it: "Expect poison from the standing water.") Then one night, fighting off some robbers who have entered the house, Caleb gets wounded—which breaks the spell—and magically turns into *himself*. And having scared off the thieves, "Caleb and Kate leaped into each other's arms and cleaved together for a long time."

As Jeremy Steig says about the book: "I like the fact that it's about a middle-aged couple and that you can feel the physical relationship between them (Kate does take the dog to bed with her). In most stories you have Wrigley's chewing gum people, and in movies you hardly ever see a couple like Caleb and Kate. But love goes on a very long time, it's not just for twenty-year-olds."

In 1978 Steig published his picture book *Tiffky Doofky*, which depicts the adventures of a garbage-collector hound who, after consulting a fortune-telling goose, excitedly anticipates a meeting with the female of his dreams that very day. "Maybe I'll find her at the dump," he muses. And there, depicted in the brilliant two-page drawing of the country dump, Tiffky discovers—like the doll found by Dominic—"a necklace agleam with emeralds on a bed of sauerkraut." He then comes across a villainous chicken, and in a series of anxiety-inducing encounters is led astray by a lady scarecrow, an evil cat, and a lunatic butterfly collector. Dreaming at the side of a road of his love-to-be, the hero wakes up to find himself being strangled by a boa constrictor, which releases its grip at the arrival of Estrella, the snake-trainer dog. He gives her the necklace she has lost, and they gaze lovingly at each other in the sunset.

Although it contains some of the wittiest of his picture-book illustrations, *Tiffky Doofky*, as Steig admits, is not one of his most successful works. "I labored over it too long, and it wasn't inspired enough," he says. "People think that writing or painting is hard work, but that's because of our armor. When we function naturally, it becomes a joy. If we fail, it's because we're not functioning well."

Steig was certainly functioning at the height of his powers when he created his recent picture book, *Gorky Rises* (1980), which tells of Gorky the frog's attempt to concoct a magic potion in the kitchen sink. The result is a bottle of "reddish-golden liquid full of tiny bubbles that glinted like particles of fire." (Liquefied orgone energy, perhaps!) Like Pearl, who dawdles dreamily through the spring woods in *The Amazing Bone*, Gorky saunters joyfully through the early summer fields ("The world was all magic, and he had a special bottle of it in his right hand"). As he lies stretched out on the grass—the bottle resting on his hip—an entranced Gorky seems at one with all aspects of the universe ("The wide, open sky outside him was bright with brilliant sun, but the sky inside him shimmered with stars"). And as we turn the page, we see Gorky's slumbering body floating up into the gentle blue sky "like a bubble rising in water."

Just as Amos on the deck of his little boat in *Amos and Boris* stares up in wonder at the immense starry sky, so Gorky sails through the air in some of Steig's most spacious drawings, feeling the "brilliant bubbles flow into his arm from the bottle he held in his hand," soaring past kites and passing over creatures and towns. But just as Amos gets thrown into the open sea, so Gorky finds himself caught in the midst of storms, and he escapes to the heights of the sky where we see him, in an extraordinary illustration, limned helplessly against the cold, starlit heavens, looking for all the world like one of Steig's Lonely Ones, as he clutches in terror onto what now seems to be a baby's bottle. Like Sylvester, he feels motherless, fatherless, homeless. But finally he decides to remove the bottle's stopper and to release the magic liquid drop by drop, thereby allowing him to fall gradually down to earth. He lands on Elephant Rock—which, in a very child-like turn of events, turns into a real elephant—where Gorky's anxious parents find him at last and take their much-adventured son home to bed.

Rarely have the ecstasies and terrors of flying been so simply and beautifully suggested as in Steig's illustrations for *Gorky Rises*. Connected to the freedom of flying is, of course, the fantasy of sexual potency, suggested in Steig's depiction of the slumbering Gorky with the magic bottle on his hips. When I pointed this out to him, Steig agreed. "It's an erection," he said, "and it's interesting that I only noticed it after I drew it—it wasn't consciously intended at all. . . . I suppose librarians wouldn't appreciate it," Steig added, smiling, "but I'm sure they won't blame me for what you find there."

Also connected to the freedom of flying is the freedom of drawing—the kind of freedom one finds in Steig's most recent cartoon collection *Drawings* (1980). "Illustrating," Steig asserts, "is hard work for me because it's very unspontaneous. *Gorky Rises* was closer to drawing because in most of the pictures there was only one character, and I didn't have to repeat landscapes very much: If you have just a blue sky, you don't have to worry about where it is. So I felt freer and less constrained. The only way I can draw is by working so quickly that I don't know what I'm doing. I draw what wants to come out." And Jeanne Steig states: "When Bill draws, he doesn't sit down with an idea. He sits down, his *hand* draws, and he looks and he laughs and he sees what's happening."

When I ask him which of his children's books are his favorites, he mentions *Sylvester and the Magic Pebble* and *Abel's Island* because "I remember doing them with excitement." It is the *doing* of things that excites Steig and reveals him to be a true Reichian. And it is this sense of doing—along with Steig's Reichian notion that "the artistic activity of human beings is creative, form-making energy exercising its fullest powers, just as it does throughout the universe—without 'practical' intention"—that suggests an affinity between Reich's ideas and the work of some of the greatest creative artists of the century: Igor Stravinsky ("My knowledge is activity. I discover it as I work, and I know it while I am discovering it, but only in a very different way before and after"); Charlie Chaplin ("Life is a desire, not a meaning"); George Balanchine ("Choreography is like cooking or gardening. Not like painting, because painting stays. Dancing disintegrates. Like a garden. Lots of roses come up and in the evening they're gone. Next day the sun comes up. It's life. I'm connected to what is part of life"); and Pablo Picasso ("The picture is not thought out and fixed in advance; while it is being made it follows the mobility of one's thoughts").

Steig's children's books are all filled with shining suns. And it was Picasso who said: "Any man can make the sun into a yellow ball. Ah, but to make a yellow ball into a sun!" Jeanne Steig says: "Bill talks about Picasso, and Reich, and his father in the present tense—they *love*, they *do*, they *say*; they're really important people to him and they're really with him."

William Steig is with us, too (his most recent picture book, *Doctor De Soto*, published in 1982, shows a mouse-dentist high-spiritedly outfoxing a foxy patient), reminding us—as he writes in his "Notes"—that "painters do not help us shed our tears, but demand of us joy in creation. . . . The active, ardent spectator re-creates the painting, following the paths of energy laid down by the artist. He experiences again what the artist experienced in making the painting: movement, emotion, a glorying in man's boundless creative power, and wonder—which is respect for life."

THE HAPPY
CHILDHOODS OF
PIPPI LONGSTOCKING
AND
ASTRID LINDGREN

PHOTOGRAPH BY JAN COLLSIÖÖ. BY PERMISSION OF BILD A-B

$\mathcal{I}$n *The Children of Noisy Village*, Astrid Lindgren narrates the adventures of six nine- to-eleven-year-olds (three boys, three girls) living in the Swedish farming area of Småland, where the author herself grew up. The children play in the linden tree's branches that connect two of three neighboring farms, celebrate holidays, visit grandparents, make huts by the lake, mingle with the animals (horses, cows, pigs, sheep, chickens, rabbits), and meet up with villagers like the shoemaker Mr. Kind, who thinks that "youngsters are a wild lot who should get spanked every day." It is a book that recalls and celebrates a kind of childhood that has become increasingly rare today. "Does Noisy Village really exist?" a young reader once wrote Astrid Lindgren. "For if it does," she added, "I don't want to live in Vienna anymore."

In *The Children of Noisy Village*, Lisa—the girl through whose eyes we see this childhood world—informs us:

> Britta and Anna gave me a storybook, and Olaf gave me a chocolate bar. He sat down next to me, and my brothers started teasing us.
> "Boyfriend and girlfriend, boyfriend and girlfriend!"
> They say that just because Olaf is not one of those silly boys who won't play with girls. He doesn't care if Karl and Bill do tease him; he plays with both boys and girls anyway. Karl and Bill want to play with girls, too, although they pretend they don't.

And this episode suggests one of the unfortunate facts about the way one reads children's literature as a child: Girls will read "boys'" books, but boys will refuse to read about girls. It is this immemorially ingrained categorization and segregation of children's books by sex that made me, when I was young, forego the experience of reading classics like *Little Women*, *What Katy Did*, *Rebecca of Sunnybrook Farm*, *Anne of Green Gables*, *Caddie Woodlawn*, and *Strawberry Girl*. And it is only as an adult that I chanced to discover the *Pippi Longstocking* books by Astrid Lindgren.

I became curious about them after four of my closest women friends told me of the strong impression the character of Pippi Longstocking had made on them when they were young. Since the child is mother of the woman, I decided to find out about Pippi (and therefore about my friends) by reading the books, and thereby came upon one of the greatest characters in children's literature.

Like the name of Peter Rabbit, Pippi Longstocking's name is legion—e.g., Pippi Långstrump (Swedish), Pipi Gūrāb-baland (Persian), Peppi Dlinnyjčulok (Russian), Ochame-na Pippi (Japanese)—and Astrid Lindgren's books about her have been translated into more than twenty-five languages. She is certainly one of the most curious (and subversive) immortals of world literature. A freckled nine-year-old with carrot-colored hair worn in two tight braids, Pippi gets her name from the way she wears one black and one brown stocking with black shoes that are twice as long as her feet. When we meet her, she is living alone—her mother died when Pippi was very young and is now "an angel . . . up in heaven," and her father, a sea captain, has been blown overboard in a storm; but Pippi is sure he floated to shore on an island and is now king of the cannibals. Her little home, a ramshackle house called Villa Villekulla, is surrounded by "an overgrown garden with old trees covered with moss, and unmowed lawns, and lots of flowers which were allowed to grow exactly as they pleased." And this is the way Pippi lives her life—exactly as she pleases. She provides for herself with a suitcase filled with gold pieces and a chest of drawers that contain an illimitable supply of gifts. She tells herself when to go to bed, sleeps with her feet on the pillow and her head way under the covers, and because she doesn't receive letters, writes them to herself. Her motto is: "Don't you worry about me. I'll always come out on top."

Pippi's only companions are a horse, which lives on her porch, and a monkey named Mr. Nilsson. She also befriends her next-door neighbors' children, Tommy and Annika—"good, well brought up, and obedient." When they first see Pippi, she is walking backward because she doesn't want to turn around to get home. "Why did I walk backward?" asks Pippi. "Isn't this a free country? Can't a person walk any way she wants to?" And Tommy and Annika realize that "this was not going to be one of those dull days."

There isn't a dull day in all the three *Pippi Longstocking* books (*Pippi Longstocking, Pippi Goes on Board, Pippi in the South Seas*) as Pippi turns into a Thing-Finder ("When you're a Thing-Finder you don't have a minute to spare") who uncovers articles like a rusty tin can and an empty spool of thread ("The whole world is full of things, and someone has to look for them"). She and her new friends

Tommy and Annika become inseparable as they hide in a hollow oak tree, where they mysteriously find soda pop to drink, and go on picnics. Pippi is always leading the way to new adventures, and she is the possessor of great physical strength—she calls herself "the strongest girl in the world"—lifting up her horse with her hands, overpowering two policemen who come to take her to a children's home, wrestling with and defeating the strongest man in the world at the circus, exhausting and warding off two burglars, and taming a tiger at a fair.

Pippi Longstocking as drawn by Louis Glanzman, from *Pippi Goes on Board*

Pippi lives completely outside bourgeois conventions. The teacher at school asks her to leave the classroom and come back only when she learns to behave. At a coffee party given by Tommy and Annika's mother, she eats all the cakes and shocks the ladies present with dramatically acted-out stories of her grandmother's maid who never swept under the beds. She washes her hair in a pool and has thereby "saved a visit to the hairdresser." She steps into a gutter—"I love gutters," she says—and wonders what's wrong with being soaked. To a teacher who asks: "You want to be a really fine lady when you grow up, don't you?" Pippi answers: "You mean the kind with a veil on her nose and three double chins under it?" When a supercilious, rich old lady named Miss Rosenblom gives out gifts only to the good and hard-working schoolchildren, demeaning all the others, Pippi does her own corrective examining, judging, and awarding of gold pieces.

She is, moreover, contemptuous of money. After winning a hundred dollars in a wrestling contest, she says, "What would I want with that old piece of paper. Take it and use it to fry herring on if you want to."

When her sea-captain father shows up unexpectedly, he and Pippi immediately arm-wrestle, then dance and wrestle some more. And after climbing a tree in order to save two children from a burning building, she climbs back up the tree, raising her arms to the night sky while a shower of sparks falls on her, and dances wildly while singing a song:

> The fire is burning,
> It's burning so bright,
> The flames are leaping and prancing.
> It's burning for you,
> It's burning for me,
> It's burning for all who are dancing!

But Pippi always uses her powers wisely. When she, Tommy, and Annika visit her father on a South Sea island—spending "wonderful days in a warm wonderful world full of sunshine with the blue sea glittering and fragrant flowers everywhere"—she is chosen to be a princess by the natives, but renounces her position immediately, saying, "I'm through with this throne business." She consistently refuses to join the compromised adult world, commenting: "Grown-ups never have any fun. They only have a lot of boring work and wear silly-looking clothes and have corns and minicipal [sic] taxes."

At the conclusion of the third volume, Pippi gives Tommy and Annika some pills (they are actually ordinary peas) which, she tells them, when taken in the dark after repeating a rhyme ("Pretty little chililug,/I don't want to get bug"), will make it impossible for them to grow up. And after this little ritual, Tommy and Annika return home, where they can see through the window of Pippi's kitchen. And there, in a beautiful farewell—similar to that of Mary Poppins's final ascent into the heavens—we find Pippi sitting at the table with her head leaning against her arms:

> She was staring at the little flickering flame of a candle that was standing in front of her. She seemed to be dreaming.
> "She—she looks so alone," said Annika, and her voice trembled a little. "Oh, Tommy, if it were only morning so that we could go to her right away!"

They stood there in silence and looked out into the winter night. The stars were shining over Villa Villekulla's roof. Pippi was inside. She would always be there. That was a comforting thought. The years would go by, but Pippi and Tommy and Annika would not grow up. That is, of course, if the strength hadn't gone out of the chililug pills. There would be new springs and summers, new autumns and winters, but their games would go on. Tomorrow they would build a snow hut and make a ski slope from the roof of Villa Villekulla, and when spring came they would climb the hollow oak where soda pop spouted up. They would hunt for treasure and they would ride Pippi's horse. They would sit in the woodbin and tell stories. Perhaps they would also take a trip to Kurrekurredutt Island now and then, to see Momo and Moana and the others. But they would always come back to Villa Villekulla.

And the most wonderful, comforting thought was that Pippi would always be in Villa Villekulla.

"If she would only look in this direction we could wave to her," said Tommy.

But Pippi continued to stare straight ahead with a dreamy look. Then she blew out the light.

As the philosopher Gaston Bachelard wrote in *The Poetics of Reverie* (as if to describe this scene): "There are moments in childhood when every child is the astonishing being, the being who realizes the *astonishment of being.* We thus discover within ourselves an *immobile childhood,* a *childhood without becoming,* liberated from the gear-wheels of the calendar." And, Bachelard continues: "In every dreamer there lives a child, a child whom reverie magnifies and stabilizes. Reverie tears it away from history, sets it outside time, makes it foreign to time. One more reverie and this permanent, magnified child is a god."

Certainly, Pippi Longstocking shares the physical strength of mythological and legendary child heroes like Hercules and Cúchulainn —the latter of whom contested with a hundred and fifty other youths and beat them all, calling himself "a boy with a difference!" And Pippi is indeed "a girl with a difference!" But, moreover, with her gold coins, her unending supply of presents from her chest of drawers, and her peas of immortality, she also resembles the Norse goddess of spring, the ever-young Iduna, possessor of the golden apples of immortality which she kept in a golden treasure chest that always remained full—apples that gave youth to the deities of Asgard.

On a less exalted but more important level, however, it is interesting to notice how the *Pippi Longstocking* books broke with the
centuries-old tradition of depicting girls in children's literature. Generally speaking, girls in eighteenth- and nineteen-century children's
books were advised to be docile, submissive, self-sacrificing, pious,
grateful, obedient, clean, virtuous, dutiful, modest, and retiring creatures. Rousseau set the familiar tone in *Emile* with his sententious
comments concerning how Sophie should behave:

> A man has no one but himself to consider, and so long as he does
> right he may defy public opinion; but when a woman does right her
> task is only half finished, and what people think of her matters as
> much as what she really is.

> Women should be strong enough to do anything gracefully; men
> should be skillful enough to do anything easily.

> Women should not be strong like men but *for* them, so that their
> sons may be strong.

> A man seeks to serve, a woman seeks to please.

> It is amusing to see her occasionally return to her old ways and
> indulge in childish mirth and then suddenly check herself, with silent
> lips, downcast eyes, and rosy blushes; neither child nor woman, she
> may well partake of both.

> A virtuous woman is little lower than the angels.

Benighted as the author was with regard to Sophie's educational possibilities—he simply prescribed and subscribed to what in fact was the
prevailing, obtuse point of view of his time—Rousseau was an inspired utopian prophet when he wrote of his educational ideas for
Emile:

> Teach him to live rather than to avoid death: life is not breath, but
> action, the use of our senses, our mind, our faculties, every part of
> ourselves which makes us conscious of our being. Life consists less in
> length of days than in the keen sense of living.

> There is only one man who gets his own way—he who can get it
> single-handed; therefore freedom, not power, is the greatest good.
> That man is truly free who desires what he is able to perform and

does what he desires. This is my fundamental maxim. Apply it to childhood, and all the rules of education spring from it.

The education of the earliest years should be merely negative. It consists, not in teaching virtue or truth, but in preserving the heart from vice and from the spirit of error.

You are afraid to see him spending his early years doing nothing? What, is it nothing to be happy, nothing to run and jump all day? He will never be so busy again all his life long.

He does not know the meaning of habit, routine, and custom; what he did yesterday has no control over what he is doing today; he follows no rule, submits to no authority, copies no pattern, and only acts or speaks as he pleases. So do not expect set speeches or studied manners from him, but just the faithful expression of his thoughts and the conduct that springs from his inclinations.

He has reached the perfection of childhood; he has lived the life of a child; his progress has not been bought at the price of his happiness, he has gained both.

It is clear that Pippi Longstocking *is* Emile—the perfect fictional embodiment.

Needless to say, there were books earlier than *Pippi Longstocking* (first published in 1945) that presented fearless and free-thinking heroines: Susan Coolidge's Katy (who hated sewing and "didn't care a button about being called 'good'"), Louisa May Alcott's Jo (who had "blunt manners" and a "too independent spirit"), and Carol R. Brink's Caddie Woodlawn (who liked to run through the woods with her brothers). But each one of these girls ends up by having or deciding to renounce her tomboy ways. As Jo's father says on his return home: "I don't see the 'son Jo' whom I left a year ago . . . I see a young lady who pins her collar straight, laces her boots neatly, and neither whistles, talks slang, nor lies on the rug as she used to do. . . . I rather miss my wild girl; but if I get a strong, helpful, tender-hearted woman in her place, I shall feel quite satisfied."*

* In an essay entitled "Sexism in Children's Literature," published in the early 1970s, a collective called the Feminists on Children's Media criticized works such as *Caddie Woodlawn*—and I'm sure *What Katy Did* and *Little Women* could have been included—as being "Cop-out Books," stating: "The Cop-out Book is often the most insidious. At its worst, it promises much and delivers nothing. But the better ones are the most infuriating, for often they are only

Pippi Longstocking shares many of the qualities of the above characters; and, surprisingly, she also might be seen to derive certain of her characteristics and spirit from the nineteenth-century tradition of ministering evangelical child waifs who were written about in Religious Tract Society stories like *Little Meg's Children, Jessica's First Prayer*, and *Christie's Old Organ*—God-fearing, motherless orphans who were morally superior to the adults around them. (As Gillian Avery states in *Childhood's Pattern:* "Mothers have a constricting effect on the plot and on the children's activities; their love is so embarrassingly obvious that it can't be overlooked, it stands in the way of that independence that children like to imagine.")

But Pippi never compromises and always remains unreconstructably herself,* for she is free of what the anarchist educator Max Stirner called "wheels in the head"—the knowledge which used and owned the individual rather than that which was used *by* the individual. Pippi exemplifies what Stirner thought of as "self-ownership" —the state in which the person is free from those dogmas and moral

---

a step away from being the exact kind of literature we'd like to see for girls *and* boys *about* girls.. The actual cop-out may be only a crucial line, a paragraph, the last chapter. But somewhere a sexist compromise is made, somewhere the book adjusts to the stereotyped role of woman, often for the sake of social pressure and conformity. The compromise brings with it a change, and this change is not only disturbing, but often distorts the logical development of the character herself. Suddenly her development is redirected—or, rather, stunted. . . . Young readers of such grievous cop-outs are forced to believe that the spunk, individuality, and physical capability so refreshingly portrayed in tomboy heroines must be surrendered when girls grow up—in order to fit the passive, supposedly more mature image of a young woman. But where is that earlier energy to be spent? Is depression in the adult woman perhaps linked to the painful suppression of so many sparks of life?" My only objection to these statements is that they overlook the fact that works like *Little Women* and *Caddie Woodlawn* contain in them the seeds of revolt that can and have inspired girls—regardless of the final compromises called for by the books. As Gillian Avery reminds us, Angela Brazil—author of the famous English girls' school books—once wrote that in her childhood she had been given R. M. Ballantyne's book *The Robber Kitten* about a kitten who ran away, proclaiming "I'll never more be good," and went to live a bandit's life. "Of course," Avery writes, "he came to grief and limped home to repent, but this point passed over Miss Brazil's head. She was infected by his magnificent and fascinating independence, and she too resisted all authority and stamped round chanting 'I'll never more be good.' She omitted the repentance, naturally."

* In this sense, she presages the more recent independent heroines whom we find in Scott O'Dell's *Island of the Blue Dolphin*, Louise Fitzhugh's *Harriet the Spy*, and Jean C. George's *Julie of the Wolves*.

imperatives that made him or her a "subservient and cringing" being —as well as what Wilhelm Reich called the "self-governing" character. Reich saw the patriarchal family structure as the ideological factory of the ruling order. (Think of Mr. Fairchild in Mrs. Sherwood's influential children's novel *The Fairchild Family*—published in 1818—who, after whipping his son, says: "I stand in place of God to you, whilst you are a child.") But among the Trobriand Islanders, Reich happily discovered a nonauthoritarian family structure that allowed young children either to remain with their parents during the day or to join with their friends in their own community—a miniature republic that functioned according to its own needs and desires. (Think of Pippi and Tommy and Annika on their various outings and voyage to the South Seas.) And like the dog-hero of William Steig's *Dominic*, Pippi Longstocking also partakes of what Reich saw as Jesus' true nature. As he wrote in *The Murder of Christ*: "Children who gleam with happiness are also born leaders of other children. The latter flock around them, love them, admire them, seek their praise and counsel. . . . Jesus knew that children have 'IT.' He loved children and he was childlike himself; knowing and yet naive; . . . streaming with love and kindness, and yet able to hit hard; gentle and yet strong, just as the child of the future is."

And this, too, is Pippi Longstocking.

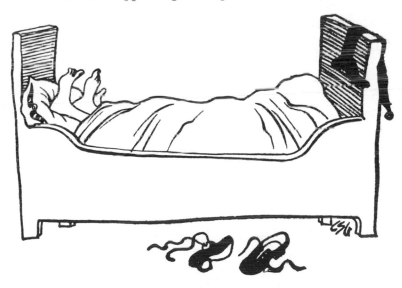

Pippi in bed, by Louis Glanzman, from *Pippi Longstocking*

· · ·

I visited briefly with Astrid Lindgren in May 1981. She greeted me at the door of her Stockholm apartment wearing a blue pantsuit, a blue scarf, and a necklace of colored baubles. "They make me look like a Christmas tree, don't they?" she laughed, as she took me through the foyer into the living room, which was lined with books and which had naïve and landscape paintings by Swedish artists hanging on the wall. We sat down and chatted—she gave the immediate impression of a person who is open, energetic, unpretentious, and unafraid (as any author of *Pippi Longstocking* would have to be)—and then I posed the predictable question: "How did Pippi come into the world?"

"I'm asked that all the time," she said, without impatience, in clear but hesitant English, "but I'll tell it to you as I've done before. In 1941 my then seven-year-old daughter Karin was sick in bed with pneumonia. Every evening when I sat by her bedside she would nag in that way children do: 'Tell me something!' And one evening, completely exhausted, I asked her: 'What should I tell?' And she answered, 'Tell about Pippi Longstocking!' She had come up with the name right there on the spot. I didn't ask her who Pippi Longstocking was, I just began the story, and since it was a strange name, it turned out to be a strange girl as well. Karin, and later even her playmates, showed a strong love for Pippi from the very beginning, and I had to tell the story again and again. It went on like that for several years.

"Then one day in March 1944 it snowed in Stockholm, and in the evening as I was out for a walk, there was fresh snow covering a layer of ice. Well, I slipped and fell, spraining one of my ankles. I was forced to stay in bed for a time. To make time pass, I started to take down the Pippi stories in shorthand—since my office days I've been a capable stenographer, and I still write all my books first in shorthand.

"In May 1944 Karin was to celebrate her tenth birthday, and I decided I would write out the Pippi story and give her the manuscript for a birthday present. And then I decided to send a copy to a publisher. Not that I believed for one minute that they would publish it, but even so! The fact was, I was rather upset about Pippi myself, and I remember concluding my letter to the publisher with 'In the hope that you won't notify the Child Welfare Committee'—

really because I had two children of my own, and what kind of a mother had they who wrote such books?!

"Just as I had thought, I got the manuscript back, but while I was waiting for it, I wrote another book and sent it to the publishing house of Rabén & Sjögren, which in 1944 announced a prize contest for girls' books. And it actually happened: I won second prize in the competition. I don't think I've ever been happier than on that autumn evening in 1944 when word came that I'd won. The next year, 1945, the same publishing house had a contest for children's books. I sent in the Pippi manuscript, and I received first prize.

"So maybe every children's book author should be sick in bed for a while [smiling]. And when I write, I lie in bed, put the book down in shorthand, and I have the feeling that nothing outside exists, I'm just on my bed in my little room and I can go and meet the people I want to."

"Pippi Longstocking seems as if she's always been around," I said.

"Maybe she was just waiting for someone to pick her and to write about her," Astrid Lindgren replied with a smile.

I read her Reich's statement about the child of the future.

"That's Pippi!" she exclaimed. "Pippi says: I'm going to be happy and free and stronger than anybody. She has power, but she never misuses it. She's just kind. . . . But do you think that children of the future will be like that? I'd be very happy if I could believe that. I don't know what will happen to our world if there aren't any happy leaders being born."

"You've written many children's books," I continued. "And in many of them the idea of being happy as a child in summertime occurs over and over (Pippi in the South Seas is really a glorified summer outing). In your book Bill Bergson Lives Dangerously, for instance, you write: 'There were nooks and crannies to hide in, fences to climb over, winding small alleyways where you could shake off your pursuers; there were roofs to climb and woodsheds and out-houses in the back yard where you could barricade yourselves. As long as a town had all these advantages, it need not be beautiful. It was enough that the sun was shining, and that the cobblestones were feeling so warm and comfortable under your bare feet that you felt it was summer in all your body.'"

"I think you should feel everything in your whole body—whatever there is to feel," Astrid Lindgren responded. "In Sweden we

especially need the summer. And when you look back at your childhood, you think it was always summer, in a way, because everything
was at its best then. I want to feel summer in my whole body and in
my heart."

"It's interesting," I added, "that in 1977 a controversial novel
came out in Sweden by P. C. Jersild, called *Children's Island* which
tells of an eleven-year-old boy named Reine who refuses to go to
municipal children's camp, and, since his mother has left for her own
vacation, he returns to their empty apartment in the suburbs of
Stockholm where he hides out and spends his time reading *The
Guinness Book of Records* and Donald Duck comics (apparently the
favorite reading material of Swedish schoolchildren today). On his
first day alone he fakes a letter to his mother which goes: 'Hi Mom.
It's great on Children's Island. We swim and play football. The food
is yummy. This morning I got stung by a bee on my big toe (bravo,
bravo!) but the nurse gave me some salve. Tonight we'll roast hot
dogs outside.' And Jersild comments: 'That would have to be enough
this time. [Reine] felt he'd finished with the whole summer in five
lines.'

"Things have certainly changed since the days when you wrote
Pippi Longstocking and the *Bill Bergson* series," I commented. "No
matter how lonely some of your child characters might feel, they
never seem to experience this suffocating sense of anomie and resignation and isolation."

"Things *have* changed," Astrid Lindgren replied. "I'm afraid
that children don't play the way we did as children and as they do
in my books. They participate in sports, but they don't *play*. Now
they look at television. TV broadens the mind in one way but nar-
rows it in another. It gives you more facts and words and information,
but it limits your imagination. It's on a more superficial level than
when a child reads a book, because he or she has to create his or her
own pictures, which are more lovely and beautiful than you can ever
see on TV. On the whole I think it's damaging if you can't control it.
I met a mother in America who told me that her daughter had
watched TV for eighteen hours one day! She must have been crazy
at that point. And I'm sure that there are many homes in which
parents don't speak to their children and children don't speak to their
parents. I can't write for teenagers now, I don't know enough about
them, they're completely unlike the Bergson children—there's no
resemblance at all. When I was a child we didn't have cars, TV,

radio, or even many films. So there was a lot of room for imagination!"

"You once said: 'That our Lord let children be children before they grew up was one of his better ideas.' And I wanted to know something about your own childhood, since you've also said that 'it is my childhood that I long to return to . . . and if I dare to be so bold as to speak of inspiration, I must say that it is there in my childhood home that I get many of the impulses that can later appear in a story.' "

"My father, Samuel August Ericsson," she explained, "was a peasant, a renter of a vicar's farm, and fell in love with my mother, Hannah from Hult, when he was thirteen and she was nine—and she remained his 'devotedly little beloved one' throughout their life together. She died eight years before him—we thought he'd die, too. But no, he said that some leave ahead, others leave later, there's nothing you can do. He enjoyed living, and he was sure that one day he'd meet her again; and he continued to love her and talk about her and to praise all her virtues. They were strong believers, which my brother and sisters and I were not. In the Bible we read that there is no marriage in heaven, just angels. So I told my father about the 'little angel Hannah,' and he got quite angry at the thought that Hannah should be there as an angel and not belong to him!

"And I've written a memoir about my parents' love affair and about my childhood," Astrid Lindgren said as she got up to find a copy in one of the bookshelves [*Samuel August från Sevedstorp och Hanna i Hult*]. "It's never been translated into English, so perhaps you could find someone to do that, and then you can find out everything." (Thanks to Ann B. Weissmann I did!)

Astrid Lindgren, the second of four children (three girls, one boy), was raised on a farm called Näs near the little town of Vimmerby in Småland. Her extraordinarily happy childhood was, as she tells us, filled with security and freedom: "security in having those two there, those who cared so much for each other and who were there all the time if we needed them, but who—if we did not need them—left us free to roam around the fantastic childhood playground we had at Näs. Surely we were disciplined with order and the fear of God, as was the tradition of the time, but in our playful life we were wonderfully free and never controlled. And we played and played and played, and it is a wonder we didn't play ourselves to

The farmhouse at Näs, Astrid Lindgren's childhood home, in the summer of 1915

death. We were climbing like apes in trees and on roofs, we jumped from lumber piles and hay lofts so that our innards complained, we crawled through our dangerous subterranean tunnels in the sawdust heap, we were swimming in the river long before we knew how to swim, totally forgetting the imperative by our mother not to 'go further out than the navel.' But all four of us survived."

Free from nagging and free to play, the children, at age six, were still expected to learn how to thin fodder beets and cut nettles for the poultry. "Just go on, don't stop" was their mother's admonition when they started dreaming over the dish pail—a piece of advice Astrid Lindgren says she has taken to heart throughout her life. And the children, far from being sheltered from adult reality, learned about life from the servant girls and farmhands: "It was fun and it was instructive for a child to grow up as I did with people of varying habits and types and ages. Without them knowing it and without me knowing it myself, I learned something from them about the conditions of life and how problematic it can be to be a human being. I learned other things as well, for this was an outspoken sort of people who did not keep anything back just because children happened to be around. And we were there, my siblings and myself, for we had to bring them coffee while they were working the fields. That is what I remember best, the coffee breaks when all were gathered, sitting there at the edge of a ditch, drinking coffee and dunking their rye-bread sandwiches and exchanging thoughts about this and that."

Astrid and her siblings, moreover, often used to run through a little stretch of forest and wind up visiting Stenbäcksroten, a group of small cottages where many outcasts of society lived—paupers, "coffee bitches" (women who were supposed to have gone mad from drinking too much coffee), and the village prostitute. There were vagabonds in their hayloft every night (probably the models for Paradise Oscar the Tramp, who befriends the orphan boy Rasmus in the author's moving *Rasmus and the Vagabond*) who arrived in the twilight and bought some milk and bread for the night. And Astrid, always curious, often investigated local lore: "Our cow-tender told us that if we walked around the coffin house in the cemetery twelve times at twelve o'clock at night, the devil would appear in all his hideousness. 'And then it happens, then "Knös" comes to fetch one,' that was the saying. And of course we had to find out if that was really true, just as we had to find out about the coffee bitches and their wickedness toward children. I believe that we spent a great deal of our time exploring what was true and what was not true in this world."

Sundays were begrudgingly devoted to Sunday school and church, for which Astrid was forced to wear "freshly washed, coarse, black wool stockings" that she detested. (Perhaps the refusal of the author's five-year-old heroine of *Lotta on Troublemaker Street* to wear an itchy, striped sweater—Lotta cuts it to pieces with scissors and then runs away—is her author's fantasy revenge for having had to wear those hated stockings as a child!) But she looked forward to traveling to family parties at her grandmother's in a horse-driven *vurst*, the journey there smelling of "horses and sunbaked leather and the resin of the pine trees". . . while the homebound journeys found her "half asleep watching the black forest under the light summer sky; and perhaps I remember even better going home from the Christmas parties, bedded down in the basketweave sleigh listening to the sleigh bells and looking up into the starry sky. . . . Yes, it was good to be a child in the age of horses." And then there were the fall and spring fairs in Vimmerby, when the streets were taken over by itinerant menageries and carnivals and were filled with candy-women, merchants, farmers, and horse dealers.

But even more than the people she grew up with, Astrid Lindgren most of all remembers nature: "The strawberry patches, the hepatica hills, the meadows with primulas, the blueberry lands, the woods where the linneas tinkled their pink bells in the moss, the pastures around Näs where we knew every path and every rock, the stream with the water lilies, the ditches, the creeks, and the trees—I remember those more than I remember the people. Rocks and trees were as close to us as living beings, and nature protected and nurtured our playing and our dreaming. Whatever our imagination could call forth was enacted in the land around us, all fairy tales, all adventures we invented or read about or heard about, all of it happened there and only there, even our songs and prayers had their places in surrounding nature."

But while she was "soaking up nature," Astrid was also introduced to "culture" when she was about five years old, by a little girl named Edith, the daughter of a cowhand and his wife, Kristin: "This girl Edith—blessed be she now and forever—read to me the fairy tale about the Giant Bam-Bam and the fairy Viribunda, and thus set my childish soul into a movement which has not yet completely ceased. The miracle occurred in the kitchen of a poor farmhand, and from that day on, there is no other kitchen in the world."

Eventually, Astrid learned to read herself and ordered books for Christmas. Her first volume was *Snow White* "with a chubby, black-tressed princess by Jenny Nyström on the cover; later, I bought *Among Leprechauns and Trolls* with the unforgettable illustrations by John Bauer. Imagine, to be the sole owner of a book—a wonder I didn't faint for pure happiness! I can still remember how these books smelled when they arrived, fresh from the printer; yes, I started by smelling them [N.B.: Maurice Sendak's similar response as a child], and there was no lovelier scent in all the world. It was full of foretaste and anticipation."

At ten, Astrid went to a school that had a library, and began "devouring" everything: the *Iliad, Robinson Crusoe, Uncle Tom's Cabin, The Count of Monte Cristo, The Jungle Books, Huckleberry Finn,* among others. "And then all the wonderful books for girls. Imagine, there were so many girls in the world who were suddenly as close to oneself as ever any beings of flesh and blood! There was Hetty, the Irish whirlwind, and Polly, a jewel of a girl from New England, Pollyanna and Katy, not to mention Sara, the one with the diamond mines who became so wondrously poor and was freezing in her attic until Ram Dass came climbing across the roof with soup and warm blankets. And then of course Anne of Green Gables: Oh, my unforgettable one, forever you will be riding the cart with Matthew Cuthbert beneath the flowering apple trees of Avonlea! How I lived with that girl! A whole summer my sisters and I played at Anne of Green Gables in the big sawdust heap at the sawmill; I was Diana Barry, and the pond at the manure heap was the Dark Reflecting Waves." She also confesses to having read mysteries, "tear-dripping" love stories, and religious books—"in my opinion, all of these books were good books, please notice that! But then, of course, I do not believe in the system of using children as literary critics."

She found it hard to find time to read as much as she wanted to since "it was assumed that the children would help around the house. I was frequently put to rocking and singing to my youngest sister, who refused to go to sleep otherwise, and that was an ordeal if one had just come across a good book. But I managed. I sang from the book, page after page. It took more time than usual, of course, but I could do it. 'There is a woman alone in the woods and crying, tralalala'—my sisters still repeat that as an example of my exercises in singing and reading."

In school her classmates used to say, "You'll turn out to be an author when you grow up" or, more sarcastically, "You'll be the Selma Lagerlöf of Vimmerby." "That scared me so much," Astrid Lindgren recalls, "that I made a firm decision—never to write a book! It says already in Ecclesiastes that there is no end to the making of books, and I didn't feel that I would be the right person to increase the stacks of books further. I stuck to my decision until March of 1944. But then that snow fell and made the streets slippery as soap. I fell, I sprained my ankle, I had to stay in bed, and I had nothing to do. So what does one do? Maybe write a book? I wrote *Pippi Longstocking.* . . . That's why I write children's books. And it is all nothing but a continuation of what started in Kristin's kitchen that long ago."

Back in Astrid Lindgren's living room, I asked her about the old red farmhouse, surrounded by apple trees, where she was born and raised. "That house," I said, "must have been the archetype of all the houses that appear in your children's books: the little gray house by the lake in *Rasmus and the Vagabond,* the old white house with lilacs and cherry trees in *The Brothers Lionheart,* the white thatched cottage in the Garden of Roses in *Mio, My Son,* and, of course, Villa Villekulla in *Pippi Longstocking.* As Bachelard writes in *The Poetics of Space:* 'There exists for each one of us . . . a house of dream-memory that is lost in the shadow of a beyond of the real past. . . . The places in which we have *experienced daydreaming* reconstitute themselves in a new daydream, and it is because our memories of former dwelling places are relived as daydreams that these dwelling places of the past remain in us for all time.' "

"That's wonderful!" Astrid Lindgren responded. "I love houses and I hate them when they go against what my dream house ought to be. I used to go to a place called Tällberg where there are wonderful old houses—peasant houses that seem as if they came up from the ground by themselves. And now there is one terrible, ugly house that destroys everything around it. Also, I bought the house where I was born, but now the town has spread into the wooded pasture land, and my old house is surrounded by things I don't like. But inside it's exactly as it was, since I've restored it—it's just as it was when I was a child."

"I've noticed that trees are also important in your books—the ones that connect the farmhouses in *The Children of Noisy Village,* the linden tree in which Rasmus perches in *Rasmus and the Vagabond,* and, of course, Pippi Longstocking's hollow oak."

"Trees mean a lot to me," Astrid Lindgren replied. "I once wrote an essay—it's in the book I just gave you—called 'Are There Different Trees?' A professor once asked that question—that's how close he was to nature! To me, there's nothing more personal or alive on earth than trees—with the exception of people and animals. And in my essay I quoted a number of verses by different poets about trees—we have trees in poems and songs and tales and myths.

"I also mentioned my favorite childhood trees: grandmother's whiteheart cherry tree covered with big, yellowish-red berries, the equal of which might have grown in paradise but nowhere else. Then there was a particular apple tree outside our house, and we used to wake early and be the first outside to eat whatever apples had fallen down during the night. And then there was the 'owl tree,' for the owls had their nests there. But during the day it was our climbing tree. It was hollow, just like Pippi Longstocking's tree, but it was an elm, not an oak as in the *Pippi* books. And we loved it, even without the soda pop inside. My brother once put a hen's egg in the owl's nest, and the owl hatched a chicken for him. I even taught my little son when he was three years old to climb that tree; and he wanted to go up it every day, otherwise he'd cry in the evening. That tree is still there, though it's now aged and battered."

And at the conclusion of her essay, she writes: "Even better, I know an ash tree that grew at the church of Vimmerby when this century was young. For under that tree they were sitting, my father and my mother, one April evening when snow was whirling around them, and my father asked my mother if she would share his life. Who knows what would have happened if that ash had not been standing there with a bench beneath it! Perhaps there would never have been a proposal, and that would have been sad for me." And the author adds: "Far away in our unknown past we might have been creatures swinging from branch to branch, living in trees. Perhaps in the deepest depths of our wandering souls we long to return there, perhaps that without knowing it we regret having ever left the crowns of the trees and stepping down onto earth. Who knows, perhaps it is pure homesickness that makes us write poems and songs of the trees and makes us dream of all the green forests of earth."

"I don't write books *for* children," Astrid Lindgren commented to me. "I write books for the child I am myself. I write about things that are dear to me—trees and houses and nature—just to please myself."

"Listen to what Bachelard writes," I said. " 'The water of the child, the child's fire, the child's trees, the child's springtime flowers . . . what a lot of true principles for an analysis of the world!' "

"How beautiful!" she exclaimed.

"And he also says: 'When the human world leaves him in peace, the child feels like the son of the cosmos.' And I've noticed that you've depicted many orphaned or foster children—Rasmus, Mio, Karlsson in *Karlsson-on-the-Roof*, and Pippi—all of them alone but in touch with what is real. I read somewhere that you once said: 'To be alone is best. There is no loneliness that frightens me. Deep down we all remain alone. Without loneliness and poetry I believe I could hardly survive,' "

"Did I say that?" Astrid Lindgren asked, laughing. "I don't remember, but it does sound like me. I think, however, that a great many children are lonely, even if they aren't orphans. It's a pity when the child has no adult—at least one—close to him or her in order to help the child to be happy and to develop."

"But all these children in your books do belong to someone," I commented. "Pippi has Tommy and Annika, Mio has the King in Farawayland, Karlsson has his friend Eric, Rasmus has Paradise Oscar the tramp, and Jonathan and Karl have each other in *The Brothers Lionheart*. I wanted to ask you about this last work because along with the *Pippi* books it's your most controversial, since it's about death—a subject children's literature, in this century at least, has tended to shy away from. Each of the brothers sacrifices himself for the other; and after their deaths, they find themselves together, first in the heavenly land of Nangiyala—where they have to battle evil forces that live outside their valley paradise. And when one of them has again to die, because he has been mortally wounded in battle, they both decide to die again in order that they can be together in another heavenly land where they will never be apart. . . . And I'm sure your father would have understood this book that reminds us that love is strong as death," I added.

"Yes, the book came about in a very strange manner," she replied. "You know how you walk around with very diffuse thoughts, waiting for something to grow and be real? And I like to walk in cemeteries; it's very peaceful to go there and read the inscriptions. And one day I saw one that said: Here lie two little brothers. And then I found other dead brothers lying together—never sisters—and that made me think of what happened to them, why they had to die so young. So I had this feeling and didn't know what to do about it. And then one early winter morning, on a train trip through Sweden, seeing a beautiful rose-colored sunrise over the snow, I suddenly knew what I wanted to write—more or less.

"I thought this book might be a comfort for children who were afraid of death, which many children are. When I was little and was told that after you die you go to heaven, I didn't find that very amusing, but thought it better than lying down in the earth and just being dead! But my grandchildren have no such belief. I felt that one of them was afraid of death, and when I showed him the manuscript he smiled and said, 'Well, we don't know how it is, it could just as well be like that.'

"And I get lots of letters about *The Brothers Lionheart*—many from adults, too. One from a German woman doctor who had lost her nine-year-old daughter to leukemia. And this little girl had lived with the book the last years of her life, and it was her only comfort. When her two little rabbits died, the girl said, 'Oh, they're in Nangiyala now.' Many children have written me saying, 'Now I'm not afraid of death anymore.' Even if it's just a tale, why shouldn't they have some comfort?

"Incidentally, I just got a letter yesterday from a Korean soldier who studied Swedish at the university there and who plans to translate *The Brothers Lionheart* into Korean. He writes: 'Spring rain falls

Astrid Lindgren's family. Samuel and Hannah Ericsson, with their children. *Left to right:* Lugegard, Stina, Astrid, and Gunnar

outside the window and spring flowers growing outside the gray walls whisper to me in my ear: Throw away your green uniform, let us go out. But I can't, because I'm a twenty-five-year-old Korean soldier.' It's wonderful to get a letter that begins that way. And I think that all soldiers should throw away their uniforms.

"I know, too, that people have told me that the *Pippi* books have changed their lives. But the best compliment came in a message on a scrap of paper that was given to me once by an unknown woman. All it said was, 'Thanks for brightening up a gloomy childhood.' And that satisfied me."

"Memory," concludes Astrid Lindgren in her essay on her childhood, "holds unknown sleeping treasures of fragrances and flavors and sights and sounds of childhood past! . . . I can still see and smell and remember the bliss of that rose bush in the pasture, the one that showed me for the first time what beauty means, I can still hear the chirping of the landrail in the rye fields on a summer evening and the hooting of the owls in the owl tree in the nights of spring, I still know exactly how it feels to enter a warm cow barn from biting cold and snow, I know how the tongue of a calf feels against a hand and how rabbits smell, and the smell in a carriage shed, and how milk sounds when it strikes the bottom of a bucket, and the feel of small chicken feet when one holds a newly hatched chicken. These may not be extraordinary things to remember. The extraordinary thing about it is the intensity of these experiences when we were new here on earth.

"How long ago that must be! Otherwise, how can the world have changed so much? Could it all really become so different in just one short little half-century? My childhood was spent in a land that no longer exists—but where did it all go?"

("But Pippi continued to stare straight ahead with a dreamy look. Then she blew out the light.")

CHINUA ACHEBE:
AT THE
CROSSROADS

PHOTOGRAPH BY DIANE DAVIS

                        "Literature," states I. B. Singer, "is completely connected with one's origin, with one's roots." And in his first children's book, *Chike and the River*, the Nigerian writer Chinua Achebe describes the adventures of his young, village-born hero—an eleven-year-old named Chike who, one day, reflects: "So this is me . . . Chike Anene, alias Chiks the Boy, of Umuofia, Mbaino District, Onitsha Province, Eastern Nigeria, Nigeria, West Africa, Africa, World, Universe." And it is this reflection that reveals the roots and the trajectory of all of Achebe's writing for both children and adults.

Born in 1930 in Ogidi, Eastern Nigeria, of devout Christian parents who baptized him Albert Chinualumogu, Achebe "dropped the tribute to Victorian England," as he puts it, when he went to university, and took his first name from his last. "On one arm of the cross," he remembers in his autobiographical essay "Named for Victoria," "we sang hymns and read the Bible night and day. On the other, my father's brother and his family, blinded by heathenism, offered food to idols. . . . If anyone likes to believe that I was torn by spiritual agonies or stretched on the rack of my ambivalence, he certainly may suit himself. I do not remember any undue distress. What I do remember was a fascination for the ritual and the life on the other arm of the crossroads. And I believe two things were in my favor—that curiosity and the little distance imposed between me and it by the accident of my birth. The distance becomes not a separation but a bringing together, like the necessary backward step which a judicious viewer may take in order to see a canvas steadily and fully."

It is this canvas that Achebe brilliantly creates and displays for us in his four novels—*Things Fall Apart, No Longer at Ease, Arrow of God,* and *A Man of the People.* The first and third of these describe Igbo village life in the days just before and during the first encounters with Christian missionaries and British colonial authorities; the second and fourth of the novels depict the rise and fall of two contemporary, village-born, university-trained intellectuals, each enmeshed in big-city Nigerian bureaucratic and power politics, each overcome by the ironies attendant on his ambivalent and problematic existence. As Achebe describes his protagonist Obi in the second of these novels: "Having made him [Obi] a member of an exclusive club whose members greet one another with 'How's the car behaving?' did they expect him to turn round and answer: 'I'm sorry, but my car is off the road. You see I couldn't pay my insurance premium'? That would be letting the side down in a way that was quite unthinkable. Almost as unthinkable as a masked spirit in the old Igbo society answering another's esoteric salutation: 'I'm sorry, my friend, but I don't understand your strange language. I'm but a human being wearing a mask.' No, these things could not be."

But it is Okonkwo, Obi's grandfather and the tragic hero of *Things Fall Apart*—a man whose whole life is dominated by the fear of failure and weakness—who emerges as one of Achebe's most powerfully realized characters. Having raised a young boy named Ikemefuna, who had been sent from a neighboring village as a peace offering, Okonkwo one day learns from the Oracle of the Hills and the Caves that he must kill this boy whom he and his son Nwoye have grown to love. Achebe narrates Ikemefuna's forest death walk:

> Thus the men of Umuofia pursued their way, armed with sheathed machetes, and Ikemefuna, carrying a pot of palm-wine on his head, walked in their midst. Although he had felt uneasy at first, he was not afraid now. Okonkwo walked behind him. He could hardly imagine that Okonkwo was not his real father. He had never been fond of his real father, and at the end of three years he had become very distant indeed. But his mother and his three-year-old sister . . . of course she would not be three now, but six. Would he recognize her now? She must have grown quite big. How his mother would weep for joy, and thank Okonkwo for bringing him back. She would want to hear everything that had happened to him in all these years. Could he remember them all? He would tell her about Nwoye and his mother, and about the locusts. . . . Then quite suddenly a thought came upon him. His mother might be dead. He tried in vain to force the thought out of his mind. Then he tried to settle the matter the way he used to settle such matters when he was a little boy. He still remembered the song:

> *Eze elina, elina!*
>   *Sala*
> *Eze ilikwa ya*
> *Ikwaba akwa oligholi*
> *Ebe Danda nechi eze*
> *Ebe Uzuzu nete egwu*
>   *Sala*

He sang it in his mind and walked to its beat. If the song ended on his right foot, his mother was alive. If it ended on his left, she was dead. No, not dead, but ill. It ended on the right. She was alive and well. He sang the song again, and it ended on the left. But the second time did not count. The first voice gets to Chukwu, or God's house. That was a favorite saying of children. Ikemefuna felt like a child once more. It must be the thought of going home to his mother.

In a passage such as this we are led into the world of Abraham and Isaac, of Greek tragedy, and of fairy tales like "Hansel and Gretel."

Achebe informs us that his mother and elder sister used to tell him tales when he was a child—folk stories that had "the immemorial quality of the sky and the forests and the rivers." And like other West African writers such as Amos Tutuola, Wole Soyinka, J. P. Clark, and Christopher Okigbo, Chinua Achebe has drawn literary sustenance from folk tales as well as from legends, jokes, riddles, and, especially, proverbs. As Ralph Waldo Emerson states in a passage strikingly applicable to Achebe's own writing:

> Proverbs, like the sacred books of each nation, are the sanctuary of the intuitions. That which the droning world, chained to appearances, will not allow the realist to say in his own words, it will suffer him to say in proverbs without contradiction. And this law of laws, which the pulpit, the senate, and the college deny, is hourly preached in all markets and workshops by flights of proverbs, whose teaching is as true and as omnipresent as that of birds and flies.

Among the Igbo, Achebe tells us in *Things Fall Apart*, "the art of conversation is regarded very highly, and proverbs are the palm-oil with which words are eaten." "Wherever something stands, another thing stands beside it," proclaims a character in *No Longer at Ease*. "Living fire begets cold, impotent ash," Okonkwo realizes in *Things Fall Apart*. And in *A Man of the People*, the narrator Odili, reflecting on the proverb "It is better that water is spilled than the pot broken," says: "Of course as soon as I grew old enough to understand a few simple proverbs I realized that I should have died and let my mother live."

"Walk where we will, we tread upon some story," Cicero once said . . . and "upon some proverb or myth," he might have added. In his essay "Language and Destiny of Man," Achebe quotes the beginning of a creation myth from the Wapangwa people of Tanzania:

The sky was large, white, and very clear. It was empty; there were no stars and no moon; only a tree stood in the air and there was wind. This tree fed on the atmosphere and ants lived on it. Wind, tree, ants, and atmosphere were controlled by the power of the Word, but the Word was not something that could be seen. It was a force that enabled one thing to create another.

And in another myth that he quotes—this one from the Igbo people (though, as Achebe points out, there are more than 700 different versions of it throughout Africa)—we read that when death first entered the world, men sent a dog as a messenger to Chuku, asking that the dead be restored to life. But a toad, desiring to punish mankind, overheard the mesage; and while the dog dallied he reached Chuku first, telling him that men, after death, had no desire to return to the world. Chuku declared he would respect men's wishes, and when the dog arrived with the true message, Chuku refused to alter his decision. In one case, then, the word is the force of life itself; while in the other, its distortion—its going astray—leads to death. And thus we can see how creation and death are both connected to the power of language.

"In small and self-sufficient societies such as gave birth to these myths," Achebe writes, "the integrity of language is safeguarded by the fact that what goes on in the community can easily be ascertained, understood, and evaluated by all." In his autobiographical essay he tells us: "I have always been . . . intrigued by language—first Igbo, spoken with such eloquence by the old men of the village, and later English, which I began to learn at about the age of eight." And like the other West African authors mentioned before, Achebe writes in English. "Let us give the devil his due," he states in "African Writer, English Language": "colonialism in Africa disrupted many things, but it did create big political units where there were small, scattered ones before. . . . And it gave [people] a language with which to talk to one another. If it failed to give them a song, it at least gave them a tongue, for sighing. . . . I feel that the English language will be able to carry the weight of my African experience. But it will have to be a new English, still in full communion with its ancestral home but altered to suit its new African surroundings."

Whatever his given or chosen language, the artist, in Achebe's view, is the protector of language; and he insists that "a spiritual bond exists between the true artist and his community." Just as John Miller Chernoff, in his fascinating book *African Rhythm and African*

Sensibility, states that most people in Africa do not conceive of music apart from its community setting and cultural context ("Africans use music and the other arts to articulate and objectify their philosophical and moral systems which they do not abstract but which they build into the music-making situation itself"), so Chinua Achebe is at pains in his essay, "Africa and Her Writers," to demonstrate the interdependence and indivisibility of art and society. His lengthy description of the Owerri Igbo ceremony called *mbari*—performed at the behest of the Earth goddess Ala—is worth quoting at length:

> Every so many years Ala would instruct the community through her priest to prepare a festival of images in her honor. That night the priest would travel through the town, knocking on many doors to announce to the various households whom of their members Ala had chosen for the great work. These chosen men and women then moved into the seclusion in a forest clearing and, under the instruction and guidance of master artists and craftsmen, began to build a house of images. The work might take a year or even two, but as long as it lasted the workers were deemed to be hallowed and were protected from undue contact from, and distraction by, the larger community.
>
> The finished temple was architecturally simple—two side walls and a back wall under a high thatched roof. Steps ran the full width of the temple, ascending backward and upward almost to the roof. But in spite of the simplicity of its structure, *mbari* was often a miracle of artistic achievement—a breathtaking concourse of images in bright, primary colors. Since the enterprise was in honor of Ala, most of the work was done in her own material—simple molded earth. But the execution turned this simple material into finished images of startling power and diversity. The goddess had a central seat, usually with a sword in her right hand and a child on her left knee—a telling juxtaposition of formidable (even, implacable) power and gentleness. Then there were other divinities; there were men, women, beasts, and birds, real or imaginary. Indeed the total of the community was reflected—scenes of religious duty, of day-to-day tasks and diversions, and even of village scandal. The work completed, the village declared a feast and a holiday to honor the goddess of creativity and her children, the makers of images.
>
> This brief and inadequate description can give no idea of the impact of *mbari*. Even the early Christian missionaries who were shocked by the frankness of some of the portrayals couldn't quite take their eyes off! But all I want to do is to point out one or two of the aesthetic ideas underlying *mbari*. First, the making of art is not the exclusive concern of a particular caste or secret society. Those young

A river goddess with two children modeled in clay in the *mbari* to Ala, Unugoet Orishaeze, Imo state, Nigeria

men and women whom the goddess chose for the re-enactment of creation were not "artists." They were ordinary members of society. Next time around, the choice would fall on other people. Of course, mere nomination would not turn everyman into an artist—not even divine appointment could guarantee it. The discipline, instruction, and guidance of a master artist would be necessary. But not even a conjunction of those two conditions would insure infallibly the emergence of a new, exciting sculptor or painter. But *mbari* was not looking for that. It was looking for, and saying, something else: *There is no rigid barrier between makers of culture and its consumers. Art belongs to all and is a "function" of society.* When Senghor insists with such obvious conviction that every man is a poet, he is responding, I think, to this holistic concern of our traditional societies.

All this will, I dare say, sound like abominable heresy in the ears of mystique lovers. For their sake and their comfort, let me hasten to add that the idea of *mbari* does not deny the place or importance of the master with unusual talent and professional experience. Indeed it highlights such gift and competence by bringing them into play on the seminal potentialities of the community. Again, *mbari* does not deny the need for the creative artist to go apart from time to time so as to commune with himself, to look inwardly into his own soul. For when the festival is over, the villagers return to their normal lives again, and the master artists to their work and contemplation. But they can never after this experience, this creative communal enterprise, become strangers again to one another. And by logical and physical extension the greater community, which comes to the unveiling of the art and then receives its makers again into its normal life, becomes a beneficiary—indeed an active partaker—of this experience.

Ibo *mbari* house dedicated to the earth goddess Obiala, at Ndiama Obute Olakwo, Imo state. The goddess, with two children, is at the corner of the most accessible side of the *mbari*. Two married Igbo couples flank her on either side.

Just as the goddess Ala holds a child on her knee, so the community always includes its children, who nourish and sustain it. In addition to his poems, stories, essays, and four novels, Achebe has written four works for children. The first of these, *Chike and the River* (1966), is an adventure story about a young boy who goes from the country to the big market town of Onitsha, dreams of crossing the big river (the Niger), finally does so, meets up with a gang of thieves whom he exposes, and in the end becomes a hero.

"The Flute" (which Achebe presents in a slightly different version in his novel *Arrow of God*) is the author's retelling of a folktale about a young boy who, trying to recover something precious to him—a plain, ordinary bamboo flute (a sign of creativity and praise) —goes to the spirit land to reclaim it; and because he is truthful and unselfish he is rewarded, whereas another boy—selfish, proud, greedy, and trying to fool the spirits—winds up destroying himself, his mother, and his brothers and sisters.

Most effective of all are Achebe's two animal stories. *The Drum* is a trickster tale about the wily and ubiquitous Tortoise who, one day, chasing after some fruit that has fallen into a hole in the earth, comes upon the land of the spirits and winds up the owner of a magic drum that, when played, produces an endless supply of food for the drought-stricken animal kingdom. When the drum is accidentally broken, Tortoise—the now self-proclaimed king—returns to the spirit-land, but, as with the second boy in "The Flute," his newly developed greed and pride lead to his obtaining a drum that wreaks havoc and destruction for him and his community.

Achebe's *How the Leopard Got His Claws*—a story that takes its place as one of the most powerful and starkest fables in the tradition that runs from Aesop and Bidpai to Kipling and Orwell—tells of a time "in the beginning" when all the forest animals live as friends; only the dog, with its sharp teeth, acts selfishly and spitefully. Leopard, clawless and gentle, is king. To protect the animals during the rainy season, he suggests that all the animals build a common shelter. But the dog and the duck refuse to help and turn away from the community. Later, one stormy night, when Leopard is out roaming, the dog attacks the animals in their shelter, wounding them severely. Leopard returns, the dog attacks him, too, and when Leopard urges that all the animals stand up to the aggressor as one, they turn into cowards and decide to make the powerful dog their king. Leopard goes into exile, and the new king orders the animals to find Leopard and force him to return to the new totalitarian society. They throw stones at the wounded leopard, chanting: "No one has a right to leave our village! No one has a right to leave our village!" And "although some of the stones hit the leopard and hurt him, he did not turn round even once. He continued walking until he no longer heard the noise of the animals." Traveling for seven days and seven nights, Leopard meets a blacksmith, who makes deadly bronze claws for him. From Thunder he receives the sound for his voice. And he returns to the village, this time to terrorize, and again becomes king. The dog escapes and servilely offers himself as a slave to the first hunter he meets, promising to help the hunter kill his fellow animals, who have now begun to behave like "animals" to each other. "Perhaps," the story ends, "the animals will make peace among themselves some day and live together again. Then they can keep away the hunter who is their common enemy."

As Achebe explains in the following conversation, both *The Drum* and *How the Leopard Got His Claws*, aside from being striking and enjoyable tales for both children and adults, are connected to the realities of Igbo life and history. And they were written both to delight and to instruct. It is this dialectical tension between delighting and instructing that is at the heart of Achebe's writings (as it is of much of children's literature). "Our ancestors," Achebe affirms, "created their myths and legends and told their stories for a human purpose (including, no doubt, the excitation of wonder and pure delight). . . . Their artists lived and moved and had their being in society and created their works for the good of that society. . . . In a recent anthology, a Hausa folk tale, having recounted the usual fabulous incidents, ends with these words: 'They all came and they lived happily together. He had several sons and daughters who grew up and helped in raising the standard of education of the country.' As I said elsewhere, if you consider this ending a naïve anticlimax, then you cannot know very much about Africa."

Today, as Nigeria (the most populous and one of the most prosperous countries in Africa) becomes increasingly developed economically and technologically (symbolized by the Nigerian External Telecommunications Network tower in Lagos), we are continually reminded in Achebe's writings that as we inevitably move forward, we must at the same time remember where we began; and that if the adults forget, then the children and the stories they like best will remind them.

Chinua Achebe is currently in the Department of English at the University of Nigeria, Nsukka. The recipient of many awards, including an honorary Doctor of Letters degree from Dartmouth College, he has traveled and lectured in countries all over the world. As unafraid and unashamed of gentleness as of strength, he has a bearing and voice that bespeak an unusual mixture of quietness, intensity, humor, and commitment. Our conversation took place in London in the summer of 1980.

. . .

In your fable How the Leopard Got His Claws, *you first describe the animals of the world at peace with one another. "They sat," you write, "on log benches in the village square. As they rested they told stories and drank palm wine." But later, after selfishness and cowardice have upset the animals' communal harmony, the leopard—now forced into the role of violent avenger—says: "From today I shall rule the forest with terror. The life of our village is ended." And this reminds me of the conclusion of* A Man of the People, *in which you write: "The owner was the village, and the village had a mind; it could say no to sacrilege. But in the affairs of the nation there was no owner, the laws of the village became powerless." It seems to me that the idea of the "village"—connected as it is with the notions of the possibilities of community, truthful language, and the attainment of real individuality—is central to all your work.*

My world—the one that interests me more than any other—is the world of the village. It is one, not the only, reality, but it's the one that the Igbo, who are my people, have preferred to all others. It was as if they had a choice of creating empires or cities or large communities and they looked at them and said, "No, we think that what is safest and best is a system in which everybody knows everybody else." In other words, a village. So you'll find that, politically, the Igbos preferred the small community; they had nothing to do—until recently (and I'll come back to this later)—with kings and kingdoms.

Now I'm quite convinced that this was a conscious choice. Some people look at the Igbos and assert that they didn't evolve to the stage of having kings and kingdoms. But this isn't true—the Igbos have a word for "king," they have words for all the paraphernalia of kingship—it isn't as if they don't know about kings. I think it's simply that, looking at the way the world operates, they seem to have said to themselves: Of all the possible political systems, we shall insist on the one where there are only so many people. So that when a man gets up to talk to his fellows they know who he is, they know exactly whether he is a thief, an honest man, or whatever. In a city of eight million people, you can't know your neighbor. And that means you have to set up a system of representation: You choose a delegate to speak for you. But the Igbos didn't want someone else to speak for them.

And this is quite central to my fiction and to my analysis of the problems of creating a new nation today. Obviously, we can't go back to the system in which every man is turning up in the village square—

.

that's in the past. But we have to find a way of dealing with the problems created by the fact that somebody says he's speaking on your behalf, but you don't know who he is. This is one of the problems of the modern world.

In Arrow of God *you write: "The festival brought gods and men together in one crowd. It was the only assembly in Umuaro in which a man might look to his right and find his neighbor and look to his left and see a god standing there." So your idea of the village seems to include the possibility not only of political participation but of a spiritual one as well.*

Definitely, you're absolutely right. It's a world of men and women and children and spirits and deities and animals and nature . . . and the dead—this is very important—a community of the living and the dead and the unborn. So it is both material and spiritual, and whatever you did in the village took this into account. Our life was never compartmentalized in the way that it has become today. We talk about politics, economics, religion. But in the traditional society all these things were linked together—there was no such thing as a irreligious man. In fact, we don't even have a word for religion in Igbo. It's simply *life.*

As a person who grew up with the values of a village and who now lives in a country that is rapidly being modernized, you seem to be in the position of someone who has found himself standing at the crossroads.

Those who live at the crossroads are very lucky, and it seems to me that there will never be this kind of opportunity again. My generation belongs to a group whose fathers . . . my father, for instance, although a converted Christian, was really a member of the traditional society—he was already full grown in the traditions of Igbo life when he decided to become a Christian; so he knew all about our culture. My children, however, belong to the world culture to which American children belong. They went to school in America for several years, and liked the same kind of music that children in America and England enjoy. But I'm in between these two. And we can talk about "transitions"—it's a cliché, of course, since every day's a transition— but I think that I'm much more a part of a transitional generation than any other. And this is very exciting. Of course it carries its penalties, since you're in a no man's land, you're like the bat in the folk tale—neither bird nor mammal—and one can get lost, not being one or the other. This is what we are, we can't do anything about it. But it does help if you have the kind of temperament I have, which tries to recover something from our past. So you have one foot in the past—my father's tradition—and also one in the present—where you try to interpret the past for the present.

The folklorist Richard M. Dorson states: "Two main conditions for the study of folklore are just being realized in Africa: the appearance of an intellectual class with a culture partly different from that of the mass of all people, and the emergence of national states. In the tribal culture all the members share the values, participate in the rituals, and belong fully to the culture, even if some hold privileged positions as chiefs and diviners. In the national culture a schism divides the society. The intellectuals in the professions, on the university faculties, and in the government seem sometimes to have more in common with intellectuals in other countries than with their tribal countrymen." Now, the sociologist Philip Slater has written about the difference he sees between the "community" and the "network." By the former he means the people whom we live with, and by the latter he is referring, like Dorson, to the people we communicate with professionally throughout our own particular country or even throughout the world —just as you have a readership and attend conferences in many different countries.

Let me touch on the difference between the network and the community, for this is what I meant by the challenge and the risk of being at the crossroads. I think there's a certain strength in being able to have one foot in the network and another foot in the community. But if one forgets the foot that's in the community—and this is quite possible—one can get carried away into the network system. And this is a real problem for us—for the African intellectual, the African writer. I've sometimes complained about African writers who blindly follow Western fashions with regard to what an author should be writing, saying, or even looking like . . . what ideas he should be expressing, what attitudes he should be having toward his community, and so on—all of them taken from the West—while we forget about the other part of our nature which has its roots in the community. So I think we have the responsibility to be both in the community and in the network. This is a challenge—it's very exciting and also very perilous.

You yourself are at the crossroads on many levels—spiritual, political, intellectual—and you have chosen to write for both adults and children. It's as if you've decided to balance and integrate all of these levels and activities.

Yes, I do that consciously. I think this is the most important and fascinating thing about our life—the crossroad. This is where the spirits meet the humans, the water meets the land, the child meets the adult—these are the zones of power, and I think this is really where stories are created. Noon—the middle of the day—is a very potent hour in our folklore. It is the time when morning merges into afternoon, the moment when spirits are abroad. When the adults go to the farm and leave the children at home, then the spirits can come into the village.

I've talked about the "crossroad hour" in one of my poems—this hour when the spirits appear—and it is this transitional period that manifests, I think, the great creative potential. It's an area of tension and conflict. So I deliberately go out of my way to cultivate what I call the crossroad mythology, because I think it's full of power and possibility.

In Things Fall Apart, *Okonkwo tells his son Nwoye "masculine" stories of violence and bloodshed, but the boy prefers the tales his mother tells him about Tortoise the trickster, about the bird who challenged the whole world to a wrestling contest and was finally thrown by a cat, and about the quarrel between Earth and Sky— stories for "foolish women and children," as Okonkwo thinks of them. But in* No Longer at Ease, *Nwoye—now the father of the protagonist Obi—forbids the telling of folk tales to his son because he himself has become a Christian, and doesn't want to disseminate what he now thinks of as "heathen" stories. All of this reminds me of the constant attacks against fairy stories in Europe by Enlightenment spokesmen and by any number of rigid moralists and educators during the past two centuries.*

I think that stories are the very center, the very heart of our civilization and culture. And to me it's interesting that the man who thinks he's strong wants to forbid stories, whether it's Okonkwo forbidding the stories of gentleness, or whether, later on, it's a Christian who, so self-satisfied in the rightness and superiority of his faith, wishes to forbid the hidden pagan stories. It is there in those despised areas that the strength of the civilization resides—not in the masculine strength of Okonkwo, nor in the self-righteous strength of the Christian faith. The stone the builders reject becomes a cornerstone of the house. So I think a writer instinctively gravitates toward that "weakness," if you like; he will leave the "masculine" military strength and go for love, for gentleness. For unless we cultivate gentleness, we will be destroyed. And this is why you have poets and storytellers.

The psychologist James Hillman has talked of the importance of "re-storying the adult."

This is what I've been trying to say when I talk about weakness and strength. You see, "re-storying the adult" is a very interesting phrase. What, in fact, is the adult as distinct from the child? The adult is someone who has seen it all, nothing is new to him. Such a man is to be pitied. The child, on the other hand, is new in the world, and everything is possible to him. His imagination hasn't been dulled by use and experience. Therefore, when you restory the adult, what you do is you give him back some of the child's energy and optimism, that ability to be open and to expect anything. The adult has become dull and routine, mechanical, he can't be lifted. It's as if he's weighted down by his experience and his possessions, all the junk he's assembled and accumulated. And the child can still fly, you see. Therefore the story belongs to the child, because the story's about flying.

In your autobiographical essay "Named for Victoria," you've mentioned that, like Nwoye, you were told stories by your mother and older sister. So you were lucky enough to be "storied" at an early age.

I was very fortunate, but I would say that this was traditional. Any child growing up at that time, unless he was particularly unlucky, would be told stories as part of his education. It doesn't happen anymore. The stories are now read in books, and very rarely is there a situation in which the mother will sit down night after night with her family and tell stories, with the young children falling asleep to them. The pace of life has altered. Again, this is what I meant by saying that our generation is unique. And I was lucky to have been part of the very tail end of that older tradition. Perhaps we may not be able to revive it, but at least we can make sure that the kind of stories our children read carry something of the aura of the tales our mothers and sisters told us.

In traditional oral societies, the storyteller would employ intonation, gestures, eye contact, pantomime, acrobatics, and occasionally costumes, masks, and props in his or her dramatic presentation.

Yes, that's right and the loss is enormous. And all I'm saying is that, rather than lose everything, we should value the written story, which is certainly better than no story at all. It's impossible in the modern world to have the traditional storytelling. But I think that perhaps in the home we should not give up so quickly. I find, for instance, that when I write a new children's story the best thing I can do is to tell it to my children, and I get remarkable feedback that way. My youngest child, incidentally, writes stories of her own! . . . But the storyteller today has to find a new medium rather than regret the passing of the past. Television is there, we can't do anything about it, so some of us should use this medium, we should do stories for television.

You once wrote that "our ancestors created their myths and legends and told their stories for a human purpose (including, no doubt, the excitation of wonder and pure delight)." And you've often stated that stories impart important messages to us and that they are repositories of human experience and wisdom. Your children's stories are, of course, excellent examples of this notion.

I realize that this is an area where there is some kind of uneasiness between us and the Western reader concerning just how much of a "message" is suitable for a story. I'm not talking about "preaching," which isn't the same thing as telling a story. But to say that a good story is weakened because it conveys a moral point of view is absurd, because in my view all the great stories do convey such a point. A tale may be fascinating, amusing—creating laughter and delight and so forth—but at its base is a sustaining morality, and I think this is very important.

In the Igbo culture, the relationship between art and morality is very close, and there's no embarrassment at all in linking the two,

Left to right: They mythical ape-man Okpangu, a lion, and a leopard in the cloister of a large *mbari* containing seventy-five sculptures, in the village of Umuofeke Agwa, Imo state, Nigeria

as there would be in Western culture. The earth goddess Ala—the most powerful deity in the Igbo pantheon—is also the goddess of the arts and of morality. I would say that Ala is even more powerful than the supreme god because of her nearness to us: The earth is where our crops lie, where we live, and where we die. And any very serious offense is called an "abomination"—the literal translation of "abomination" in Igbo is *nso ani* (*nso* = taboo, *ani* = earth)—*that which the earth forbids.* That's how you refer to the worst kinds of crimes, like murder and rape. But Ala is also, as I said, the goddess of art.

You've given a beautiful description of the mbari—*a ceremony performed at the bequest of Ala—and I imagine someone like Tolstoy would have loved this ceremony. I mention him also because his children's fables reflect his deep-seated notion of the connection between morality and aesthetics.*

Tolstoy, coming out of the great Russian tradition, is an excellent example of an artist who proves that purpose does not destroy art.

Your children's tale "The Flute" might also have come out of this tradition, too.

That's right. This story is, as you know, really a traditional folk tale, and what I've done is to retell it . . . while adding a few details—such as the one where the boy himself makes his own flute. I'm very much concerned about our consumer culture in which few people make anything themselves anymore. Our ancestors made things, and so I put this detail in the story, and I think that one is entitled and expected to do that. Of course the purist collector of folk tales would say this is terrible. But my concern is that stories are not only retrieved and kept alive but also added to, just as they always were, and I think this is really what a living, traditional storyteller would do. I loved the stories my mother and elder sister told me, but there were always little changes here and there. And this was part of the entertainment—you heard a tale a hundred times, but each day there was one additional little twist, which was expected.

This also suggests the personal style of the storyteller.

Yes, there's that combination of stability and change. You mustn't alter the story so much that you don't recognize it. The child won't accept tinkering with the folk tale to the extent that it becomes something else. But little twists now and then . . . yes.

In The Drum, *the tortoise, when retelling to the other animals the story of how he descended into the spiritland to find his magic drum, improvises little dramatic changes in order to make his tale sound more heroic and convincing—which is, of course, what people do quite often in everyday conversation.*

To serve their own ends [laughing].

It's strange but obvious that it is children—the seemingly least significant members of society—who are given stories about the most important matters: selfishness, pride, greed, the meaning of life and death.

That's right, and this is wonderful for children. I think the adult sometimes loses sight of the nature of stories. But these great fundamental issues have never changed and never will. I mean, children always ask the same questions: Who made the world? How come some people are suffering? Who made death? And to think that we have somehow moved on to more "adult" subject matters is simply self-deception. What we do, of course, is quite often get trapped in trivia masked in highfalutin language. But the basic questions are still the same, and this is what children's stories particularly deal with.

I think that mankind's greatest blessing is language. And this is why the storyteller is a high priest, and why he is so concerned about language and about using it with respect. Language is under great stress in the modern world—it's under siege. All kinds of people— advertisers, politicians, priests, technocrats—want to get a hold of it and use it for their own ends; these are the strong people today; the storyteller represents the weakness we were talking about. But of course every poet is aware of this problem. . . . And this is where children come into it, too, because you can't fool around with children —you have to be honest with language in children's stories; mere cleverness won't do.

In your essay "Language and Destiny of Man," you quote several haunting lines from an Eskimo poem called "Magic Words": "That was the time when words were like magic./The human mind had mysterious powers./A word spoken by chance/might have strange consequences./It would suddenly come alive/and what people wanted to happen could happen—/all you had to do was say it." It seems that the only people who are supposed to believe this are members of oral societies and young children everywhere.

Yes, and they're right, they are blest. We lose belief at our cost. These lines take you right back to the beginning of things. "And God said, Let there be light"—he didn't do anything, he just said it. And you can also look at the aborigines in Australia, who are somehow closer to the beginning than ourselves: You have the same feeling there that the word has power.

To go for a moment from the power of the word to the problems of translation: in No Longer at Ease, *you describe the homesick hero, Obi, in England, feeling happy when he comes across another Igbo-speaking student on a London bus, but discomforted at meeting a Nigerian student from another tribe: "It was humiliating to have to speak to one's countryman in a foreign language, especially in the presence of the proud owners of that language. They would naturally assume that one had no language of one's own. He wished they were here today to see. Let them come to Umofia now and listen to the talk of men who made a great art of conversation. Let them come and see men and women and children who knew how to live, whose joy of life had not yet been killed by those who claimed to teach other nations how to live." You write in English, but which language— English or Igbo—do you use with your children?*

Both English and Igbo—even when we were in America. The youngest girl was just over a year old when we left Nigeria and went to America. And when she went to nursery school—she was just two— she refused to speak English, even though she was already bilingual like everybody else in the family—she had a few words of each language. She refused to talk to her teachers, and we realized that she was putting up a fight for her language. And it lasted a couple of months. Incidentally, one of the conditions she exacted from me for going to school was that I had to tell her a story in Igbo as I drove her there. And another coming back every day, too [laughing]. I didn't quite know what to make of it, but I think that it reveals the importance both of language and of stories. And if a child is deprived of these things I think he or she will be unhappy. The imagination becomes stiff. A lot of cruelty, in fact, comes from a lack of imagination—I think it's all very much connected. And I really feel that stories are not just meant to make people smile, I think our life depends on them.

I wanted to ask you about the background to your powerful fable How the Leopard Got His Claws.

That story was made at a very difficult time politically—at the beginning of the Biafran struggle. A good friend of mine, a very fine poet named Christopher Okigbo, who was killed fighting for Biafra, had set up a publishing house. We had fled from different parts of Nigeria because our lives were in danger—he fled from Ibadan, I fled from Lagos, and we returned to Enugu. (He had been West African representative for Cambridge University Press, so he knew about publishing . . . and, in fact, he asked me to do my first children's book, *Chike and the River,* for Cambridge.) So when we both arrived back in Enugu, he suggested that we set up a press. I said, Well, you set it up, you know about it, and I'll join. He said, You'll be chairman and I'll be the managing director [laughing], so the Citadel Press was formed. The name came from the idea of the fortress—you flee from a foreign land, in danger, and return home to your citadel. Little did we know that Enugu wasn't safe—anyway, that's another story. We were going to concentrate on children's books, and so we told our friends we were planning on publishing and asked for manu-scripts from all the writers around. And a man named John Iroaga-nachi sent in a story called "How the Dog Became Domesticated"—it was a charming, traditional-type story, but it was rather weak. So I decided to edit it, and as I edited it, it grew . . . it grew until it just turned into something else, it wasn't about the dog at all anymore but rather about the leopard. And it was now a parable about Nigeria—the common house that had been torn apart.

I was possessed by that story, which works on very many levels. Biafra was represented by the leopard . . . but let's not talk about whom the dog represents; I think a good story remains valid even beyond the events described. It is however, interesting to mention that when the city where we were working fell to the federal troops, we had that book in press. In fact, the last time I saw Christopher Okigbo was when he came to discuss it with me. That day a bomb fell on my house. And the end of it was that Enugu was sacked, and we fled and abandoned the book.

Now, at the end of the war, we went back to the site of the publishing house, and it had been razed to the ground—it seemed to me that whoever did it didn't like publishing or at least this particular publishing house and perhaps this particular book. Fortunately, there was one proof copy that somehow survived—I think a friend of ours, a relation of Christopher Okigbo's who had a copy of the galleys, fished it out and brought it to me. And so I made a few more changes, not major ones, and it was published. Later on, one chap who was working as an intelligence officer with the federal troops said to me, "You know, of all the things that came out of Biafra, that book was the most important."

What a background to a children's book!

Children read the book and love it. Not only in Nigeria, but also in East Africa, where they did a special edition of it. In Nigeria it sold out very quickly—it was out of print for a long time—but a Nigerian publisher has just reissued it, and it's used as a supplementary reader in schools.

I don't believe children get all the levels—they're not supposed to—but I think they get the main point about the ingratitude and opportunism of the animals, and about the danger of not working together when they have a common problem. Of course, the villain, is the dog . . . which is a problem, I understand, for readers in the

West—it's very difficult for them to see a dog in the role of a villain, but I did that that deliberately. John's original story had the dog as the nice guy, a wonderful fellow who became a slave. But I don't like slaves, so this is why I turned the plot around 180 degrees.

It was a very interesting experiment. I asked Okigbo to write the lamentation of the deer—the song it sings when it's thrown out of the house by the dog. So in fact there were three people involved in making this story. Actually, four, because of the illustrations. What happened is that at the end of the war Biafra was in very bad shape, and some friends of mine in Enugu set up a publishing house. And they said that they wanted to do what I and Okigbo had tried to do before the war. They knew some Norwegian people, who in fact had shown interest in Biafra during the war—the Scandinavian countries had been very sympathetic to Biafra. So it was through that connection that a Norwegian firm decided to publish the story, and they commissioned Per Christiansen, a leading illustrator of Norwegian children's books, to do the pictures. And then the Norwegians printed the book, though it was published in Nigeria.

I wanted to ask you, too, about your children's story The Drum, *which begins: "In the beginning when the world was young . . ." Here you conjure up a kind of fairy-tale setting in which animals and trees talk to each other. . . . By the way, the number seven seems to come up in your children's books all the time. In* The Drum, *for example, there are seven steps to the underworld, seven times that the drum thanks the tree, and so on.*

Seven is a magical number. And this is almost a formula—crossing the seven rivers and the seven savannas in order to go beyond the world of the human to the world of the spirits. The Igbo week is four days, and seven weeks is one month. Seven weeks is a crucial measure of time. When a child is born, it's not really regarded as fully here until it has lived seven weeks. Then it is human and is given a name.

The tortoise, who's the protagonist of the story, follows the fruit he's let fall into the underworld abode of the spirits. And when he returns to his family and friends, he begins to make a grand speech.

Yes, it's like an Igbo meeting. He's trying to become a king, which is anathema to the Igbo.

So here again we discover a parable. And when the tortoise has to repeat his journey to the underworld—since the magic drum has been destroyed and he wants to get another one from the spirits—

He fakes it. So here is a way in which the story of *The Drum* and "The Flute," have the same theme. A true adventure isn't a faked adventure, and there's no mercy shown to the faker. You do something the first time, you do it honestly, that's okay. But then you go back and you plan something which doesn't arise out of necessity— that's fakery. And children understand this because they know about faking. Adults think that they can fool children [laughing], but they don't really succeed.

In "The Flute," the "faked" situation is set up by the greedy first wife, who wants to get something for her son and herself.

Yes. Stories often become far more evil when human characters move in—there's a greater possibility for evil. Somehow there's a limit to how evil the tortoise can be—you know that. He's a rogue, but he's a nice kind of rogue. And in the end he's punished, and that's it.

The Igbo tortoise trickster has been compared to Spider of the African Hausa, Fox of the Toba of Argentina, Maui of the Polynesians, and Rabbit of Afro-American folklore. And their common characteristics, as described by Brian Sutton-Smith, are as follows: "violation of taboo; impulsiveness; a lack of close, caring relationships; apparent disregard for the feelings of others; an inability to learn from past mistakes; lack of anxiety or remorse; an exhibitionistic narcissism; constant use of pretense and trickery; and a demeanor of childlike, innocent charm" —characteristics that Sutton-Smith suggests are reminiscent of the symptoms of the psychopath.

I have to say that the picture painted there doesn't fully account for the role of the tortoise in the Igbo folk tales. As I said, he's a nice rogue, because nobody hates him in the end. If you see someone who's always around when something happens, you say "a story is never complete without a tortoise"—that's one of our proverbs. So Tortoise is a character around whom stories are built. And he tries to get away with more than his fair share. He's smart, sometimes over-smart, and he gets punished. But he's not an evil creature. Certainly not a psychopath! That's too strong.

*I've recently read a number of Tortoise stories from the Cameroons—
there seems to be an interchange of folk tales between Cameroonians
and Igbos—and in one of my favorite of these tales, Tortoise decides
to collect wisdom—since it's more valuable than gold—so he goes
around obtaining it from everyone he meets and puts it all in a pot,
which he carries around with him. One day he decides to hide the
wisdom pot in a tree so that no one will get to it. He starts to climb
up with it, but the pot proves too cumbersome. Finally, his baby son
notices his father struggling, and he advises him to tie the pot to his
back. Up on the tree, Tortoise realizes that his child possessed wisdom
that he himself had failed to recognize, so he pushes the pot off the
branch; it smashes on the ground below, scattering wisdom all over
the world.*

In a way, it's an anticapitalistic story, isn't it, suggesting that everyone
should have his share? And we share stories with the Cameroonians—
the Ibibios are a major tribe between us and them, plus a number of
smaller tribes that merge finally into the Cameroons.

*A number of Cameroonian stories concern themselves with the dangers
of misusing magic—a woman, in one tale, uses a magic potion to
make her husband unattractive to other women (his body turns into a
snake's body), and she becomes miserable. And in "The Flute" and
The Drum, you also suggest that one shouldn't tamper or fool around
with the spirit world.*

The question of frontiers is very important—you must not overstep
them—and these frontiers are set up in every space and time: there's
even a frontier to ambition. One of the most typical Igbo tales is
about a proud wrestler who has thrown every challenger in the world,
and so he decides to go and wrestle in the land of the spirits. This is
rashness. His praise-singer (a very good wrestler would have a man
playing the flute for him, singing his praises on the flute) begs him
not to go to the spirit world. But he says, No, I'm bored; there's
nobody in the world who can challenge me, I must go there. So they
go. And when they arrive there the spirits come out to wrestle with
him—one after the other—and he beats them all. And then he begins
to boast. He says, What sort of spirit world is this? The famous spirit
world, and it can't find somebody who can give me a proper fight!
Is there nobody else? The spirits have a consultation and tell him,
Well, there is somebody, but we think you shouldn't fight him. He

responds, No, if there is anybody at all here now, I must wrestle with him. And this person is his *chi*—his personal spirit—and when he comes out he's very unimpressive, as you would expect, very weak and hungry-looking, thin as a rope. Who is this? the wrestler asks. They tell him that this is the man who will challenge him, and he laughs. But his *chi* moves toward him and with one finger picks him up and smashes him on the ground. And that's the end of our great wrestler.

This is a great story about frontiers. Because Igbo people are very ambitious; you see, they have these cautionary tales about the frontier—you must not try to become the greatest of the greatest, you must not go beyond a certain point.

You once wrote: "A man is never more defeated than when he is running away from himself." And here, a man is never more defeated than when he fights his personal spirit.

It comes to the same thing; you can't win. We create these tales and fables, like God creating man in his own image. These folk tales aren't just decorative things—they tell us so much about the people who make them. And when told to children, they're intended for their safety, for their survival in the world.

You create the stories to curb yourself. The Igbos are so ambitious that everyone wants to be a king, in fact—this is the strange thing about it. And I'm not being facetious, because what happened at the end of the Biafran war was that somebody in the Nigerian government thought of the idea of letting the Igbos have chiefs.

The British tried the same thing.

Exactly. It's what the British tried and failed to do. But this time it worked. In every village now there's a king—they call themselves *kings*—these illiterate traders who made money at the Onitsha market! So the Igbos now have more than six hundred chiefs throughout Igboland. And we are a people who are reputed, who are *famous* throughout the world for not having kings. I'm saying it to make the suggestion that there must obviously have been a predilection in our character for ruling others, and it was that instinct, if you like, that the culture was fighting. I think a good culture fights against the instincts of destruction. And this held as long as we had the initiative to control our own history. In recent times this has changed, and the situation is different. Now, the kings we have today aren't going to do any harm; they have no real power, they're really clowns. But the fact is that in the Igbo language, "king" means enemy. The culture was right.

It's like Tortoise in The Drum *who wants to become king. Yet Tortoise is usually very egalitarian—if there's a bigger or faster creature, he brings him down to size.*

He's an egalitarian, and the idea of his becoming king is something I created based on our current situation—a contemporary "folk" situation, if you like, because I don't think it would have occurred to my ancestors to make a tortoise aspire to kingship.

Children seem to have a special affinity with Tortoise.

Yes, they love him. He's a nice, unreliable kind of rascal, and the village is all the happier for that kind of character—as long as there aren't too many like him in any one community [laughing]. You know the kind of character he is, and when he appears everybody immediately knows that Tortoise is up to his tricks, and they protect themselves. Remember the story in which Tortoise wants to go with the birds to heaven and have a feast? They give him wings, and though he says he's converted, he actually intends to cheat them. As the Chinese say: If you fool me once, shame on you; fool me twice, shame on me. That's a very wise statement. Unfortunately the birds let themselves be fooled three, four, or five times. And so do we.

But getting back to why children, especially, like the trickster: Perhaps it's because this figure is very lively, like a child; he's always doing something unexpected. There's a difference between the kind of roguery Tortoise is guilty of and evil. I don't think children like an evil character, they prefer a lively and vivacious one. Even if he's not very honest, they know that anyway, so he can't fool them. And there's room for this kind of person in all stories. Even in adult fiction. Think of a villain like Chief Nanga in *A Man of the People*, who has an attractive character—yes, a trickster, he's really a Tortoise figure. And you're attracted to him in spite of yourself, in spite of what you know. There's always drama around him, something is always happening where he is. As with Tortoise, he isn't going to simply walk down the street and disappear, he's going to start something.

Finally, I think that children like Tortoise because he's a very small fellow—he's weak in relation to the giants of the animal world. The tortoise is the slowest of all slow creatures, and yet he wins the races.

I wanted to ask you about your first children's book, Chike and the River. *The name Chike has* chi *in it, and so does your first name,* Chinua. *About* chi, *you've written:* "There are two clearly distinct meanings of the word chi in Igbo. The first is often translated as god, guardian angel, personal spirit, soul, spirit double, etc. The second meaning is day, or daylight, but is most commonly used for those transitional periods between day and night or night and day. . . . In a general way we may visualize a person's chi as his other identity in spiritland—his spirit being complementing his terrestrial human being; for nothing can stand alone, there must always be another thing standing beside it."

When we talk about *chi,* we're talking about the individual spirit, and so you find the word in all kinds of combinations. Chinwe, which is my wife's name, means "*Chi* owns me"; mine is Chinua, which is a shortened form of an expression that means "May a *chi* fight for me." My son is named Chidi, which means "*Chi* is there." So it's almost in everybody's name in one form or the other. Our youngest girl asked me why she didn't have *chi* in her name [laughing], she thought it was some kind of discrimination, so she took the name Chioma, which means "Good *chi.*"

What does Chike mean?

Chike is a shortened form of Chinweike, which means "*Chi* has the strength or the power." And that's what that frail-looking character has—he has the power.

Chike comes from Umofia, the village that is the main setting for Things Fall Apart *and* No Longer at Ease. *And this village seems to me to be as rich an imaginary geographical setting as Faulkner's Yoknapatawpha County.*

I had the idea of its being more like Thomas Hardy's Wessex—someplace in the mind, occurring again and again . . . and thus in that way creating a geographical solidity for that zone of the mind. There's

actually no place called Umofia, but its customs and its people are
clearly those of Ogidi in Eastern Nigeria, which is where I'm from.

*You've written: "As my forefathers said, the firewood which a people
have is adequate for the kind of cooking they do."*

In fact, that was an understatement, because the firewood the people
have is the *only* kind they can cook with—and even if it wasn't, they
couldn't do very much about it.

In Chike, *the young hero thinks: "So this is me . . . Chike Anene,
alias Chiks the Boy, of Umuofia, Mbaino District, Onitsha Province,
Eastern Nigeria, Nigeria, West Africa, Afrioa, World, Universe."*

[Laughing] We did that kind of thing in school. If you had a new
book, you wrote down your name, and just went on looking at yourself
in a widening gyre.

Illustration by Prue Theobalds from Achebe's *Chike and the River.* Reprinted by permission of Cambridge University Press

Chike goes from his village to Onitsha, a famous market town which you've written about elsewhere, stating that "it sits at the crossroads of the world. . . . Because it sees everything, Onitsha has come to distrust single-mindedness. It can be opposite things at once. It was both a cradle of Christianity in Igboland and a veritable fortress of 'pagan' revanchism." It was always the "marketplace of the world," a place where "riverine folk and the dwellers of the hinterland forests met in guarded, somewhat uneasy, commerce; old-time farmers met new, urban retail traders of known and outlandish wares." And it always attracted "the exceptional, the colorful, and the bizarre."

It's almost a mythical city, with all those extraordinary people, not the least of them Dr. James Stuart-Young—a scholar, mystic, and trader—a crazy Englishman who arrived, it seemed, from nowhere early in the century and who claimed to be a Ph.D. And he was an egalitarian! In those days he fought on the side of the people against the big British and French commercial concerns—multinationals, as we now call them. He was a one-man band who lived and died in Onitsha. I saw him once when I was a child—a tall, bald-headed Englishman. . . . I loved Onitsha then and I love it still. It's different now, of course. It was bombed, and it's been rebuilt, but it's still very vital. And I think that this vitality is the main quality of the "crossroads."

So this is the setting for the book, an adventure story that seems to have been written especially for ten- or eleven-year-old kids.

Yes, it's a "children's novel," if you like. And it came about, as I mentioned before, thanks to Christopher Okigbo who really made me do it. It was my first children's book. I enjoy writing for children, it's very important for me. It's a challenge I like to take on now and again because it requires a different kind of mind from me when I'm doing it—I have to get into the mind of a child totally, and I find that very rewarding. I think everybody should do that, not necessarily through writing a story, but we should return to childhood again and again. And when you write for children it's not just a matter of putting yourself in the shoes of a child—I think you have to be a child for the duration. It's not easy to begin with, and I didn't know if I could do it, it never occurred to me until Christopher Okigbo said I must do a children's story.

It seems that, in the African tradition, the infant is generally thought
of not as a kind of tabula rasa *but rather as a messenger whose presence*
is a gift from the other world.

I think that the idea of the child as messenger is certainly prevalent.
Now, my wife has been doing some work on the notion that some
children who are born, die, to come back, and to repeat cycles of birth
and death—this is a very common and popular belief among the Igbos.
In the past, of course, this was meant to explain the high rate of
infant mortality. And in doing this research, my wife encountered
stories about how children come from the world of "over there" into
the world of men. It's very interesting to discover the attributes they're
supposed to come with. The fact is that there's a bargain made, there's
a discussion concerning what you'd like to be and what you'd like to
do that takes place before the child comes over here. So the child is
not a *tabula rasa,* he or she is someone who has already negotiated
its entire destiny *over there.* And the child comes to the borderline,
and there is somebody there—perhaps a group of people—who tries
to talk him out of what he has agreed to be—they want to discourage
the child from aspiring too greatly. So what I am saying is that the
child comes with a whole realm of experience. Of course, these are
really metaphors for explaining reality. But a child isn't a clean slate,
it's got all its genes from its ancestors—what he or she is going to be
is more or less fixed in the genes, among other things.

In Childhood and Cosmos: The Social Psychology of the Black African
Child, *Pierre Erny writes: "The consciousness of receiving into earthly*
existence a new life which comes from elsewhere, of receiving it much
more than molding it, is the very basis of the relationship with the
child, who can be made an object of almost fearful respect and grati-
tude. . . . If an 'angel' . . . is seen in the child, education takes a very
specific direction. It becomes humble; it gives way to the revelation of
this being who comes to bring eternally young life to the living. . . .
The child brings along with it more than can be given to it. It renews
those who welcome it, rejuvenates them, regenerates them. Childcare
is composed of piety, admiration, freedom, confidence, and gratitude
more than authority or a spirit of domination and possessiveness."

It's true, and had better be, too. What Erny is talking about here concerns the attitude of the *adult* to the child, and I believe that in bring-

ing up children it's the adult who learns. As a parent I know that, and so this leads to the humility Erny mentions—I think this is very real. Now, that's not permissiveness, that's not to say you must never correct a child, because we're not talking about the years of experience the child cannot possibly have. But if you accept that the child comes from somewhere else, you can renew your acquaintanceship with that world through the child. I think this is a very good way of putting it, because these are metaphors for our experience. We really don't know. We're simply trying to use words as images to convey vague but insistent notions that visit us. In the past, when a child was born, our people would go to a diviner, to find out which of the ancestors it was who had come again. So this child was not new. And once they established who the child was, they gave him all that respect.

In Things Fall Apart, *you suggest that Nwoye, the son of Okonkwo, is the reincarnation of Okonkwo's father, Unoka.*

Yes, that's what I was saying. But this was a metaphor. I don't know how it operates, I don't know whether it means that this is exactly the same person or just somebody who has aspects of the character. It is a mystery to me, and it must remain a mystery. But I'm saying that, as a metaphor, people do come around in that way—children are supposed to be reincarnations of their grandfathers, not of their fathers. And quite often there *is* a very close relationship between grandparents and their grandchildren.

Among a number of African tribes, according to Pierre Erny, both young children and old men are considered ritually pure. And Erny writes: "There is . . . a special familiarity between children and old men, and especially between grandfather and grandson; this is explained by the fact that they are in a similar position in relation to intervening age categories, that of parents and procreators, and there is thus a kind of complicity between the two. The Bambara compare the old man-child couple to a tree covered with mistletoe, for one announces the decrepitude of the other."

It's very true. I have a poem called "The Generation Gap," which talks about that specifically, in terms of the pattern of the coming and going of the moon. There's usually some friction between father and son, and that would explain why there should be complicity between the child and the grandfather—they have one common enemy [laughing].

The Ijo of the Niger Delta have a proverb that goes: "He's of goblin ancestry who knows not whence he came." And this might imply that there is and should be a connection not only between grandfather and grandchild but also between the adult and his sense of his own childhood, since both connect one to one's past.

Yes, that's right, because if there is a constant coming or going between us and the world of the ancestors, which is what my people believe, then it's in fact the child who can tell you about that world since it's coming from there—it's not the old man who's *going* there but the child who's *coming* from there.

In all your work, the grandfather casts his shadow on the grandchild, the village on the city, and the pagan tradition on the Christian one.

The duality. Things come in twos. "Wherever something stands, something else will stand beside it"—this is another very powerful Igbo statement. It's absolutely true, and it's when someone refuses to see the "other" that you have problems. To my mind, one of the worst and most unimaginative of states is that of single-mindedness. This is the state of a man like Okonkwo in *Things Fall Apart*. In certain limited and restricted spheres this is admirable. But beyond that it becomes a real liability—he cannot see that things come in twos, and in that respect he resembles the British missionaries more than his own people—the way, the truth, and the life. But the old men in the village have no problem with that. They understand that you should have your own God, because it's only natural that if there's one God there must be another. For such people it's easier to accept and appreciate other people. But the single-minded, missionary type, whether he's the Englishman Smith or Okonkwo, doesn't operate on the level of this duality.

Ezeulu, the hero of Arrow of God, *seems to represent this twofold system.*

Yes, I had to do Ezeulu because I had "done" Okonkwo, if I may put it that way. Now, I wanted to do Okonkwo the way I did him because he does represent something, but what he represents is a kind of mind that could obtain anywhere—it happens to be that of the Igbo community. But I wanted to say something deeper about the community itself, not through the eyes of a simple-minded defender like Okonkwo, or of a simple-minded opponent like the district commissioner, but of a man of title and importance within the community—a ruler in fact, a priest, an intellectual. And to see the crisis through his eyes. Ezeulu's failing—his priestly arrogance—could apply to any priest, and it's really not very harmful or fatal. But the situation he was dealing with couldn't have been solved by anybody anyway. So the important thing was to have a complex sensibility tackling that crisis, that's all. Not to have him succeed. And that's part of our history.

Igbo history seems now to be unalterably connected to Nigerian history, and history has brought Nigeria to a critical point—as a country it, too, seems to be at the crossroads. What role do you think stories— and particularly stories for children—can have in these rapidly changing times? And might it not be possible for those of us in the West to learn something from your experience?

Whether or not the West learns anything from the African experience is a matter for the West to decide. I can only say that a major prerequisite to learning is humility; and that on present showing this virtue is extremely difficult for the West, thanks to its immense material success.

But to the main part of your question. Igbo and Nigerian fortunes seem to be indissolubly linked again—for good or ill. Our responsibility as Nigerians of this generation is to strive to realize the potential good and avoid the ill. Clearly, children are central in all this, for it is their legacy and patrimony that we are talking about. If Nigeria is to become a united and humane society in the future, her children must now be brought up on a common vocabulary for the heroic and the cowardly, the just and the unjust. Which means preserving and refurbishing the landscape of the imagination and the domain of stories, and not—as our leaders seem to think—a verbal bombardment of patriotic exhortation and daily recitations of the National Pledge and Anthem.

THE WISDOM
OF
MARY POPPINS:
AFTERNOON TEA
WITH
P. L. TRAVERS

PHOTOGRAPH BY JERRY BAUER

"*I*'m a mere kitchenmaid in the house of myth and poetry," P. L. Travers has said. And it was in this house that she discovered (the author dislikes the word "created") one of the most extraordinary characters of twentieth-century literature—the proper, prim, unexplaining, and unexplainable nanny, Mary Poppins.

Appearing as if heaven-sent at the front door of the Banks family's Cherry Tree Lane house (blown in with the wind) and flying home- and heavenwards in several ascensions (the last in an apotheosis of light), this Oddity, this Misfit, this Great Exception—as Mary Poppins is variously referred to throughout the five volumes that reveal her unsettling activities and uncanny being—is nothing less than a cosmic nanny. Whether she is showing the Banks children the Park inside the Park or the world turned upside down, talking to a dog or a starling, or dancing with the starfish or the sun, Mary Poppins has the character of a functionary incarnated from above, appearing as a kind of combination fairy godmother, guardian angel, shamaness, priestess, witch, and guru who, using every moment as a moment of instruction, teaches us to watch, to wait, to wake up, and to strive to become what we are. As a Gnostic text says of Mary Magdalene, "She speaks as a woman who knows the All."

"If you are looking for autobiographical facts," P. L. Travers once said, "*Mary Poppins* and my other books are the story of my life." The author has always expressed an aversion to biography and autobiography ("What porridge John Keats had doesn't matter"). But when we realize that Mary Poppins and P. L. Travers are both, in fact, *servants*, we might begin to see in the above statement a certain truth beyond its seeming willfulness. In any case, the "real" house in which the mythical and poetic Mary Poppins came to light was one that P. L. Travers lived in sometime during the early thirties, when she was convalescing from an illness—a house the author describes briefly in her autobiographical note for *The Junior Book of Authors*:

The house was a small old thatched manor, mentioned in Doomsday Book and the Sussex countryside that spread out round it was full of history and legend. But I did not need these to excite in me the atmosphere of fairy tale for I had soaked myself in that all through my childhood and had, as it were, borne it along with me till my grown-up years. I have always thought Mary Poppins came then solely to amuse me and that it was not till a friend saw some of her adventures written down and thought them interesting that she decided to stay long enough for me to put her into a book. I never for one moment believed that I invented her. Perhaps she invented me, and that is why I find it so difficult to write autobiographical notes!

To convalesce in this context means to return to childhood (isn't that in fact what we do psychologically when we rest after illness?), becoming smaller in order to grow stronger. And it must have been with the heart and mind of a child that P. L. Travers came across Mary Poppins (who, for her part, seems to have discovered her author at the same time), for she is a character who apprehends the world with, in Elizabeth Barrett Browning's beautiful phrase, an "infantine familiar clasp of things divine."

Significantly, it is from the perspective of the Banks children, not of the adults, that we observe Mary Poppins flying up the banister in her first appearance, only to realize that, just a few chapters later, these same children, are no longer able to fathom the language of their newborn twin brother and sister and, in *Mary Poppins Comes Back*, of their infant sister Annabel ("Slowly I moved at first, always sleeping and dreaming. I remembered all I had been and I thought of all I shall be. And when I had dreamed my dream I awoke and came swiftly"). The Taoists considered infancy to be the perfect moment, since a baby was identified with the Tao. The rest of us quickly forget the way and language of sunlight and stars, of starlings and wind; only the Great Exception remembers, and, as one of the children affirms in *Mary Poppins Opens the Door*, "she's a fairy tale come true."

To P. L. Travers, fairy tales are myths "fallen into time and locality." And this, in fact, is the way Mary Poppins appears, falling from the skies with her parrot-headed umbrella, white gloves, and carpetbag. "Had she lived in another age, in the old times to which she certainly belongs," the poet Æ once told P. L. Travers, "[she] would undoubtedly have had long golden tresses, a wreath of flowers in one hand, and perhaps a spear in the other. Her eyes would have been like the sea, her nose comely, and on her feet winged sandals.

Mary Poppins as illustrated by Mary Shepard, from *Mary Poppins Opens the Door*

But, this being Kali Yuga, as the Hindus call it—in our terms, the Iron Age—she comes in the habiliments most suited to it."

Like all fairy tales, Mary Poppins seems to have been always present and with us—"She who is before all things." The author writes in her "Afterword" to *About the Sleeping Beauty*:

> Perhaps we are born knowing the tales for our grandmothers and all their ancestral kin continually run about in our blood repeating them endlessly, and the shock they give us when we first hear them is not of surprise but of recognition. Things long unknowingly known have suddenly been remembered. Later, like streams, they run underground. For a while they disappear and we lose them. We are busy, instead, with our personal myth in which the real is turned to dream and the dream becomes the real. Sifting all this is a long process. It may perhaps take half a lifetime and the few who come round to the tales again are those who are in luck.

And in her essay "Only Connect," she adds: "The tales have to be told in order that we may understand that in the long run, whatever it may be, every man must become the hero of his own story; his own fairy tale, if you like, a real fairy tale." Since fairy tales reveal us to ourselves—just as the character of Mary Poppins, the "fairy tale come true," does—we return to them in order to remember and redis-cover who we are. We must wake to and awaken the stories within us, much as the fairy-tale prince rouses the princess from her sleep, thereby fulfilling what P. L. Travers sees as the essential mythical requirement—"the reinstatement of the fallen world."

This, simply, has been P. L. Travers' task. And she has gone about it by allowing the truths of story and rhyme to speak for them-selves and to dawn on and in us in ways we might never have ex-pected. The author instinctively understands that that which is often considered insignificant and despised may unexpectedly prove itself to be what is most valuable and revealing (Cinderella, the Youngest Brother, the Fool). As she has discovered: "The stories have to be loved for themselves before they will release their secrets." And like the most devoted of spiritual maids, P. L. Travers attends to the stories through service and stillness—pondering, questioning, wondering— waiting on and for them, but never forcing them, to reveal their noumenon. (Forcing someone to explain, as the Grimms' "Faithful John" suggests, petrifies one's being and meaning.)

In *About the Sleeping Beauty*, P. L. Travers asks:

> Are we dealing here with the sleeping soul and all the external affairs of life that hem it in and hide it; something that falls asleep after childhood, something that not to waken would make life meaningless? To give an answer, supposing we had it, would be breaking the law of the fairy tale. And perhaps no answer is necessary. It is enough that we ponder upon and love the story and ask ourselves the question.

In "Only Connect," she speculates:

> Doesn't it seem to you, too, that there is more in the tales than meets the eye? Think of all those stories of the three brothers who go off in search of various treasures. As a child, naturally, I thought of them as separate entities—the eldest so handsome, always delayed at the crossroads, or prevented from going farther because of some tempta-tion. He's handsome and brave, and relying on this, he assures himself that when the time comes, he'll find the treasure. Then the second, sure of his cleverness, a cleverness that proves to be groundless, also

fails in the quest. Lastly, the third brother sets out, realizing his ignorance, knowing himself a simpleton. And so he is. Simple and humble, willing to accept help from anyone who will give it. . . . Nowadays, however, I think of the brothers, not as single adventurers, but as three stages of one man.

And in her essay "The Shortest Stories in the World," she looks at the rhyme "Green Grow the Rushes-O"—which she sees as a manual of traditional instruction—and, turning to its famous culminating lines ("One is one and all alone/And ever more shall be so"), she writes:

> When I was a child, I brooded long upon that One. Was it God? Was it myself? I have now come to the conclusion that it is both. Essential aloneness is to be found at either end of the spectrum. "I'll sing you one-O" is a riddle that takes a lifetime to find the answer.

The poet Kenneth Rexroth once commented: "There are two ways of knowing, under standing and over bearing. The first is called wisdom. The second is called winning arguments." P. L. Travers follows the first way. As she herself tells us in her essay "The World of the Hero":

> To understand; for years I pondered on that word and tried to define its effect on myself. At last I came to the conclusion that what it means is the opposite of what it says; to understand is to stand under. Later I discovered that this was, in very fact, its meaning in Middle English. So, in order to understand, I come to something with my unknowing —my nakedness, if you like: I stand under it and let it teach me, rain down its truth upon me. That is, I think, what children do; they let it make room in them for a sense of justice, for the Wicked Fairy as well as the Sleeping Beauty, for dragons as well as princes.

And from the vantage point of "standing under" and "unknowing," she observes things from a source and center that lie in the country the old Scandinavian stories call East of the Sun and West of the Moon, at a moment beyond time—never and always—that the fairy tales refer to as "once upon a time."

P. L. Travers' five Mary Poppins books—*Mary Poppins, Mary Poppins Comes Back, Mary Poppins Opens the Door, Mary Poppins* *in the Park*, and *Mary Poppins in Cherry Tree Lane**—appeared in 1934, 1935, 1943, 1952, and 1982. (Along with these five major volumes in the canon are two ancillary bibelots, *Mary Poppins from A to Z* and *Mary Poppins in the Kitchen*, in 1962 and 1975.) In 1962, P. L. Travers published her Christmas tale *The Fox at the Manger* (in which a fox makes an offering of its cunning to the infant Jesus, wildness and tameness coming together as two parts of a cosmic unity), and in 1971, she brought out her moving, undeservedly neglected novel *Friend Monkey* (in which the Linnets, a family much like the Banks; Miss Brown-Potter, a woman much like Mary Poppins; and a cast of incongruous and endearing characters and creatures—especially Monkey, the all-compassionate, over-loving hero of the book—seem to lose but finally find themselves and each other in a community of love).

Throughout these years, she has also been presenting and publishing a series of lectures and essays that attest to a lifelong habitude—her profound love for myths, fairy tales, nursery rhymes, legends, parables, and proverbs—all those oral tatters and literary scraps that adults, during the past three centuries, have discarded and allocated to their children. And these beautifully and dramatically written lectures and essays, many of which first appeared in *Parabola* magazine and which the author plans eventually to collect in one volume, are illuminating in the connections they make, adamant in the values they

---

* The most recent book, *Mary Poppins in Cherry Tree Lane*, is a short (ninety pages), beautiful coda to the entire series—a gathering together of the earthly and heavenly luminaries of the Mary Poppins universe (the Park Keeper, Miss Lark, Mr. Banks, Castor and Pollux, Orion, and Mary Poppins and her charges, among others) who find each other on Midsummer's Eve in the Herb Garden of the Park. And on this night of music, cherries, and magical herbs, when everything is possible ("even the impossible"), all the characters—"insubstantial luminous boys hand in hand with substantial children"—form a Grand Chain, "each hand taking the hand of each, and the big Bird flying among them. The top spun and the circle spun round it, and the Park round the circle, the earth round the Park and the darkening sky round the earth. . . . The song would never be done, it seemed, and the top would never stop spinning. The circle of humans and constellations would go on turning forever." And as the night ends and Mary Poppins leads the Banks children home, they—knowing she will leave at any moment—ask her, "How shall we know how to find you?" while realizing, of course, that "wherever she was, she would not be lost." Because as Mary Poppins says, "All that's lost is somewhere." And just as the number five is said symbolically to comprise the four cardinal points together with the center, so this fifth Mary Poppins book might be seen to be the center and distillation of the entire canon.

promote, haunting in the depths they touch, and courageous in the wisdom their experiences draw upon. As P. L. Travers writes in "Letter to a Learned Astrologer":

> I throve on what was difficult, the difficult man, the difficult child; the arduous exploring of the Empty Quarter—your Nadir, where no planets were—where, perhaps, (dear Brutus!) it was necessary that I should become my own planet; the discovery that in lack lies treasure if you are willing to find it; and that by confronting the Unknown—not as though it were knowable but as an absolute—one receives, oh, intimations; the hard-won realization that life, like Coyote, is a trickster, conning one into expectations that have no basis in reality; that there is nothing to expect, nothing to be gained, and nobody to blame; that there are no rights of any kind but only a purpose to be served—was that my "something else"? I had to learn that to be vulnerable, naked and defenseless is the only way to safety; that the sieve knows a lot about water, emptiness of plenitude, the Erinyes of kindliness. This is easy to say, less so to accept. But one can grow ripe on difficulty as a plum grows ripe on sunlight.

P. L. Travers lives in a quiet, small period house in the Chelsea section of London, and everything in her home contributes to a visitor's sensing the emptiness of plenitude and the plenitude of emptiness—exemplified, in her upstairs study, by several beautiful Japanese scroll and screen paintings, mostly by Sengai: a willow almost breaking in the wind; six persimmons; a cock crowing to the morning and a little hen bird nearby; the depiction of the syllable *mu* (literally meaning "not" or "without" and referring to a famous Zen koan); and the extraordinary "Ten Oxherding Pictures" (attributed to the twelfth-century Chinese Zen master Kaku-an Shi-en). This allegorical series, composed as a training guide for Chinese Buddhist monks, shows the progress of a man searching for his ox (for that which a person is or has in his or her self), and at the same time, with gravity and grace, conveys a sense of the meaning and transparency of meaning and transparency themselves: "1) Searching for the Ox, 2) Seeing the Traces, 3) Seeing the Ox, 4) Catching the Ox, 5) Herding the Ox, 6) Coming Home on the Ox's Back, 7) The Ox Forgotten, Leaving the Man Alone, 8) The Ox and the Man Both Gone out of Sight, 9) Returning to the Origin, Back to the Source, 10) Entering the City with Bliss-bestowing Hands." "This last is the ultimate aim," P. L. Travers says, "the bringing back to the market place—and to others—what one has found." (Reproductions of these pictures and accompanying texts can be found in *Manual of Zen Buddhism* by D. T. Suzuki.)

At the time I visited P. L. Travers in July 1979, I was feeling perplexed and confused about several things in my life, whose murkiness contrasted sharply with the clarity of the pictures in her study. Everything she showed me in her house somehow seemed to help me put things in perspective—especially the photographs of various Buddhas. "I assimilate myself to this gesture," she said, pointing to one of these—Maitreya, with the raised hand. " 'Silence!' he says. 'Don't explain. It cannot be explained.' " She also took me to her garden in the back, where she was growing more than twenty varieties of herbs, many of which appear in her recent *Mary Poppins in Cherry Tree Lane* ("Taste all of them," she suggested, "they will do you good"). Then, as a friendly gesture, she cut off some rosemary sprigs and gave them to me ("This will last forever and bring you good luck. It means 'To Remember' ").

As we conversed over tea—her voice peremptory but gentle, her words precise but lustral—she saw through my confusion (with eyes "so blue they go back to God"), channeled my loquaciousness, and gave me some suggestions ("Not for you to repeat, it's meant just for yourself"). Then, more generally, she said: "Accept everything that comes and make jewels of it. Truly, I don't want to sound pious, but I feel like that. And that's what I call the hero nature—you can only be the hero of your own story if you accept it totally."

I knew that in 1978 she had received an honorary degree from Chatham College in Pittsburgh and that she had lectured extensively at Smith, Radcliffe, and Claremont, yet she protested: "I'm not a scholar or a teacher, I'm not anything very much. I'm just somebody who remembers and links things up. Things link themselves within me." When she liked a particular quotation I read her, she immediately wrote it down on a scrap of paper, saying: "A note is written on the back of an envelope, say, or the back of an old bill; then I pay my bill and I've lost it. But it is remembered in me." And at the conclusion of our tea, her last words to my final question were: "Maybe. Maybe is enough to live with."

In his *Essays in Idleness*, the fourteenth-century Japanese writer Kenko comments: "Three kinds of people make desirable friends. First is the friend who gives you things; second, a doctor; and third, the friend with wisdom." To me, P. L. Travers, as a person and writer, is all three in one: giving, healing, and wise. And doesn't *Sophia*— the Greek feminine term for "wisdom" and the personified Divine

Mother of the Gnostics (teacher, guide, and source of insight)—
suggest many aspects of both Mary Poppins and P. L. Travers?

Although I consider P. L. Travers, like Mary Poppins, to be a
teacher, it is rather as one who serves that she would like to be known.
As she told me: "C. S. Lewis has a wonderful phrase to the effect
that 'there is only one Creator, and we merely mix the elements he
gives us.' I never use the words 'creator' or 'creative,' because I know
that I'm neither. I'm a sort of apprentice, perhaps." On the bottom
of the last page of *Mary Poppins Open the Door* we find, printed in
capital letters: GLORIA IN EXCELSIS DEO. And, similarly, at the
conclusion of *Friend Monkey* and *Mary Poppins in Cherry Tree Lane*
we discover the initials: A. M. G. D. (*ad majorem Dei gloriam*).

It is known that P. L. Travers has been (and in a true sense still
is) a pupil of Æ, Gurdjieff, and a Zen roshi, among others. And I
have even heard it said—only half-jokingly—that Mary Poppins is
simply a disguised version of Gurdjieff. "This," she says scoffingly,
"is ridiculously untrue—two of the *Mary Poppins* books were written
before I had ever met him. I owe them to Nobody, not Somebody."
And it should be clear to any reader that characters with the divine
concreteness of Mary Poppins or Friend Monkey's Miss Brown-Potter
are like only themselves:

> ". . . Oh, Mary Poppins, tell me truly! [said Michael Banks]
> You aren't anybody in disguise? I want you just as you are!"
> A faint, pleased smile puckered her mouth. Her head gave a
> prideful toss.
> "Me! Disguised! Certainly not!"
> With a loud sniff at the mere idea, she disengaged his hands.
> "But, Mary Poppins—" Jane persisted. "Supposing you weren't
> Mary Poppins, who would you choose to be?"
> The blue eyes under the tulip hat turned to her in surprise.
> There was only one answer to such a question.
> "Mary Poppins!" she said.

Our tea and conversation finished, I took my leave, and on my
way out past the bay tree growing on the doorstep, P. L. Travers
pointed to a photograph of Æ ("the tutelary deity of the house," she
announced) and, hanging next to it, several drawings by him—one of
them showing a young woman reclining in a tree ("I was in Donegal,
Ireland, sitting in that tree, thinking of the birds and the bees—who
knows what I was thinking—and Æ was drawing and loudly reciting
from the Bhagavad-Gita").

Hanging alongside this sketch was another drawing—a simple and powerfully conceived Tree of Life done by one of P. L. Travers' young students. And it seemed fitting that, in this servant's dwelling, the famous and the humble, the adult and the child, were side by side. I almost bumped into a rocking horse, standing mysteriously next to the front door, on my way out. And as I left, I remembered something P. L. Travers had said in her essay "I Never Wrote for Children":

> To be aware of having been a child—and who am I but the child I was, wounded, scarred and dirtied over, but still essentially that child, for essence cannot change—to be aware of and in touch with this fact is to have the whole long body of one's life at one's disposal, complete and unfragmented. You do not chop off a section of your imaginative substance and make a book specifically for children for— if you are honest—you have, in fact, no idea where childhood ends and maturity begins. It is all endless and all one.

Sketch of P. L. Travers by the poet Æ. "I was in Donegal, Ireland, sitting in that tree, thinking of the birds and the bees . . . and Æ was drawing and loudly reciting from the Bhagavad-Gita."

I wanted to mention to you that when I was feeling depressed recently, I found that reading both the Mary Poppins books and Friend Monkey *was very healing to me.*

That's the kind of thing I'd rather have said than anything. My lawyer says that he keeps the books by his bed to help him with his cases. Of course he's a great flatterer. But you know, I'm always happy when grown-ups like the books because their substance is really grown-up, as all children's themes, I think, should be. How could I possibly think of writing for children? It's ridiculous. They know so much more than we do.

Incidentally, I must tell you that I don't give a damn for the Year of the Child [UNESCO designated 1979 as the International Year of the Child] because to me *every* year is the year of the child. What are they going to do at the end of it? Drop the children over the edge of the world? This fragmentation of life! I think that *Mary Poppins* and *Friend Monkey*, if they do anything, celebrate the whole of life—nobody is separate from anyone else. I hope they're life-celebrating books.

In his study entitled Once Upon a Time, *Max Lüthi writes these powerful words: "Everything can enter into relationship with everything else: that is the actual miracle and at the same time the simple foregone conclusion in the fairy tale. . . . The fairy tale sees man as one who is essentially isolated but who, for just this reason—because he is not rigidly committed, not tied down—can establish relationships with anything in the world. And the world of the fairy tale includes not just the earth, but the entire cosmos."*

It's so right. But that's the only way to live. And that's why I don't have any time for *acquaintance*. Either a person is my friend or I let him go. . . . I see you're seeing significance in that.

Well, I . . .

But you *should* see significance in it—you're a friend already! Acquaintance—what is it? A little sip of something at a cocktail party. I refuse to go to them now, nobody goes away with anything; they're nothing but confetti. I can't bear the noise of conversation. But two voices together . . . how marvelous. Three, four, five—just a handful, how lovely!

How about an Englishwoman and her adopted African son and an Indian monkey and a parrot [the main characters in Friend Monkey] . . .

You mustn't go wrong there. Miss Brown-Potter didn't adopt Stanley Fan. When one character says, "Your servant answered the door," she replies, "He's not my servant, he's my friend." They're not mother and son, they're just pieces of the universe which have been brought together by their mutual . . . sympathies is too small a word. What's a better one?

Affinities.

Affinities. That's right.

Or maybe aloneness.

Maybe aloneness. And only aloneness can bring togetherness. Too near is too far. But go far and you'll find the near. If you're too near something, you can't see it very well, you can't find the relationship. Go some distance from it—idea or person—and there you're immediately joined together. You know how it is when you love somebody, and you look at him across the room—a crowd of people—and that exchange is much closer than an embrace.

I once was thinking of someone I cared about, and what came to me were the words: "I'm thinking of you, but you're too close."

Yes, quite right. . . . I've only come to see these things by hindsight, but Mary Poppins is always at a distance, and therefore she can be intimately precious and close, never to be lost.

Speaking of which: Skylab fell across the Australian desert recently; and its disintegrating descent was described in the English papers as "glowing fragments . . . white-hot debris . . . a long bank of twisting, spectacular orange and blue lights leaving a sonic boom behind." That would be an apt modern-day reentry for Mary Poppins, don't you think?

Oh dear, no! Anything connected with machinery would be well away from her—any man-made thing, except the umbrella and the carpetbag, which are inevitabilities. But a man-made invention, no. That's to misunderstand her.

It's interesting that Mary Poppins carries a bar of Sunlight Soap in her handbag.

In her *carpet*bag. Don't get it mixed up. Handbag is the English word for what you call a pocketbook, where she keeps her purse and her money. It's in her carpetbag that . . . *Sunlight Soap!* I never thought of that! Oh, I do thank you for telling me.

Yes, I thought of it in the sense of its cosmic significance, but perhaps it's a brand name.

Of course it's a brand name. In my childhood I remember those large bars—at least a foot long—of solid, thick, yellow soap. Everyone had them, they were the most commonplace items. The great mistake many people make when they think about Mary Poppins is to imagine that she works for a rich family. But the household helpers are there for the same reason Max Lüthi suggested in the quotation you read me before: They are there as part of the universe. And you have to remember that Mary Poppins is *essentially* a servant, in every sense of that word. The so-called workers in the Banks house are so absurd: Ellen, who never lifts a hand to help, always has a bad cold and a sneeze. Robertson Ay, who's he? What is he paid for? He does nothing but sleep.

He turns out to be the Fool.

Yes, he does, but I didn't know he was going to turn out that way when he first cropped up in my mind. And then there's Mrs. Brill, who's always having to go away—one imagines her as part of some enormous extended family—her niece's cousin's sister's aunt's daughter is probably having a new baby. It's a peculiar collection of people, you must admit.

But getting back to Sunlight Soap . . . it's the commonest, coarsest soap there is. It washes floors, it washes clothes and children, there's nothing it doesn't do . . . or, rather, didn't do in my childhood. . . . You see, I don't know much about Mary Poppins, but other people constantly make me aware of things that are connected with her. It's wonderful to be given what one had thought was one's own book by other people. But I never really thought it my own, you know. I always thought of it as something given or lent.

You once described the book's genesis, saying that you were convalescing in the Sussex countryside and that Mary Poppins sort of appeared to you.

Yes. But her name occurred a long while before that. When I was in my teens, I wrote a small story about someone named Mary Poppins putting children to bed. I can't remember what paper the story appeared in, but the name was a long time a-growing, a long time in existence, perhaps. And then it came back when I was ill and recovering from what was thought to be TB—it wasn't. So the story goes, I've mostly forgotten it. Because to me it's not important. What porridge John Keats had doesn't matter. He had to eat to live, and thank God he did, that's all.

In Wordsworth's "Immortality" Ode—whose sentiments are at the heart of Mary Poppins *(". . . every common sight/To me did seem/ Apparell'd in celestial light")—there is a stanza that seems to describe her . . . and the Swedish writer Staffan Bergsten, in his fascinating* Mary Poppins and Myth, *seems to feel the same way, when he quotes it:*

> *Thou, whose exterior semblance doth belie*
> > *Thy Soul's immensity;*
> *Thou Best Philosopher, who yet dost keep*
> *Thy heritage, thou Eye among the blind*
> *That, deaf and silent, read'st the eternal deep,*
> *Haunted for ever by the eternal Mind,—*
> > *Mighty Prophet! Seer blest! . . .*

And have you noticed the first initials of the words "Mighty Prophet"?

Oh, I never thought of that! How interesting that is! I'm reminded of a letter I received from a young woman threatened by a fatal disease who apparently had been deeply affected by Mary Poppins. And she said: "I've never written a fan letter before. All I can say is, 'Dear Mother Nature, thank you for altering my life. Dear Snowstorm, thank you for beautifying the world'." Marvelous. I'm not those things, it's just that her beautiful mind reached out to something she felt for and immediately related it to something else that seemed to her to be true.

At the conclusion of Mary Poppins Opens the Door, *you write: "The bright shape speeding through the air above them would forever keep its secret. But in the summer days to come and the long nights of winter, they would remember Mary Poppins and think of all she had told them. The rain and the sun would remind them of her, and the birds and the beasts and the changing seasons. Mary Poppins herself* had flown away, but the gifts she had brought would remain for always."

Yes. A little boy, after coming to end of the third volume, wrote to me: "Madam, you have sent Mary Poppins away. Madam, I will never forgive you. You have made the children cry." What a reproach! And I wrote back to him to say that I, too, had cried because I had no idea Mary Poppins was going away for good. I just cried all over the typewriter, I wept and wept.

In that concluding chapter, there's a passage about Jane's premonitions: "Jane turned away. What was the matter with her heart? It suddenly felt too big for her chest. 'I'm lonely,' she said in a whisper to Michael. . . . 'It's not that kind of loneliness. I feel I'm going to lose something'." And at the conclusion of Friend Monkey, Mr. Linnet—having left England and now alone with his new communal and spiritual family on the deserted shore near the forest in which Monkey had originally found himself abandoned—reflects: " 'I'm a castaway!' he thought, for a moment feeling lost and lonely." And I feel that connection there.

Do connect them, please. *You* must make the connection for me. It's quite true. I hadn't realized, until I'd written all the books, that *Mary Poppins* and *Friend Monkey* are very alike in many ways. The Banks family could perfectly easily be the Linnet family transposed—except that in *Mary Poppins* the little girl Jane is the sensitive one, and in *Friend Monkey* it's the boy Edward. And, of course, I see, after reading the books, that Miss Brown-Potter does have something of Mary Poppins in her.

And Mr. Linnet and Mr. Banks are similar. The former senses and finally discovers what's true. The latter understands Mary Poppins and her ways almost in spite of himself.

You've hit on something. Mr. Banks is the complement of Mary Poppins because he *almost* knows. Mrs. Banks never knows. Neither does Mrs. Linnet.

He's the one who tells the children to wish on the star that Mary Poppins has become. He's the one who, sleepwalking on Halloween eve, finds his shadow.

Yes, he understands more than he knows. But I didn't intend it—I only saw that afterwards, just as I only saw the connections between *Mary Poppins* and *Friend Monkey* much later.

I wonder whether you know a poem by William Blake called "William Bond." Do you have a volume of his poetry here?

My dear, of course I have! It's upstairs in the study. Go in at the door, and on the top shelf in the third section nearest the window you'll find Blake; he's in a little, worn, red-leather binding. [I go upstairs, find the book, return downstairs with it, turn to the poem and show it to her.] This one I don't know. [She reads the fifty-two-line poem aloud, ending with the final two stanzas:]

> I thought Love liv'd in the hot sun shine,
> But O, he lives in the Moony light!
> I thought to find Love in the heat of day,
> But sweet Love is the Comforter of Night.
>
> Seek Love in the Pity of others' Woe,
> In the gentle relief of another's care,
> In the darkness of night & the winter's snow,
> In the naked & outcast, Seek Love there!

When I hear that poem, I think about some of your characters— naked and outcast—who seem to reveal and realize more than many obvious heroes and heroines.

The comic ones, the strange ones, those who own nothing, like Robertson Ay or the Park Keeper who, in "The Children in the Story" [*Mary Poppins in the Park*], says, after warning the Three Princes not to touch the flowers: "Oh, I'm picking all the roses, I'm breaking the bye-laws, and I'm *giving* them to you." It's those minor characters with their sudden vivid moments that I love. . . . That's a beautiful poem, my dear.

And I'm reminded of something you once wrote in "Only Connect" about your childhood in Australia: "My body ran about in the south- ern sunlight but my inner world had subtler colours, the greys and snows of England." And in "Letter to a Learned Astrologer," you tell of how you received a special issue of the Children's Encyclopedia, *sent by a relative from England, with an accompanying form letter addressed "Dear Child." The letter invited you to subscribe to the encyclopedia and to "explore the worlds that were opening up" before you. And it was signed Arthur Mee. So you wrote to Arthur Mee, asking him to send you the fare to England, assuring him that he wouldn't have to provide for you since you planned to sweep crossings, like Little Joe.*

When I read that essay over, I wept because I saw this child from the outside. I *was* the child writing to Arthur Mee and expecting a note from him. And I fully intended to sweep crossings. But Arthur Mee didn't want me.

And neither, according to your essay, did the Gypsies you came across one day, who, you hoped, would certainly steal you.

No, the Gypsies didn't want me either. But they were more than Gypsies—they must have been traveling Mohammedans, with their peaked tents and a browsing camel. So ceremonial and hieratic and ritualistic it all was, and I thought: "They'll take me, they'll take me." Not that I was unhappy. Not at all. I was perfectly happy where I was, but I knew that I had to go somewhere else. I've never not known it.

I've written before about how I used to have, and still have, a certain feeling at sunset that brings back to me that lonely, melancholy, very rich *something*. "There must be something else." Those were the words I gave this feeling full of sorrow and longing I had when I was a child. As I've said, it wasn't as if I didn't laugh and enjoy and be happy in what I had. But always that phrase came. The sunset was something that you couldn't escape from, it had to be confronted. I'm never happy in a house that doesn't look out on the sunset.

In a biographical reminiscence, you wrote: "My childhood, in a house overlooking sweeping fields of sugar cane, was full of reef's tokens— shells, palm fans, sprays of coral. My earliest memory is of walking through the green forests of the cane, as if through a jungle, and of making nests—which I hoped a bird would inhabit—between the juicy stalks. I chewed cane, when it was ripe, as modern children chew gum."

That's really not quite so exact. There are memories of two different places mixed up in that passage. Alongside our house grew a great field of weeds—members of the *Siderum* family. It had masses of leaves on the outside, but when they fell down and dried up, they became the material for a nest inside the stems. And I used to nest there, thinking I was a bird. About six I was, and while I knew I was a child, I also knew that I was a bird. And I'd sit there brooding—it seemed like hours—my arms tightly clasped around me. And the others would say, "She can't come, she's *laying*," just as you might say of a blackbird, "She's brooding." Then my mother would come and undo my limbs—this knotted little body that was busy in its nest. "I have told you once," she would say, "and I've told you twice—no laying at lunchtime." She never said: "No laying!" She never said: "You're not a bird!" She never thought: "Oh, my God, she must see a psychiatrist—my child thinks she's a wren or a kiwi!"

This reminds me of the scene in Friend Monkey *in which the house is quiet and you hear the song "Greensleeves" in the distance. Then you see Monkey, with his long arms wrapped closely around himself, feeling alone, as he remembers the forest where he was first left alone by the other monkeys. And suddenly, "Miss Brown-Potter at the age of ten, mumpish in her white muslin, stepped down from her portrait frame and came and stood beside him. For a long time or a short time —neither could have measured it—the two of them communed together, motionless as a painted child beside a painted monkey." At that point, the ominous Professor McWhirter, who is trying to steal Monkey away, tiptoes in. . . . So you have Monkey, wrapping his arms around himself—the way* you *did when you were nesting as a child— remembering the forest, its green leaves.*

[Sings] "Greensleeves was all my joy/And, oh, Greensleeves was my delight,/Greensleeves was my heart of gold,/And who but my Lady Greensleeves?" . . . Again you've made the link. What I meant that he was hearing was "Greensleeves" sung by Miss Brown-Potter's parents. And *you* suggest that it refers to the green of the forest? Ah, think of that!

And also the nesting image of the arms around the body.

Right, yes. You've hit on something so true—that the body remembers. We always think that memory is in the mind, and possibly also in the heart. But we forget that the body is the prime remembrancer. Put yourself in this gesture [puts arms around herself].

Wilhelm Reich believed that our body contains our past, and that when you release its tension, the past, too, is released.

I'm sure it's true. From my own experience. Sometimes I can find myself lying so *still* in my bed, so still, and yet so sensing the whole of my body in its quietude that I could be a plant. I could, in a way, know—though not with my mind—that my *body* knows what it's like to be a plant. I've never known what it's like to be an animal— I haven't got there yet. But I've had this extraordinary stillness quite recently in which so much inward life is flowing . . . like Dylan Thomas's "The force that through the green fuse drives the flower/ Drives my green age." So still and yet so vivid. Strange that it's come to me to know this so late in life. Perhaps I knew it as a child but didn't really know that I knew it. One does not, then, need to know.

The word "truth" in ancient Greek has as one of its meanings "no forgetting."

No forgetting. . . . How marvelous! If I had to choose a motto—and I don't have anything as my special motto (though my family motto is "*Fier sans lâche*": Proud without stain")—I'd choose that: No forgetting.

It's in all of your books. Monkey is remembering. And throughout the Mary Poppins volumes, almost everyone is remembering or forgetting to remember. "Slowly I moved at first, always sleeping and dreaming," says the newborn infant in Mary Poppins Comes Back. "I remembered all I had been and I thought of all I shall be. And when I had dreamed my dream I awoke and came swiftly."

You've given me a real gift. You see, I get gifts everyday from everywhere, and that's more precious to me than rubies. . . . But along with no forgetting, I continually sense myself as knowing less and less. To become an *unknower* would be wonderful. I sometimes think that when Henry Moore makes one of his reclining women full of holes, that he has me in mind. I just feel the holes, and the air going through, not knowing anything! A nitwit!

A television producer once came to me and said: "The Mary

Poppins books are not invented." And I was so pleased. I'm not going to pretend that there's anything occult about them or that they were borne upon the wind of fancy—not at all. They just came in through the holes of those reclining women.

There is a story going around that Henry Moore offered a sculpture to some Town Council who were flattered, but even so begged that it should not be one with holes in case some little boy put his head in a hole and couldn't get it out again! I would like to have reminded that Town Council that what goes in must also, by law, come out, and that any little boy could do no better thing than to put his head into that kind of emptiness. He would come out knowing a lot!

To return to your childhood and your essay "Only Connect": You write: "In a world where there are few possessions, where nobody answers questions, where nobody explains—I say this with joy, not sorrow!—children must build life for themselves. One child is forced this way, one another. I went into imagination and poetry." . . . Now, in Friend Monkey, *Miss Brown-Potter is described as having lived, as a child, in an attic with a nurse and then a governess—"a shy child in a white dress, isolated, plain, dreaming of far-away places." And I'm struck by the resemblance here between the passage I quoted from "Only Connect" and the childhood lives of Miss Brown-Potter and Beatrix Potter (two Potters, incidentally!).*

Yes, I made that connection—not in my mind but in my "no forgetting," and it came out in Miss Brown-Potter. (In fact, we knew a family of Brown-Potters when I was a child.) And instinctively, with my not-knowing, I gave her the same kind of childhood as Beatrix Potter had. But she also relates to Mary Kingsley, the niece of Charles Kingsley, who went to West Africa and explored it—as an anthropologist—wearing elastic-sided boots, flowing skirts, a cape, and a bonnet. She made great friends with a Scottish missionary woman, similarly dressed, and she lived contentedly amongst the tribes—in particular the Fan tribe (now called the Fang tribe). She would give the tribal women her high-necked blouses as presents, and the men wore them! When Miss Brown-Potter tells Mrs. Linnet that all she has to do to leopards is to give them a poke with her foot and they'll move on, well, I took this from Mary Kingsley. A leopard one day came sniffling around her skirts, and she said, giving it a poke with her boot, "Get along, you idiot!" and it got along at once. This to me was so marvelous. What a woman! And they honored her by burying her at sea, just as she had wished. Of her bones are coral made!

There's something very lonely about the childhoods of Beatrix Potter and Miss Brown-Potter. And Louis, too—the cockatoo in Friend Monkey—*is described as being "far from home and a stranger in the world of men." It reminds me of an extraordinary statement by Meister Eckhart: "Pity them, my children, they are far from home and no one knows them. Let those in quest of God be careful lest appearances deceive them in these people who are peculiar and hard to place; no one rightly knows them but those in whom the same light shines."*

Please let me have a copy of that. Meister Eckhart is one of the greatest, greatest teachers. We're *all* far from home. Make no mistake about that. But I might as well be a clod in a forest with grass growing out of it, so at home do I feel in this world. I think it's a most beautiful world. This is something like what the Buddha, on the way to his Paranirvana—his death—said. Though he was aware that his true home was elsewhere, he knew this world was his home while he lived in it. I want no other planet, I don't want to move to a space colony. The farther I go, the more I like being here. But that doesn't prevent me from knowing full well that I'm far from home.

"Do not fight,/But help one another/On your way—/Dear migrating birds," wrote the Japanese poet Issa. And it seems that the little community of Friend Monkey *is one in which each creature helps the other. Except, perhaps, the cantankerous, incorrigible, stubborn Uncle Trehunsey.*

I wasn't going to change or sentimentalize that uncle. He was going to live and die as himself.

Friend Monkey, *with all its fantastic characters, would make a wonderful film, don't you think?*

And I see how it could be done. They could disguise a very small man as a monkey, as they did with those animals in *Peter Rabbit and Tales of Beatrix Potter*—a tiny man or boy in fur and a monkey face. I'd like it so much to be done as a film—but certainly not as a cartoon, for you must show the sorrow and the grief and the endless love that is in Monkey . . . it never fails. He brings disaster in his train until the very end. . . . You know, I didn't realize that Professor McWhirter wasn't a bad guy until that very end, I had no idea! It came upon me as a shock—in a garden in Virginia—and I lifted up my hands and said, "To have given me such an idea, how marvelous, where could I have got it from?" He was *not* a villain, after all, but the rescuer. Perhaps, in a sense, the villain is always the rescuer, the one who throws the story forward, like the Wicked Fairy in the Sleeping Beauty story.

It's in this approving sense that you write about the Wise Women of fairy tales—"sisters of the Sirens, kin to the Fates and the World Mothers"—each of them an aspect of Kali, "who carries in her multiple hands the powers of good and evil." You often talk about what you call "the necessary antagonist."

The necessary antagonist is always the one who brings to fruition the essential ending. What would we do without any nay-sayers?

Having discovered that Professor McWhirter is not a villain, Mr. Linnet thinks to himself: "What use is the right fact when the point of view is wrong?"

Yes, I'm so grateful to D. H. Lawrence—I've quoted this again and again, and think he should be canonized for saying that there's the truth of truth as well as the truth of fact. You see, everybody sees Professor McWhirter collecting and stealing the animals—that's the truth of fact—but they don't know till the end of the story that he's taking them to the secret islands in order to protect them. That's the truth of truth.

In one tradition, the Indian monkey god Hanuman, who is the inspiration for Friend Monkey, is said to be the son of Shiva. And I noticed that on one of your walls you have a poster of a nineteenth-century Indian painting showing Hanuman carrying Shiva and Parvati in his heart. In this regard, there's a text I like very much which I wanted to read to you: "For one cycle of creation Shiva dances. For the next cycle he dreams. We think we are living in the real world and Shiva is dancing. We are not. He is dreaming."

It's wonderful. I must have that quotation.

I read it to you because everywhere in the *Mary Poppins* books are dancers and dancing: "With a little push, Michael spun them round. And again a push, And again a spin. And soon they were all revolving gently in the middle of the room" [Mary Poppins in the Park]. Even the world dances: " 'It's love that makes the world go round!' yelled Eenie, Meenie, and Mynie. And, indeed, the world did seem to be spinning, turning for joy upon its axis, as the little Park spun round its buttercup tree. Round and round and round it went in a steady, stately movement" [Mary Poppins in the Park].

James Stephens said: "The first and last duty of man is to dance." And I agree with that. In my childhood, at any moment of despair or joy, I danced. And in a way I do it still. I once saw a fox dancing— thought it was a fox, prancing on its hind legs at the edge of the wood. (I put this scene into my book, *I Go by Sea, I Go by Land* [1941].) And there was the farmer standing by. "Look," I said to him, "the fox is dancing." "No, it's a vixen," he replied slyly, looking at me. "Women and vixen are two of a kind—dancing alone with their secrets."

Here's a scene from Mary Poppins Comes Back—Mary Poppins's and the Banks children's evening out with the moon, sun, planets, and constellations:

> "Then," said Jane wonderingly, "is it true that we are here tonight or do we only think we are?"
> The Sun smiled again, a little sadly.
> "Child," he said, "seek no further! From the beginning of the world all men have asked that question. And I, who am Lord of the Sky—even I do not know the answer. I am certain only that this is the Evening Out, that the Constellations are shining in your eyes and that it is true if you think it is. . . ."
> "Come, dance with us, Jane and Michael!" cried the Twins. And Jane forgot her question as the four of them swung out into the ring in time with the heavenly tune.

Who, where, and what are we? Are we dreaming or dancing?

Maybe both! I must tell you about an eight-year-old child, the grand-daughter of close friends of mine in America. Her elder sister used to come to my apartment—she had always been the one who had written letters to me and who thought I was her special friend. And this second child felt left out—I didn't know it or else I wouldn't have left her out. And one day she spoke up and demanded: "Why can't *I* go to tea with her?" So I asked her specially, all by herself. We had tea, played games, told stories, and on the way to the elevator, she took my hand, stood in front of me like a fierce little avenging goddess, and said: "Tell me, and don't give me any guff—is Mary Poppins real?" So I gave it the silence and the contemplation that I thought the question required. "Well, she's real to me anyway." I said. She hugged my arm and joyfully cried: "She's real to me, too."

And, quite recently, I got a letter from this child, now twelve years old. In it she told me that she had been feeling rather depressed, and so decided to put on a Mary Poppins record—the Caedmon records, beautifully spoken—"It is true if you think it is"—she remembered what I'd said to her and felt it would last her all her life. "I knew how to go through the world," she wrote. . . . I so much wanted to give something special to this child!

Jane asked the sun a question, and the child asked you a question. But where does a scene like that come from?

I just put the scene down as it arrived. It comes out of something in me, but it isn't as though I invented it, as I said before. Because all this is in the human bloodstream. I've talked about this many times: I think that everything that's known is in the bloodstream, which gathers itself, for three score years and ten, perhaps, into a reservoir, whose physical location is about two inches below the navel, in the great bowl of the abdomen. Japanese Zen masters call it *Hara*—the original, the vital center of the man. In Celtic legend it's the Cauldron of Plenty, the Water of Life, and among the Australian aborigines it's "the dreaming."

I've asked in one of my lectures: "Where does the psyche live?" And answered the question by saying—you and I touched on this before—that unless a thing is known organically it isn't known at all, or known only partially. That the body, through which this endless river courses—and specifically that reservoir I just spoke of—is the essential alchemical vessel in which thought and memory ferment . . . where instinct, sensation, and emotion act as the mind's transforming leaven, and the opposites confront each other in an everchanging dance. All that ever was is there, and all that ever will be.

Tolkien had something of the same idea when he talked about

the "soup" of memory, the seething pot, and how cooks dip in their ladles. But I don't agree with that—it's too much like intention and choosing. Yeats wrote, in "The Song of Wandering Aengus":

> I went out to the hazel wood,
> Because a fire was in my head,
> And cut and peeled a hazel wand,
> And hooked a berry to a thread;
> And when white moths were on the wing,
> And moth-like stars were flickering out,
> I dropped the berry in a stream
> And caught a little silver trout.

You see, he didn't ask for any specific thing. He took what came. I think it's a matter of . . . fishing. You don't know what will take the hook. One merely fishes in the cauldron.

There's a story about a Taoist saint who used to fish with a pin and a single silk filament and who was so in tune with the flowing of the water that he caught a multitude of fish.

Wonderful. Yes, I must mention that the next time I give my lecture.

In the cauldron must be the Great Mother, about whom so much has been written. The poet Robert Bly says that the Great Mother is basically a union of four force fields: the Good Mother (Isis, Demeter), the Death Mother (Lilith, Hecuba), the Dancing or Ecstatic Mother (Artemis, Sophia), and the Stone or Tooth Mother (Medusa, Coatli-cue). About the third type, Bly writes: "Artemis and all the dancing mothers, all the virgin mothers, and all the visionary mothers, Diotima and Sophia, share the energy of this field. She was often called 'Virgin,' not because she avoided sexual joy, but [because she brought] ecstasy into the world." And I've felt that Mary Poppins was, in this sense, a kind of Ecstatic Mother.

A woman has all these things in her. And yes, it's possible, as I said in "Letter to a Learned Astrologer," to be profligate yet keep the secret sense of oneself—like Virgo. Virginity has the most wonderful power—if it is true virginity—of *intensity*, the intensity that can be seen in a person like St. Theresa of Avila. Well, I can't answer for Mary Poppins . . . perhaps she has a lover somewhere. But it doesn't matter. And it's her affair, so to speak, not mine! (Anyway, he is certainly not Bert, the Matchman, who is a supernumerary character, and there to point up aspects of Mary Poppins, not at all to aspire to her hand.)

No, people who call Mary Poppins "prudish" are wrong, I think. The word "propriety," perhaps, correctly conveys the delicacy of her character, her way of not giving things away. I was very shocked that, in the film version of *Mary Poppins*, Mrs. Banks—that feather-headed, silly little woman is, first of all, shown as a suffragette! . . . but worse still is seen pulling up her skirts and displaying her underwear. It was incredible to me, in a film set in Edwardian times. And again, when Mary Poppins dances a sort of cancan on the roof with the sweeps, she swirls her skirts till all her underwear is revealed. Now, Mary Poppins could, of course, dance a cancan, but her skirts would *certainly* know how to behave. They would obey her, don't you see? She would never wear her petticoats on the public's sleeve. She's not so easily bought!

No, she's not a repressed spinster, which is what people who call her "prudish" usually mean. Could such a one as we have been talking about be called that? A very close friend of mine, who's a poet, said to me, when we first met: "Look, let me tell you at the outset— I loathe children's books. Don't ask me to read *Mary Poppins*." And I said to him, "Not for my sake?" "All right," he replied morosely, "send it." And after he had read it he wrote, saying: "My God, why didn't you *tell* me? Mary Poppins with her *cool, green core of sex* has me enthralled forever!"

It's been said that the term "virgin" signifies the psychological unity of both sexes.

Maybe. Everything contained within. But, remember the power of paradox! Today, "virgin" is a dirty word. A "virgin" is "deflowered," as though the deflowering were a duty rather than a joyful falling of petals at the right moment. . . . By the way, I slipped up a little bit unintentionally in my essay about the Sleeping Beauty [in *About the Sleeping Beauty*]. Basile, in "*Sole, Luna, e Talia,*" tells how the heroine is raped and then produces twins. Perrault tastefully provides a chapel, since he was writing for court ladies. And the Grimms' rendering has her woken by a kiss. But now I've found out that in the original German version there also was a rape, and that Wilhelm Grimm, to make it more romantic, altered it to a kiss. But never mind, she is, after all, *pierced* by a spindle, so she has to be *pierced* again—kiss or rape, it doesn't matter so long as she is woken. It's like the sun bringing the seed into being with a single shaft of light. One should be intense and put one's intensity at the service of whatever wakes us. If we're to serve we have to awake in mind, body, or feeling. And that's why I'm so happy that Mary Poppins is a mere domestic and doesn't come to us as a goddess.

So you don't see Mary Poppins as a kind of Ecstatic Mother?

I don't want to assert that. I don't want to claim anything. Why make claims? Mary Poppins is a handmaiden, but in whose service I do not know.

I was thinking the other day of an incident in my childhood. My mother would play *any* game; she'd quickly jump to a game, as I do, with a child. And one day I said to her: "Mother, you be the mistress and I'll sit in the kitchen and come when you ring the bell and say 'Yes, ma'am?' " But something in her didn't want to play that game—she'd be a leopard, a turkey, Rumpelstiltskin, but not someone giving orders—not mistress and maid. Something sensitive and delicate and loving in her rejected it.

There was nothing pious in this wish of mine, or do goodish; it did not come from Arthur Mee's *Child's Book of Golden Deeds* but from the imaginary picture of myself in a cap with two tails and a frilly apron, dashing in with the soup tureen and ladling broth into everyone's bowl.

Don't start interpreting this as the Bounteous Mother element, since it was probably mere self-importance. I did once think I would like to be a nurse, but that was because, at the age of eleven, I'd seen my first stage play, where the hero was brought in wounded—his forehead covered with tomato sauce. I dreamed of bandaging his head for about two years and then faithlessly eloped, so to speak, with my first Hamlet. I knew then that a nursing career was not for me. My real job was to go mad, give everybody a sprig of some herb and drown myself in the river. It would be worth it to have Hamlet cry out at my graveside: "Hold off the earth awhile,/Till I have caught her once more in mine arms." As Yeats said, "Our friends are exultations, agonies." He was rather fat, I remember—the Hamlet, not Yeats! Perhaps it's just as well I never met him—not Yeats, the Hamlet.

But, looking back, it seems to me that there was always some man who, as it were, gave me a push along the way. Well, if I had to travel it—and I'm sure that I did indeed have to—then every push was useful.

I recall your saying: "I'm a mere kitchenmaid in the house of myth and poetry."

Yes, indeed . . . or rather that is what I would like to be: to take a stoup of wine to Homer or polish Pallas Athene's sandals! Or stir the pot on the fire.

I know you admire the "Round Dance of Jesus" from the Gnostic Acts of John—a text from the early Christian movement.

It's one of the most precious documents. And Gustav Holst made a wonderful oratorio of it [*Hymn of Jesus*, Op. 37].

The Acts describes Jesus, anticipating arrest, bringing his followers together into a circle, holding hands to dance, while he stands in the center and chants:

> *I will be saved,*
> *And I will save. Amen.*
> *I will be released,*
> *And I will release. Amen.*
> *I will be wounded,*
> *And I will wound. Amen.*
> *I will be born,*
> *And I will bear. Amen.*
> *I will eat,*
> *And I will be eaten. Amen . . .*

I quote this because I'm reminded of the speech by the Hamadryad— the serpent leader of the animals in the zoo—who tells the children in Mary Poppins *(as they watch the animals dance the Grand Chain around Mary Poppins) that "it may be that to eat and be eaten are the same thing in the end. My wisdom tells me that this is probably so. We are all made of the same stuff, remember, we of the Jungle, you of the City. . . . Bird and beast and stone and star—we are all one. . . . Child and serpent, star and stone—all one." It also reminds me that in certain primitive tribes, the hunters wear the horns of the animals they are killing, identifying with them in order to create a balance between them.*

The Grand Chain. Illustration by Mary Shepard, from *Mary Poppins in Cherry Tree Lane*.

Wonderful. Yes.

And in "Letter to a Learned Astrologer," writing about the sign of Aquarius, you point out that the pictorial zodiac shows us a man alone carrying "a pitcher, flagon, or amphora, the ultimate morphology of the feminine." And to hint at an explanation of the dual function of this man and his watering pot, you present the following formulation: "I will pour out." "I will be poured."

Yes, I was thinking of the passage from the "Round Dance of the Cross" when I wrote that. One says, "I will pour out": the other says, "I will be poured." That is my gesture in life—I'm happy to be poured. Happy to be a flagon that is poured out. The water of life—you baptize with it, it quenches thirst, it laves the newborn and the dead

—I meant it in every way. He who pours out; and she who is poured —they're reciprocal, like Yang and Yin.

It's a very deep passage, and I don't think I understand it fully.

Nor do I. Nor do I. I wait to be told.

Mary Poppins presents the children with certain situations; and as in initiations, the children enter into them and come out with a new understanding.

Well, I feel one is taught by what one does. There's a wonderful line in a poem by Theodore Roethke which says: "You learn by going where you have to go." You can't learn before you set out, can you? You go along with the road and learn as you go. Having written certain things, I sometimes think to myself, "How did *she* learn that? It's so *true*."

You mean Mary Poppins?

No, P. L. Travers. And I long to meet her. And then I wonder: Am I she?

Are you?

I don't know [smiling]. I know I'm sitting here now, but I have a deep feeling of anonymity. It's partly arrogance, since to me the best poems are written by Anon. And I think that to aim at being Nobody is setting one's sights a bit high. But the name is a mysterious thing and so intimate. I don't like mine taken until I give it. That's going to be my next lecture: "Name and No Name."

In ancient Egypt, a person was given two names at birth—the true name and the good name (the greater and the lesser). Only the latter was made public; the greater belonged to the ka, or soul, and embodied all the individual magical power. Evil spirits would direct their anger to the lesser name, leaving the person unharmed.

I didn't know that, but it has always been my instinct to think that there is a Name and a name . . . and that the one with a capital is private. It was, after all, given ritually. The surname is a kind of protection. And when you find somebody snatching your first name, you're done out of the joy of saying, "Please do call me so-and-so." Because in that way you're giving a gift . . . from my point of view, of course. Maybe it's very old-fashioned.

It's much more atavistic and archaic than old-fashioned.

I know that. During World War II I was living in America, very homesick for England, and the Secretary of Indian Affairs at that time, whom I knew, said he'd send me off to live with the Indians. I was a guest one summer of the Navajos and the next of the Pueblos and was given a secret Indian name and told I must never reveal it. I have never told a soul.

And the Gypsies don't like you to say anything that praises a child—"How pretty!" or "How clever!"—since it brings bad luck. They quickly make the finger-sign to ward off the evil eye. I feel a belonging to that world. I suppose there is something very archaic in me, but I don't want to feel like wearing my heart on everyone else's sleeve. That's why I'm so glad you have come without asking questions like: Where born, what done, what porridge, how many children, what color eyes? No, no, that doesn't matter; you've come with far greater material. I won't be dissected and I won't be analyzed. Analyze a thing and it disappears, it becomes a mere collection of parts, not the whole; you can never discover the whole.

Dreams, for instance. A dream can sometimes show us a part, sometimes a whole. Here is one of mine:

> A cock pheasant and his mate
> > Pecked at the grain by the wild dark sea
> And the cock he lifted a lordly wing
> > Across the sea-marge and said to me
> "Lady, I have a message for thee!"
> > And the little hen bird went on pecking.
>
> I crouched in the coin of my castle walls
> > Hand to my ear, lest the news should grieve
> My heart, but he rose three stories tall
> > And his blazing eyes at the window eave
> Judged and would give me no reprieve.
> > And the little hen bird went on pecking.

They ploughed and sifted and ground me to
    A speckle of dust on a pebble stone,
Those blazing eyes, and I knew myself
    Naughted by light, my trellis of bone
Pared of its flesh, my known unknown.
    And the little hen bird went on pecking

Then a footfall rang at the inner door
    And a turbaned, princeling boy came through—
Lifting towards me his open palm,
    He smiled, and I was brought forth anew.
"The message has come," he said, "for you!"
    And the little hen bird went on pecking.

O prince and cockbird, lords of life,
    It is enough, the seed has stirred,
Now it needs only the sun and the rain
    And I to go with never a word
Down to the sea-marge and pluck the grain
    Along with the little hen bird.
And the little hen bird went on pecking.

I don't know what your psychiatrists would make of this—all sorts of labels such as archetype, Id, etc., I dare say—and in the process of labeling, the idea would have been lost! But when I told the dream to my Zen teacher, he just smiled and said: "You yourself were always the little hen bird. Go on pecking. That is Zen."

Coming back to the "Round Dance of the Cross," we see Jesus telling his followers: "I am a mirror to you/who know me." In the story "The Cat who Looked at the King," which is told in Mary Poppins Opens the Door, *we find the following passage: "[The Cat] is still wandering . . . for Near and Far are alike to him. And always as he goes, he watches out for one or another who will return his gaze. A king, it may be, or perhaps a shepherd, or a man going by through the city streets. If he comes upon anyone like that, he will stay with them for a little while. Not very long, but long enough. It takes no more than the tick of a second to look down deep in his deep green eyes and discover who they are." Throughout the* Mary Poppins *books, a cow looks for her missing star, each person finds his own balloon, each child discovers his own true music. As Mr. Twigley, in* Mary Poppins Opens the Door, *says: "Everything in the world—trees, rocks and stars and human beings—they all have their own true music."*

Do you know how that last story came about? I was walking with a friend on Hampstead Heath. And an old man came stumbling toward us, muttering: "My heart aches . . . my heart aches." "We'll go get a doctor," said my friend. "No, no," I said, and then recited: "My heart aches, and a drowsy numbness pains/My sense, as though of hemlock I had drunk—" "Enough!" the old man shouted, "I have it, I'm all right!" And he strode away declaiming Keats's "Ode to a Nightingale" in the place where it was written.

But this is not the whole story. The next day, my friend, as he was going into the British Museum, met that same old man coming out. "Where is she?" the old man asked. "She gave me so much yesterday that I'll give you this secret to take to her. Tell her that the whole world is made of music." And that's what the story is based on. . . . But coming back to what you were saying with regard to the Cat: it's very, very difficult to look into anybody's eyes and to have your own looked into. Very few people look you in the eyes. Have you noticed? It takes courage!

You yourself have such intense blue eyes!

I don't *know* I have blue eyes! That's what people tell me. I don't look into my own eyes.

You once said: "Mary Poppins is the story of my life." And I took that to mean that the books reflected the readers themselves, just as Mary Poppins reveals the characters to themselves in your books.

That's a good interpretation. As I said before, I don't think that biographies are of any use at all, much less autobiographies. What people write, paint, do, *is* their biography. People are always looking around for some excuse or fundamental point from which *this* or *that* began, and I don't believe it exists. In fact, there's a great poem by Rilke called *"Ernste Stunde"* (Solemn Hour) in which each stanza repeats the phrase "without cause": "He who walks anywhere in the world,/ without cause walks in the world,/walks toward me." It's ridiculous to look for causes. We find one and feel we've solved the problem; it gives us something to lean on; the solution is now made clear, we think . . . but it never is, never is.

"No cause, no cause."

So beautiful: "No cause, no cause." It's magnificent how King Lear, so self-full, so arrogant, could become such a wonderful revealer.

To be revealed in the dance, as if in the mirror—it seems that all of Mary Poppins's little tasks and lessons and teachings, if they could be summed up, might come out as: see, know, and become yourself.

That's the first thing. And yet I did not aim. It happened.

"What I am you shall see/When you come yourself," says Jesus in the "Round Dance." "Come. Tonight" are the leaf messages Michael and Jane receive through their window on Halloween eve. And that's the night the shadows leave their owners and dance in the park.

I think that was a piece of seeing—though I don't know how I came to see it—when the Bird Woman says: "The shadow is the outside of your inside."

I remember that speech: "Through and out on the other side—it's the way they get to be wise. . . . When you know what your shadder knows—then you know a lot. Your shadder's the other part of you, the outside of your inside—if you understand what I mean" [Mary Poppins in the Park]. *According to the Second Epistle of Clement, when Jesus was asked at what moment the Kingdom would come, he said: "When the two shall be one, the outside like the inside, the male with the female neither male nor female."*

You're really teaching me my book.

Your book taught me about your book. Look at what Miss Lark's shadow says to Miss Lark that night: "I'm gayer than you think, Lucinda. And so are you, if you but knew it. Why are you always fussing and fretting instead of enjoying yourself? If you stood on your head occasionally, I'd never run away." And that speech reminds me of several episodes in which characters who are unalterably grasping and selfish are, as in fairy tales, punished by becoming what they reveal themselves to be: locked up. I'm thinking of Matilda Mo, who becomes a prisoner of the Indian chief in Mary Poppins in the Park; of Mrs. Clump, who is made little and is locked up in a tiny golden castle in Mary Poppins Comes Back; and of Miss Andrew—Mr. Banks's domineering governess—who is put into a birdcage in Mary

Poppins Comes Back. *Unlike decent and respectable Miss Tartlett, who learns to love living upside down with a new point of view, these other women are tormented by their own rigidity.*

And they're not sentimentally melted or sweetened. People have said to me that these are scary books, and I think they are . . . if you see deeply into them. Think of the "Bad Wednesday" chapter [*Mary Poppins Comes Back*] in which the old man says to Jane—caught in the world of the Doulton bowl—"Perhaps you'll *never* go back home!" And also think of the demons attacking Michael in "Bad Tuesday" [*Mary Poppins*]. It's very frightening. . . . And, remember, going back to *Friend Monkey* for a minute, Uncle Trehunsey never changes. At the end, he is forced to retreat into his own tight little house.

It seems as if you're showing that selfishness in a form of death.

Yes, I suppose so. I didn't set out to teach that, but you learn from your own books. Someone once suggested to me that I strongly dislike things to be caged. And I suppose I do. This man pointed out that *Friend Monkey* is all about freeing things from cages. It is so, now that I come to think of it. And here you are reminding me that these three women—Mrs. Mo, Mrs. Clump, and Miss Andrew—are all locked up. But no one ever is really sorry about the fates of these three. That's my training in Grimms': drop the millstone on the wicked stepmother . . . good! She *deserves* it! G. K. Chesterton said once: "Children are innocent and love justice; while most of us are wicked and naturally prefer mercy." And there's no mercy for those three women, nor for Uncle Trehunsey.

In a review of Randall Jarrell's The Animal Family, *you wrote these beautiful words: "Taking time takes one into timelessness."*

That's so, it does. If we don't take time over something, or give time to something, we never know what it is to be beyond time. We say, "I have no time for this, no time for that." Which is true. But in that way we never find timelessness. (Of course, it's also true that when we've got too much time we have no time. Paradox!)

Someone once said that time is just eternity in disguise.

I don't think I quite agree with that. Do you?

If it means that in a moment of time you can experience or comprehend eternity.

Yes, but is that moment *time*? Is it? It's a question. I'm not sure.

In Milton's sonnet "How soon hath Time, the subtle thief of youth," the poet suggests that acts in time can, with the gift of grace, conform to eternal meaning.

I'd forgotten that Milton wrote of this. Yes, I think events have to ripen. We start making decisions—"I'll do this on Tuesday" or "I'll go to Greece in September"—so nothing is left to grow ripe and ready . . . to see if Greece really is the place rather than, say, the North Pole. We have to wait . . . wait *on* something. Wait on what will be Heaven's decision, as the ancient Chinese would say. And then you'll be told, perhaps.

As opposed to "waiting for."

Yes, "wait on" has a different taste. If you're waiting for, you're expecting. But if you wait on, you're biding Heaven's time. *Then* you're really being a servant.

It's like the moment in fairy tales after a crisis, when the hero or heroine just waits . . .

I was thinking in bed the other night about "Little Bo-peep": "Little Bo-peep has lost her sheep,/And can't tell where to find them;/*Leave them alone,* and they'll come home,/And bring their tails behind them." Nothing's lost, not even the tails! So you leave a problem alone, you don't even look for its solution. And it comes home! I know where *I* leave it alone—right in here, two inches below the navel, the vital center, as I told you before. That's where everything goes and is allowed to simmer.

That's where ulcers come from, too [laughing].

No they don't. Ulcers come in the stomach. And they don't come from biding your time.

In his essay "On Love," A. R. Orage talks of three kinds of love: the chemical, the emotional, and the spiritual.

And all three can come together perfectly easily, even when it's difficult: "Love looks on tempests and is never shaken."

But what about "all for love and the world well lost"?

Yes, love has to lose the world . . . in order to gain the world, perhaps. I don't know. Remember Dante's Paolo and Francesca: "They closed the book and read no more that day." What a description of a love affair! Love, anyway, is the severest of all disciplines. It has no easy way.

Are there any of your characters who exemplify all three types of love?

Monkey does, I think.

But he loves too much.

Too much is better than too little. "Much can always be whittled down, but little can be done with little," as Miss Brown-Potter says. . . . And as I suggested before, I don't know that Mary Poppins doesn't do too much. There are deeps in her.

Mary Poppins's message to me is: Be awake! That seems to be the message of all your work. The story in The Fox at the Manger *ends: "And always, among the sleepers, there must be somebody waking— somewhere, someone, waking and watchful. Or what would happen to the world . . . ?"*

You surprise me and yet you don't surprise me. I think it's true. Isn't to stay awake the fundament of all teachings? "I say unto you: watch!" It's in the Old and the New Testaments. And I was thinking of that.

Think also of the guardians of Eastern temples—which look so furious and ferocious. They're there to ward off the man who hasn't the courage to enter and to open the door for him who is able for it. So the ferocious has that dual paradoxical aspect. Hölderlin wrote: "Danger itself fosters the rescuing power." Perhaps one should say that to oneself every morning. We are so afraid to be vulnerable.

There's a hint of this in a poem called *"Fröhlichkeit"* (Joy), which I'll read to you. Under its title is that saying from the Gospels —"The children of this world are wiser than the children of light." And the poem goes:

> Beware the children of light,
>   That riff-raff crew,
> They will pilfer your peace of mind
>   And your money, too.
> Not as thieves in the night,
>   Deeper far their offence,
> They make light of the things of this world
>   By their innocence,
> Toppling the sturdy house
>   To its basic sand,
> Reducing the diamond
>   To dust in the hand.
>
> On all your highroad journeys,
>   Wrapped against wind and snow,
> You will find them arrived before you
>   Barefoot, by the low;
> Your effect will be cause,
>   Your right, their wrong,
> Your wisdom a tattling tale
>   To be had for a song,
> And your women, hard to please,
>   Cold to you as the sea,
> They will pluck in passing
>   Like plums from a tree.
>
> Beware the children of light,
>   They will turn you away
> From all that goes by the clock—
>   "Now" they will say,
> "Is then, here, there
>   And the frost is warm,
> Sun icy and only danger
>   Can keep you safe from harm;
> Taste of the aloe's honey,
>   Give your breast to the thorn,
> Let the stone bird pluck at
>   The living fern."

Why have you been hiding this poem?

Just shy. I wasn't shy when I was much younger, but then I had an Æ, an Orage, a Yeats behind me. They backed me up.

In "Only Connect," you recount that wonderful story of your taking a boat to the Lake Isle of Innisfree in the pouring rain, cutting off a huge armful of rowan branches, then traveling without pause back to Dublin, and arriving at Yeats's door, a tatterdemelion—a drenched Gypsy girl with your offering.

[Laughing] That's what I was. But he wasn't going to deal with the situation, so he called for help. I was taken upstairs by a factotum, dried, and given some cocoa. Then he sent for me, and never a word said of my offering. Later he gave me a couple of poems—one of them was "The Song of Wandering Aengus," which I read part of to you before (he used to call me "Sapling"). And when I told him I'd put some of his poems to music—the music was not made, it just came to me—he asked me to sing them, which I did. "Beautiful, beautiful," he said. "I couldn't have imagined anything more like them."

    Well, I was rather cocky, and the next day I told Æ that Yeats was pleased with the music. "Hmmm," said Æ, "you must sing them to me too sometime . . . but remember that Yeats is tone-deaf!" [Laughing] That took me down a peg.

In the New Testament we read: "God hath chosen the foolish things of the world to confound the wise." Perhaps "the foolish persons of the world," too.

Ah, yes! The first legendary fools were women—so we read in Chambers' *Book of Days*—and a notable one was Iambe. Zeus, knowing that Demeter was wandering and hunting for what was lost, sent Iambe with her. And Iambe told her stories and ballads and legends and poems to charm the time, the waiting, the searching. And from these poems—so the legend goes—comes the form of the iambic pentameter.

In King Lear, when the Fool is onstage, Cordelia isn't; and when she is, the Fool disappears.

Notice that Lear says: "And my poor fool is hang'd." When I was a child and first read that, I grieved because I thought it was the Fool who was hanged, but of course it was Cordelia. The fools in Shakespeare carry the sorrow of the world—and sing, nevertheless.

In Mary Poppins in the Park, *we find the story of the goosegirl, in which the fool—the tramp—turns out to be an angel in disguise; and in fact everyone in the story has his or her own disguise.*

Isn't it interesting that all aspects are shown there: The pig thinks it's a woolly sheep, the donkey thinks it's an Arab steed, the goosegirl a princess, the shepherd a prince. Then along comes the tramp who tells them about the awful things that happen to these grandiose creatures. And so they settle down with their lives, and accept to be just what they are. But when they ask the tramp who he is, and he says he's an angel in disguise—which is, indeed, what he turns out to be—they're left in extremity: Are they or aren't they what they thought they were? Nothing is resolved or explained. But as you will remember, *one* person at the end of that story certainly knows who *she* is!

Another "fool" story in Mary Poppins Comes Back *is about the King of the Castle and the Dirty Rascal. There's a song which the king sings as he sleeps on a rainbow: "Say goodbye, Love,/Never cry, Love,/You are wise/And so am I, Love!" And in your essay "The Youngest Brother," you quote a couplet by Alexander Pope: "Go, teach eternal wisdom how to rule—/Then drop into thyself, and be a fool!" These stories in the* Mary Poppins *books certainly seem to exemplify that couplet.*

Yes, these are wonderful connections.

It's interesting, too, that in the Tarot deck the card of the Fool is unnumbered. And it's been said that the significance of this is that the Fool is to be found on the fringe of all orders and systems.

Not unnumbered, but Zero, which is all numbers and no numbers. The Fool is omnipresent, serenely passing through the world—as I said in "The Youngest Brother"—here and there alike to him.

You've based so much of your work and ideas on fairy tales and nursery rhymes.

Well, they were made by grown-ups who had to manifest something for themselves, and then the children purloined them. "Wee Willie Winkie runs through the town,/Upstairs and downstairs in his nightgown." Mightn't that be about a man who forgot to put on his trousers, having been drunk the night before—a man called Winkie, not very tall, "rapping at the window, crying through the lock," a bit of a fool? "Wee Willie Winkie" is a silly thing if it refers *only* to a child's jingle. . . . Rhymes and fairy tales for grown-ups gradually became children's literature, but they're the foundation of all literature in every country, which, by their very nature and unknowingness, is not ignorance by any means—the children understand.

In the "Happy Ever After" chapter in Mary Poppins Opens the Door, *we see nursery rhyme and fairy-tale characters—along with Robinson Crusoe and a few others—escaping from their books at the final moments—the "Crack"—between the old and the new year. As Sleeping Beauty tells us: "Inside the Crack all things are as one. The eternal opposites meet and kiss. The wolf and the lamb lie down together, the dove and the serpent share one nest . . . . This is the time and place, my darlings—the only time and the only place—where everybody lives happily after."*

It so interested me as a child when—at what moment—the old became the new . . . that perhaps was when everything came out of the Crack. . . . And why wouldn't you have oneness if you and every other creature are particles of the universe? How could *you* not be a particle of the universe?

We are such stuff as dreams are made on.

Do you think so? Who dreamed you?

Well, I've been thinking of that. So have many of the characters in Mary Poppins.

The whole question is not, Who dreamed me? But rather, Who am I in myself? A dream is made flesh, and I am here, solid, eating bread and butter and drinking herb tea. Don't let us get too absorbed in dreams, in the modern analytical sense. Don't let's be too contemporary, because there's nothing more quickly old-fashioned than the contemporary; nothing that goes more quickly into a dream.

Jane asks Mary Poppins: "Do you think that everything in the world is inside something else? My little Park inside the big one and the big one inside a larger one? Again and again? Away and away?" [Mary Poppins in the Park].

It's that same question. Anything I write is all question. I don't think I have the answers.*

Blake wrote: "May God us keep/From Single vision & Newton's sleep." And in "The Park in the Park," Jane learns what it means to be in two places at once.

Children ask me about that, and I always say to them: Close your eyes and think whether you can be at home and here with me at the same time. And they do and they see that they can.

I don't have an answer to the question of who I am—or at least not an answer I could speak of. But I think it's the essential question: Who am I? Why am I here? What is the world?

In the meantime, we have tea in an ancient house in London—holding our cups and saucers.

And let's see the magic and mystery in *them*—in the cups and saucers —the mystery in the most ordinary things. Again and again I've tried to say that this has everything to do with Mary Poppins. Why does she come to such an ordinary little cup-and-saucer family? Nothing she has is grand—or of value—only the gloves which she gives away. Reluctantly, I had to give her a fur coat for *Lucky Thursday*, but I thought of it as a sort of cast-off, mangy rabbit coat, come from a rummage sale.

* "They held their breaths, waiting for an answer. She looked at them for a long time and her blue eyes sparkled with it. They could see it dance on to her tongue, all agog to make its disclosure. And then—it danced away. Whatever the secret was, she would keep it." (From the conclusion to *Mary Poppins in Cherry Tree Lane*.)

In reviewing Lucy Boston's books, you wrote: "For it takes the ordinary to comprehend, even to be related to, the extraordinary, just as, in order to fly, you need firm ground to take off from. In airiness we lose all sense of air, let alone earth; in the poetic, poetry; in childishness, the child. It is solidity that gives us wings."

I'm not interested in any other miracle but the ordinary. "Extraordinary" is the quintessence of the ordinary.

You have had a number of extraordinary teachers—Gurdjieff, whom you've written about . . .

And a Zen roshi—I don't know if I would have understood anything of Gurdjieff if I hadn't had a grounding in Zen—and Æ and, indeed, other traditional teachings and myths and fairy tales.

Was Æ a teacher?

Yeats was a great poet, Æ was a great soul. And his death was an enormous event for me because I was there all the days of his dying; being with him much during his earlier sickness, but also during his last days, I watched a great man doing his own dying . . . something that comes to not very many. His death was the epitome of his life.

He never set out to teach, although he never stopped talking about and quoting the Bhagavad-Gita . . . but I learned from him continually, very much by osmosis. I took it in like sunlight and rain, as a plant does, and only much later did it become a kind of teaching for me. For instance, he taught me that true poverty means not being without the comfortable bed, the easy chair, the whole loaf—but being able to dispense with them at any moment—not being *attached* to things.

This house itself is quite unencumbered with things.

It's elegant but not sumptuous—it has only those things that are needed. I make a home wherever I live—I've been told that even when in a hotel bedroom I turn it into a bird's nest. But if fate tells me to get up and go, I'll drop it all and leave—something in the manner of this little poem:

Cast like bread upon the water
To what shore after many days
Shall she return to the sea's daughter,
What hand receive the flotsam maize
From Lord Poseidon's granaries?

Finding and losing. Losing and finding. The first sentence of the second chapter Friend Monkey *reads:* " 'Lost your friend?' a voice enquired [of Monkey], apparently from the air." *And then in the last chapter, we read:* "But what was he [Monkey] bringing in his arms? Could it be—yes, it could, indeed! The starlight made no bones about it. Something that had been thrown away—lost forever, it was hoped—was now, with anxious, loving care, being restored to the owner."

I remember. And I'm planning to write a story about this idea very soon. No, I don't want to talk about it yet. . . . But here in the paragraph you have quoted, Mr. Linnet has thrown away his boots and hat, and this *awful* over-loving creature brings them, incontinently, back. Poor Linnet! But there's something worth noting here, however, that I've seen since writing *Friend Monkey*. It is that he *has* to have back his boots and his hat, and go forward with all, good and bad, that is his own—all that makes him Linnet. Doesn't this relate to what we began with when you admitted you had been depressed? All right, so you, too, have to have your depression, your negativity, what you will, as well as the jewels at your feet—look in front of you —and also *me*. You've got a friend! So with all this *you* can go forward —see! And dance!

WHEN THE VOICES
OF CHILDREN
ARE HEARD
ON THE GREEN:
IONA AND
PETER OPIE

PHOTOGRAPH BY JOHN SIMONDS

IN MEMORY OF PETER OPIE:
November 25, 1918–February 5, 1982

When the voices of children are heard on the green,
And laughing is heard on the hill,
My heart is at rest within my breast
    And everything else is still.

"Then come home, my children, the sun is gone down,
And the dews of night arise;
Come, come, leave off play, and let us away
Till the morning appears in the skies."

"No, no, let us play, for it is yet day,
And we cannot go to sleep;
Besides, in the sky the little birds fly
And the hills are all cover'd with sheep."

"Well, well, go and play till the light fades away,
And then go home to bed."
The little ones leaped and shouted and laughed
    And all the hills echoèd.
                —William Blake: "Nurse's Song"

It is a sunny English spring day in the village of Liss, Hampshire—May 7, 1981—and I am accompanying Iona Opie on her weekly visit to the Liss County Junior School where, for the past eleven years, she has come to observe the games and listen to the rhymes of the local schoolchildren. Walking east down the main shopping street, we pass a fishmonger's shop with a Noah's Ark in imitation stone at the top of the building (Iona informs me that the original owner's name was Noah Carpenter), a bank, a newsagent, the Pixie Cafe, the Jack and Jill clothing store for children, an old forge now occupied by solicitors, and a Sunday School annex of the Evangelical Church. Crossing the street, we walk into the yard of a brick-and-tiled building with what looks like a dovecote on top—a standard 1870s schoolhouse with modern classroom blocks added on. It is a few minutes before noon as Iona and I stand outside waiting, alone, everything quiet.

Suddenly, hundreds of shouting children between the ages of seven and eleven rush out of the building like a swarm of enraged bees, spreading out in waves, bunching up into a congeries of interlocking groups, as I dizzily begin to feel like Baudelaire's "painter of modern life" who, the poet suggested, should set up shop "in the heart of the multitude, amid the ebb and flow of motion, in the midst of the fugitive and the infinite . . . enter[ing] into the crowd as though it were an immense reservoir of electrical energy." In buzzing confusion there are children rushing around—forming groups, dispersing, and regrouping—as Iona, calmly holding a reporter's spiral-bound notebook and pen, watches two boys racing over to the nearby wire fence. A girl approaches us, looks warily at me, then withdraws . . . at which point Iona suggests gently that, as the children aren't as used to me as they are to her, perhaps I should stand on the other side of the fence. So I edge my way outside, relieved to be a little distanced and distant from the madding crowd, and watch a scene straight out of Brueghel, as if his famous painting of children playing in the street had come to life.

One group of girls is shouting and chanting and clapping, several other groups—one with six girls jumping all together—are skipping rope, and a third group is twirling and spinning before breaking up and re-forming on the other side of the yard. Meanwhile, a few boys are playing leapfrog, while others are variously pushing each other and boxing and racing and playing ball and playing dead and chasing girls, as Iona—insouciantly, almost invisibly—wends her way through the hurtling mob, stopping occasionally to talk to children and take notes. A whistle blows as several teachers come out to end the play recess. Just then, three boys come running up to the fence and offer me some army insignia. "Where do you live?" one of them asks me. "America? You've come all that way to see us playing our games" he exclaims incredulously. The second boy points across the street. "There's a skinhead over there—they like to menace us." "My brother wants to be a punk," the third boy informs me. "And what about you?" I ask the first. "I want to be a human being," he says, as they all run off, a teacher calling them back to class. Then, as suddenly as it began, everything returns to stillness, as if the mind had emptied itself of all thoughts. Iona stands motionless, looking over her notes;

Peter Breughel the Elder, *Children's Games,* 1560. Reproduction courtesy of Kunsthistorisches Museum, Vienna

and as she begins to come out to meet me, I notice three starlings flying into the yard and beginning to pick up the crumbs from the potato
crisps that some of the children had just been eating.

Walking back with me through the village, Iona says: "I'm
neither fish nor fowl nor good red herring in the playground. The
children can't place me, but it doesn't bother them now because they
know I have this special role in life, which is listening to what they
explain to me. But I'm not a teacher and I'm not a parent, just an
unknown species. Occasionally, a new pupil will come up and say,
'That boy's been hitting me.' And all I do is guy it up, make a bit of
an act of writing down what she's said; and by the time I've written
it, the children think it's so funny that they've forgotten all about
their complaints.

"The best way of settling squabbles is to have everybody dissolve in giggles. If only the nations of the world could think how
funny they were being . . . just think of those medieval knights dress-
ing up with plumes on their heads—how ludicrous to stick three
feathers on yourself, take a pointed stick—slightly elaborated and now
made of metal—and launch yourself at somebody else! And when
spring comes to Liss playground, as it has now, the girls start skipping
and the boys start making war. And I'm afraid that's how it is.

"I simply go in there and the children tell me things. I'm very
passive about it, in fact; it's just that I know what to look for, I already know the games. In the early days I asked one of the teachers,
'What are they playing?' 'Nothing. They don't play games as I used
to.' And I said, 'What's that game over there? I wonder what it's
called here.' 'I shouldn't think they call it anything.' A thoroughly
negative attitude all around . . . because it's not a teacher's job to
notice games. In fact, I think the child would get very worried if the
teachers went around asking what they were playing. It's the only
time the children have to do anything they like.

"I sort of moon about, I'm a sort of typical village idiot, really;
I never even know how to play marbles, I can't always follow the
game and I have to get the children to explain. And they love explaining, they know more than I do. Playtime is the one time when
children are the 'superiors.' Adults sometimes ask us why we use the
word 'people' in our book on children's games, 'You need six people
to play a game,' for example. But that's what they themselves say. We
never like to make fun of children, because this isn't what we'd want
to have done to us. So if a child makes a mistake in saying a word,

we would never print it that way; but if it's his ordinary way of talk-
in, that's fair enough, that's the right way of saying things.

"I find that my being there has no effect on the games. I've
sometimes wondered when on earth the children were going to skip
again, because even though I have great faith in the continuity of
games, every now and then I lose faith, thinking, Has skipping disappeared forever? And then, when they think on their own that they
haven't done so for a long time, they jolly well start to skip again. It's
the period of time between strong crazes that interests me. If the
children have a violent craze for hopscotch—as they did a few years
ago, when the whole playground was covered with hopscotch dia-
grams as if it were one enormous Oriental carpet—then, all of a
sudden, they won't play it anymore. It is as if it were a disease they
have got out of their system. And then a new game will arrive—like
'Shirley Temple.' Do you know it? Some girl brought that down from
Wales, and it was previously unheard of in this playground, as far as
I know. It's a circle game, with a girl in the middle being Shirley
Temple, while the others sing, 'I'm Shirley Temple, the girl with
curly hair,' as she goes through all the motions, curling her hair with
her finger. And of course the boys, who like looking and gawking at
the girls, go 'Ooooh' and whistle, because the game involves the girls
hitching their skirts up a little at the side ('She wears her skirt to
there'). And *everyone* was playing it. I wondered what on earth had
happened when I arrived one day, because the circle must have contained fifty children. They arrange games like lightning, then play
and get tired of them. It's the speed of childhood living. . . . And now,
as always, I go home and immediately write up what I've heard and
seen."

The following is Iona's report for that day:

Liss Thursday 7 May 1981. "Dry, quite sunny, and warm," as the
weatherman said it would be; and the village was May-entranced
already, with Queen Anne's lace high by the footpath and bluebells
like dream-pools in the ditch.

Two little toughs came racing across the playground to the
roadside fence, flung their arms in the air, fists clenched, and both
shouted "First!" One, a merry coppernob, explained: "He was racing
against his class, and I was racing against mine." He sighed with
satisfaction. "We *both* won."

An eight-year-old, with a white face under her dark fringe, took
a pinch of my jacket and led me to a quiet corner. She recited a
rhyme I must have first heard when her mother was her age:

> I'm Popeye the sailor man,
> I live in a caravan;
> There's a hole in the middle
> Where I go to piddle—
> I'm Popeye the sailor man,
> Too-too!

She gave a rich, fruity chuckle, and said "There's another one that I am not going to tell you." ("Too-too!" seems to be the latest of the exclamatory endings, following "Sexy!" and Basil Brush's "Boom-boom!" They are the verbal equivalents of a dig in the ribs.) I asked my usual question, "Where does it come from?" She looked down at the dimpled darling standing by her side, who said, "My brother made it up." (Confirmation yet again, if confirmation is needed, of our observation in *The Lore and Language of Schoolchildren* that "children are, in fact, prone to claim the authorship of a verse when they have done no more than alter a word in it, for instance substitute a familiar name unknown to them; and they tend to be passionately loyal to the presumed genius of a classmate, or of a child who has just left their school, who is credited with the invention of each newly heard composition.")

Another girl had been waiting with awful persistence and no expression on her face. "Now I want to tell *my* jokes," she said. "What's green and goes up and down?—A gooseberry in a lift. I got it from my joke book. What is red, white, and black?—A sun-tanned zebra. Where do frogs leave their coats?—In the croakroom. What do Chinese frogs say?—Oke, oke." "I don't understand that last one," I muttered. "Nor do I," she said, "and it doesn't say anything in my joke book."

All the while I had been aware of the hum-and-buzz that girls make when the chanting games are "in." A girl called Jackie, who had been lingering near, started clapping with her small friend. I listened to the words, which seemed different from when I last heard the rhyme. "How does it go?" I asked. "'Si, si, my playmate'?" Jackie giggled at her friend and said with scorn "'Si, si, my playmate'!—no, it's 'Si, si, my *baby*.'" "Well, let's have all the words," I said, and they clapped and chanted:

> Si, si, my baby,
> I cannot play with you,
> Becos I've got the flu,
> Chickenpox and measles too, too, too;
> Flush down the lavatory
> Into the drainpipe,
> And that's how it goes, goes, goes.

It did not seem to me an improved version, but it was the one every-one knew today. The playground was dotted with groups of girls hand-clapping, and, as well as "Si, si, my baby" I heard the strains of "My name is Alli alli, Chickerlye chickerlye."

The joke-teller was still lingering about. I did not really want more jokes from a joke book, so I said "Skipping seems to be the thing now—is that right?" "Yeh," she said, "I'm going to do some skipping. I'm going to ask my friend." She went off and Jackie came back, saying "I've just thought of a joke. You have to say 'Behind the bush' each time." So we went into the familiar routine, though with a script that was new to me:

> There was this young man and lady.
> Behind the bush.
> And they took their clothes off.
> Behind the bush.
> They snogged.
> Behind the bush.
> Where was you last night?
> Behind the bush—

She clapped her hand to her mouth and ran off squealing with simulated horror, which left me free to go and watch the skipping.

But I was intercepted by a girl who wanted me to hear her monster jokes. (Monsters seem to have become part of the inner circle of children's acquaintance; more unruly than teddy bears, yet almost as lovable.) "What is the monsters' favourite soup?—Scream of tomato," "What did the vampire say when he left the dentist's?—Fangs very much." I tore myself away and worked towards the skipping, realising as I went that there were also numerous games of leapfrog that I had not noted. I stood by one long rope and gazed round. A boy rushed by holding up a finger with a plastic wound on it, shouting "Look, I cut my finger!" Two girls hurtled up with "A new game—it's called Blue Slime. We have this blue ball and we pretend it's slimy and it keeps on jumping into our hands and we have to keep throwing it away." When the excitement had died down I asked the girls how many skipping ropes they could see, saying I had counted four. "You can only see three now," said the bounciest of the girls, "because that one over there has just vanished, because someone tripped and hurt theirselves."

One of the awkward squad barged up and said, "Excuse me, Miss, can you shift out the way? Cos I want to do my jumps with this." He held out a large die-cast vehicle of the most expensive sort. "All right," I said, and shifted. "Oh, you're not a teacher," he murmured, and went back to the edge of the playground where the grass meets the asphalt. I was not sure whether this was a compliment—it sounded like one. I followed him. The cliff the boys were hurling their cars over was now steep and pebbly, exposed by last winter's rain. He looked up and said, "We try and get the cars off the side so they land upright. It'd be a good idea for a fête, we'd get pounds."

The bell had gone and the girls had begun to queue for the second-and-third-year classrooms, giving me a chance to talk to some of the skippers, but they said they had only been playing the usual games: "On the mountain stands a lady," "Bluebells, cockleshells," "Building up bricks," "I'm a little bumper car," and "Salt, pepper, vinegar, mustard," where, they said, "you go quickest if you land on *mustard*."

A boy with a pink, determined face asked if he could borrow my pencil and paper. "I've bin following you all morning," he complained, "I've got some picture stories." He began drawing and saying "There was a castle and a king lived in it and he went for a walk and tripped over and fell into a pond and what does it end up as?" It looked a bit rude to me, but I guessed "A key?" and it was. Some other boys gathered round and said "Do another!" so he got down on the ground and drew a circle, and added to it saying:

"This is a pond, and a man fell in the pond and a swarm of bees jumped in after him. *There's* two caves up round the top, and two long caves down the side—and it turns out to be a dog."

A boy in the group started spluttering and said, "Ponds remind me of something." He gabbled his "something" so quickly I had to ask him to say it again. "Well," he said, "you take someone's hand—it's a fortune sort of thing. You tell them 'You're going to have three wives, and two Rolls-Royces, and four houses, and—say—three sons, and a fifty-acre garden, and a pond in it'—and then you spit in their hand." He looked flushed by the time he had finished. He sat back on his heels, took a comb out of his trouser pocket and began combing his hair. "That's fun," I said, not letting on that the trick is an antique. "You'd better go in now."

About two hours later, and about two miles due west of the village, Iona's husband and collaborator, Peter Opie, is walking with me to the open cart shed that adjoins the old stables—now used for storage—on their property. "I'm bringing you here," he says as we enter the dark and damp shed, "so that you can see where the swallows live. They gather here, build here, have their young here, then they go back to Africa, but every year they come back to this particular place.

"Gilbert White, the eighteenth-century country clergyman who lived just down the road, by the way, and who wrote *The Natural History of Selborne*—it's one of my favorite books—observed the comings and goings of the village birds—swallows and swifts and martins. And in the same way, Iona goes down to the playground every single week and notices when a game starts and when it finishes its season. And it's exactly what Gilbert White was doing with the birds and animals in Selborne. In his notebooks, White noted when the children started playing marbles, but as far as we're aware, nobody has watched the children in a village week after week, year after year in order to say whether or not games appear seasonally.

"What I want to point out is this: Gilbert White found it almost impossible to believe that swallows migrated to Africa and then came back to this region. And he did everything he could to show that it wasn't true; he thought that in winter they hibernated in the village—he had all the thatch off of one house to find them!—or went into the marshland. Because, being a practical man, it was much too extraordinary for him to believe that this tiny little bird could go to Africa, live there, and then fly all the way back to exactly the same place each year.

"Now it's the same for us: Because we're practical, it seems utterly extraordinary that a children's rhyme or a nursery rhyme or a fairy tale—all the things we study—can come across half the world unchanged. Whereas, if you're a romantic, it's easy—you can just go through the centuries or around the world without bothering too much about it. The romantic can believe anything. If you tell him that something is one hundred or two thousand years old, it doesn't make any difference to him, he doesn't understand that that means one year or one generation after another. But if you're a practical person, and you're really looking at what actually happens, then the world is so much more marvelous. So, to me, it is more exciting to get a thing back a couple of hundred years than a couple of thousand. Of course, if a rhyme, say, has gone back two hundred years, then there's no reason why it might not have gone back a further couple of hundred, and so on. And if people say, Well, the rhymes and games deteriorate and change, it still seems to us much more extraordinary that they're recognizably the same after two centuries. To my mind, it's the similarities that are extraordinary, not the variations.

"Gilbert White was the first person to observe that swallows copulated in midair. He was the first to distinguish between various animals such as a stoat and a weasel. He was the first actually to look at these creatures in their natural environment and wonder how they worked and where they fed, and then he wrote down what was happening day after day. I can remember a time twenty-five years ago when it used to be said that zoölogy was a dying discipline because there was no more to learn or classify. And then look what happened: People suddenly began studying animals not in zoos but in the wild, and a whole new world was opened up.

"There are antiquarians who read and write about children's games in ancient Greece and who try to make out how they worked . . . while their very own children are playing those games outside their own homes, and it never occurs to them simply to ask their sons and daughters to help them with a classical text. But Iona and I are both library workers *and* collectors in the field—our roles are interchangeable—and this is what is so difficult for most people, since they just don't have the time. One must have read one's stuff before one goes into the field, otherwise one doesn't know what to look for: You can go down to that playground and think that the children are just 'mobbing around,' as we used to say—you don't see a structure to what they're doing. And I think Mark Twain put it best when he said: 'Supposing is good, but finding out is better.'"

In her book *The Century of the Child*, Ellen Key wrote that "The desire for knowledge, the capacity for acting by oneself, the gift of observation—all qualities children bring with them to school—have, as a rule, at the close of the school period, disappeared." And these qualities are exactly those that Iona and Peter Opie share with children, and which they have never lost.

On the simplest level, the Opies' observation of six- to fourteen-year-olds is a function of their work as folklorists. It was the Englishman William John Thoms who coined the word "folk-lore" in 1846 (as a substitute for "popular antiquities") when, as the late American folklorist Richard Dorson states, "members of the educated gentry discovered with astonishment that an alien culture of the 'lower orders' surrounded them and was expressed in collections of local tales, customs, and beliefs." Substitute the word "children" for "lower orders" and one discovers the key to the Opies' approach. "Certainly our attitude to the young has changed since the nineteenth century," the Opies have written, "when Herbert Spencer could complain that men of education felt the rearing of fine animals to be a fitter subject for attention than the bringing up of fine human beings."

Like the original pioneer members of the Folklore Society that was founded in 1878—Andrew Lang, George Laurence Gomme, Edward Clodd, Alfred Nutt, and Edwin Sidney Hartland—the Opies, who are members of this still-functioning society, are part of an increasingly smaller circle of self-supporting, independent scholars. "We had a little money in the beginning," Peter Opie told me, "less than what we would have got on a grant—but we wouldn't have received a grant anyway, because people thirty years ago didn't know that the subject we wanted to investigate even existed. And like Gilbert White, we are two of the last persons following the tradition of the private scholar, which is very strong in this country but which is no longer practical. It ceased being so after World War I, but there were still a few left. Our blessing has been that everybody else's interest in social history has increased. But, while our books aren't on the Harold Robbins level of best sellers, they are best sellers on a scholarly level, and keep us going."

As collaborators, Iona and Peter Opie resemble no one so much as the Brothers Grimm, about whom Professor Donald Ward has compendiously written: "The two complemented one another in their thoroughness in assembling data and collecting materials, in their ability to sense valuable sources, in their painstaking philological work, in their devotion toward the simpler folk of their homeland, and in their almost childlike fascination with what to others was trivia." And these words could be applied equally well to the Opies. "I'm the one who sits and stews," Peter Opie says, "and Iona is the one who does the 'action,' so to speak: She collects, records, and then says that I've got it all wrong when I've written it down. It never occurred to me that I would marry someone whom I *wouldn't* work with. The work is more important than the part either one of us plays in it. And the breakthrough comes when you don't mind the other person criticizing what you're doing."

In 1959, the Opies published the first of their major studies on "the simpler folk of their homeland"—*The Lore and Language of Schoolchildren* (hereafter referred to as *Lore and Language*), which, for the first time, thoroughly uncovered and explored "the curious lore passing between children aged about 6–14 which . . . continues to be almost unnoticed by the other six-sevenths of the population." Based on the contributions of about 5,000 children attending seventy primary, secondary modern, and grammar schools in different parts of England, Scotland, Wales, and Ireland, the Opies presented the riddles, epithets, jokes, quips, jeers, pranks, significant calls, truce terms, codes, superstitions, strange beliefs, and rites of the modern schoolchild, examining and commenting on them with fascinating historical annotation and comparative material that suggested the extraordinary continuity of the beliefs and customs of the tribe of children. As the Opies write:

> Boys continue to crack jokes that Swift collected from his friends in Queen Anne's time; they play tricks which lads used to play on each other in the heyday of Beau Brummel; they ask riddles which were posed when Henry VIII was a boy. Young girls continue to perform a magic feat (levitation) of which Pepys heard tell ("One of the strangest things I ever heard"); they hoard bus tickets and milkbottle tops in distant memory of a love-lorn girl held to ransom by a tyrannical father; they learn to cure warts (and are successful in curing them) after the manner which Francis Bacon learnt when he was young. They call after the tearful the same jeer Charles Lamb recollected; they cry "Halves!" for something found as Stuart children were accustomed to do; and they rebuke one of their number who seeks back a gift with a couplet used in Shakespeare's day. They attempt, too, to learn their fortune from snails, nuts, and apple-parings—divinations which the poet Gay described nearly two and a half centuries ago; they span wrists to know if someone loves them in the way that Southey used at school to tell if a boy was a bastard; and when they confide to each other that the Lord's Prayer said backwards will make Lucifer appear, they are perpetuating a story which was gossip in Elizabethan times.

The Opies' second work on the child tribe, *Children's Games in Street and Playground* (1969—hereafter referred to as *Children's Games*), is concerned with "the games that children, aged about 6–12, play of their own accord when out of doors, and usually out of sight. . . . We are interested in the simple games for which, as one child put it, 'nothing is needed but the players themselves.'" (Investigations of skipping, marbles, fivestones, hopscotch, tipcat, and other ball games are promised for further volumes.)

Based on a further survey of 10,000 local authority school-children, *Children's Games* studies the games not as archaeological remains—as Lady Gomme did in her classic *Traditional Games of England, Scotland, and Ireland* (1894–98)—but, in the Opies' words, as "living organisms which are constantly evolving, adapting to new situations, and renewing themselves or being replaced." The result is a book that reveals not only the continuity but also the internationality of children's amusements. As the Opies state:

These games that "children find out for themselves when they meet," as Plato put it, seem to them as new and surprising when they learn them as the jokes in this week's comic. Parties of schoolchildren, at the entrance to the British Museum, secretly playing "Fivestones" behind one of the columns as they wait to go in, little think that their pursuits may be as great antiquities as the exhibits they have been brought to see. Yet, in their everyday games, when they draw straws to see who shall take a disliked role, they show how Chaucer's Canterbury pilgrims determined which of them should tell the first tale. When they strike at each other's plantains, trying to decapitate them, they play the game a medieval chronicler says King Stephen played with his boy-prisoner William Marshal to humour him. When they jump on a player's back, and make him guess which finger they hold up ("Husky-bum, Finger or Thumb?") they perpetuate an amusement of ancient Rome. When they hit a player from behind, in the game "Stroke the Baby," and challenge him to name who did it, they unwittingly illuminate a passage in the life of Our Lord. And when they enter the British Museum they can see Eros, clearly depicted on a vase of 400 B.C., playing the game they have just been told to abandon.

When *Lore and Language* first appeared, a reviewer for *The Times* of London stated that the Opies were "the Frazers of the tribal life of children." And on the publication of *Children's Games*, the anthropologist Edmund Leach wrote in *The Listener* that "the earlier book still stayed within the conventions of orthodox folklore studies. The emphasis was on the surprising perpetuation of children's rhymes down the centuries, the plotting of distributions, the tracing of origins. . . . But now they have become anthropologists: they have come to realise that it is not so much the games that are interesting as the children who play them, so the emphasis has partly shifted towards a record of the child's astonishing 'natural' capacity for organisation and rule-making and learning and teaching."

What the Opies did in this second book was to divide the games (every one of the 2,500 names listed in the index) into twelve basic types (e.g., Chasing Games, Catching Games, Seeking Games, Hunting Games) and then to arrange each type acording to the basic motif of the individual games (e.g., The Touch Having Noxious Effect, Chaser at Disadvantage, Equal Number of Players Hiding and Seeking). The Opies' next problem was, as they state it, "to present our findings in a form in which the facts are readily available, yet not so prosaically that the spirit of street play, its zest, variety, contradictions, and disorderliness, is entirely lost." And in the captivating and beautifully written little essays that report their findings, the Opies describe, define, compare, contrast, annotate, ruminate, expatiate, and theorize with extraordinary grace, wit, and perspicaciousness about, for example, the differences between "play" and "games" ("Play is unrestricted, games have rules. Play may merely be the enactment of a dream, but in each game there is a contest"); the way in which each stage of a game—the choosing of leaders, the determining of which side shall start—is almost a game in itself . . . "more akin to cere- monies than competitions"; the possible reasons for the avoidance of the disliked role of the chasing or seeking "he" or "it" (with a discus- sion of the role's possible supernatural or satanic connotations); the origins of dips and Chinese counting formulae (used to determine the role of chaser) that begin "Eenie, meenie, macca, racca" and "Inty tinty tethery methery" (with a discussion of the "shepherd's score," the numerals supposedly used in the northwest of England in past times "by shepherds counting their sheep, by fishermen assess- ing their catch, and by old knitting women minding their stitches"); the writers' inescapable impression that "children do not really enjoy competitive athletics. The only running-race that comes to them naturally is the one that follows the challenge 'Last one there is a sissy!' (or, as Samuel Rowlands reported in 1600, 'Beshrow him that's last at yonder stile')"; the idea that "the more insignificant a game appears, the more remarkable is its history" (e.g., "Stroke the Baby"— a game that they trace back to a wall picture in a tomb at Beni Hassan in Egypt, ca. 2000 B.C., which shows "a player on his knees while two others, unseen by him, thump his back with their fists"—or the 2,000-year-old "Crusts and Crumbs"—a game in which Crusts chase Crumbs, then Crumbs chase Crusts, and which Plato refers to in a passage in *Phaedrus* when commenting upon how lovers and loved ones often exchange roles); the fact that children and adults once played the same games, and reminding us that in 1855 Palgrave, Jowett, and Tennyson diverted themselves during the Christmas gam- bols at Farringford by playing "Blind Man's Buff"—"in one form or another the sport seems to be part of the social history of the world"— after the children had been put to bed; the way in which, in the ball game "Kingy," "those who are not He have the ball hurled at them, without means of retaliation, and against ever-increasing odds (an element"—as the Opies acerbically comment—"that obviously ap- peals to the national character"); the likelihood that in Acting Games like "Old Man in the Well," "Fox and Chickens," and "Mother, the

Cake is Burning," children may be preserving "in vestigial form some of the most genuine folk-plays performed in Britain"; and the apodictic conclusion that, in their games, "the young do not commonly invent, merely imitate . . . that what passes as original is due not to art but to artlessness, to mishearings, to imperfect understanding, to the three-foot-high viewpoint which sees a palace roof in a table top, and fears a thunderstorm when the dog snores."*

In *Man, Play, and Games*, the French sociologist Roger Caillois quotes the ancient proverb: "Tell me what you play and I shall tell you what you are." Certainly, many of the games described by the Opies reveal children to be mirrors of the adult world. In the March 12, 1982, edition of *The New York Times*, for example, John Darnton, reporting from Cracow, Poland, tells of how a group of army officers, representing the ruling Military Council, went on a tour of a nursery school. As Darnton writes: "The acronym for the council, *Wron*, is uncomfortably close to the Polish word for crow, *wrona*, which has become its universal nickname. The children swarmed around the officers, chanting a ditty: 'The black crow, it crows darkly and sees the world only in black.'" And in *Children's Games*, the Opies point out that "in Berlin, when the wall was built (1961), West German children began shooting at each other across miniature walls. In the United States, after the death of President Kennedy (1963), children were found playing 'Assassination.' Throughout time, it seems, juvenile performances have varied only as their surroundings have varied. In classical Rome, where the law was administered in public, Seneca observed Roman boys playing at judges and magistrates, 'the magistrates being accompanied by little lictors with fasces and axes.' . . . And during the Second World War children in Ausch-

---

* Psychologists and educators have often noted that the expressiveness and imagination that young children demonstrate in their first songs, language, and drawings begin to disappear as soon as they enter their school years, as they move from a state of *poiesis* to that of *mimesis* ("As if [their] whole vocation/ Were endless imitation"—Wordsworth). Concerning this shift, Howard Gardner has commented: "The penchant for succumbing to convention, for conforming to one's peers, comes to permeate children's activities. Even as children at play are determined to follow the rules exactly and to tolerate no deviation, so, too, in their use of symbols they will brook neither experimentation nor novelty." But Gardner interestingly adds: "Although artistic work by children appears impoverished during this period, the common disparagement of this 'literal stage' seems to me misguided. Far from being the enemy of artistic progress, literalism may represent its advance guard. That concern with realism that pervades the literal stage may be a crucial phase of development—the time for mastering rules."

witz concentration camp, well aware of the reality, were seen playing a game that proved the most terrible indictment ever made against man, a game called 'Going to the Gas Chamber.' "

In another sense, many children's amusements seem to reflect—and preserve—the atavistic behavioral patterns of early man's hunter/gatherer way of life; and the hierarchical, territorial, and aggressive aspects of these games might be seen to derive from what Paul Mac-Lean has called the reptilian or R-complex part of the brain. (Carl Sagan has even wondered "whether the frequent ritualistic behavior in young children is a consequence of the still incomplete development of their neocortices.")

But if children's games perhaps reflect social and neurological realities, they are often also forms of human communication, types of learning situations, and symbolic models of conflict and resolution. As usual, the Opies cut through much theoretical clutter, simply observing that "in the security of a game [a child] makes acquaintance with insecurity, he is able to rationalize absurdities, reconcile himself to not getting his own way, 'assimilate reality' (Piaget), act heroically without being in danger. . . . He can be confident, too, in particular games, that it is his place to issue commands, to inflict pain, to steal people's possessions, to pretend to be dead, to hurl a ball actually at someone, to pounce on someone, or to kiss someone he has caught. In ordinary life either he never knows these experiences or, by attempting them, makes himself an outcast."

What is most significant and remarkable about the Opies' approach is that they never becloud with superciliousness or sanctimoniousness the clarity of their observations; and in no instance do they abandon their role as mediums by which to present and explain the energy and impulses behind the games that children play and the rhymes that they recite. As they affirm:

> Children seem to be instinctively aware that there is more to living than doing what is prudent and permitted. In a boy's world trees are for climbing, streams are for jumping over, loose stones are for throwing, and a high wall is a standing challenge to be mounted and walked along. . . . So it is that the juvenile tribe holds ritual games, almost as part of the process of growing up, in which the faint-hearted are goaded into being courageous, and the foolhardy stimulated to further foolhardiness. . . .
>
> We have noticed that when children are herded together in the playground, which is where the educationalists and the psychologists and the social scientists gather to observe them, their play is markedly

more aggressive than when they are in the street or in the wild places. . . . Often, when we have asked children what games they played in the playground, we have been told "We just go round aggravating people." . . .

Such behaviour would not be tolerated amongst the players in the street or the wasteland; and for a long time we had difficulty reconciling these accounts with the thoughtfulness and respect for the juvenile code that we had noticed in the quiet places. Then we recollected how, in our own day, children who had seemed unpleasant at school (whose term-time behaviour at boarding school had indeed been barbarous), turned out to be surprisingly civilized when we met them in the holidays. . . . It seems to us that something is lacking in our understanding of the child community, that we have forgotten Cowper's dictum that "Great schools suit best the sturdy and the rough," and that in our continual search for efficient units of educational administration we have overlooked that the most precious gift we can give the young is social space: the necessary space—or privacy—in which to become human beings.

If the Opies had written only *Lore and Language* and *Children's Games*, they would be regarded as two of the most important folklorists/anthropologists of our time (they have been called "the greatest living experts on the folklore, games, and beliefs of childhood," and the words Opie-esque and Opie-ise have already entered the language). But, as they assert in their preface to *Children's Games*: "Many folklorists . . . seem to be magically insulated from literature not strictly within their discipline; and neither [W.W.] Newell [author of *Games and Songs of American Children*, 1883], one of the founders of the American Folklore Society, nor Lady Gomme, seems to have been aware of the juvenile books on children's games that had long existed, even in their day, both in Britain and in the United States. This extensive literature has been examined systematically for the present work, apparently for the first time." And their involvement with children's books goes back forty years. As Justin G. Schiller of New York City—the distinguished antiquarian bookseller specializing in historical children's literature—has stated: "I can't think of anyone who can speak with more authority than they on the structural development of historical children's literature in the English language."

The Opies' first major work, *The Oxford Dictionary of Nursery Rhymes*, appeared in 1951 and has been reprinted eleven times. One of the best of all bedside books, it points to the rhymes' origins in songs, adult jests, proverbial maxims, prayers, charms, lampoons, barrack-room refrains, country ballads, mummers' plays, and political squibs—thereby questioning many folklorists' presuppositions about the "folk" making folklore; attempts, in the captivating notes to each rhyme, "to find the earliest recording of each piece no matter in what kind of literature it appeared; to offer the possible circumstances of its origin, to illustrate changes in the wording through the years, and to set it beside its forebears or companion pieces from other lands"; and lambastes and refutes what the Opies consider to be many of the "worthless" speculations concerning the meanings of the rhymes by those whom the editors call the "happy guessers" (that Little Bo-peep is Mary, Queen of Scots, for example; that "Ring-a-ring o' roses" dates back and refers to the Great Plague; that, in "Sing a song of sixpence," "the maid is a sinner; the blackbird, the demon snapping off the maid's nose to reach her soul, etc."). To this day, the *Dictionary* remains, in Justin G. Schiller's estimation, "the primary reference bibliography of English nursery rhymes." And along with their two additional collections (*The Oxford Nursery Rhyme Book*, 1955, and *The Puffin Book of Nursery Rhymes*, 1963), the Opies have pre-sented us with more than a thousand rhymes, many in different ver-sions ("because we don't want them to become solidified," Peter Opie explains).

In 1973 they brought out *The Oxford Book of Children's Verse*, which arranges 332 poems chronologically, from Chaucer to Ogden Nash, each of them traced back to its first printing or earliest known record, each of their authors and sources commented on briefly at the end of the book. The anthology gives many examples of admonitory, exhortatory, and overedifying poems—the kinds of poetry parodied by Lewis Carroll in "Speak roughly to your little boy,/And beat him when he sneezes" (*Alice's Adventures in Wonderland*). But, as the Opies comment in their preface, "children cannot be surprised by the extraordinary who have not been made aware of what is ordinary." And *The Oxford Book of Children's Verse* is an excellent historical overview and accounting of the often "ordinary," sometimes "extra-ordinary" poetry that English-speaking children have heard and read during the past seven hundred years.

In 1974 the Opies published *The Classic Fairy Tales*, consisting of twenty-four stories (including "Cinderella," "Beauty and the Beast," "Rumplestiltskin," and "Jack and the Beanstalk") as they were first printed in English or in their earliest surviving texts. In addition, the editors summarize the "history and points of interest in each tale,

Jack and Jill

AND

OLD DAME DOB

JACK and Jill
Went up the hill,
To fetch a pail of water;
Jack fell down,
And broke his crown,
And Jill came tumbling after.

Then up Jack got,
And home did trot,
As fast as he could caper;
To old Dame Dob,
Who patched his nob
With vinegar and brown paper.

When Jill came in,
How she did grin
To see Jack's paper plaster;
Her mother, vexed,
Did whip her next,
For laughing at Jack's disaster.

Now Jack did laugh
And Jill did cry,
But her tears did soon abate;
Then Jill did say,
That they should play
At see-saw across the gate.

A page from the Opies' *The Oxford Nursery Rhyme Book*

particularly from the textual point of view" and show by their selection of illustrations "how the tale has been depicted at different periods." As they write in their preface: "The reason such a work has not been attempted before is not immediately apparent. It may be that folklorists today are so preoccupied with orally communicated texts that literary research has become unpalatable. . . . The folklorist today commonly eschews texts that have come under literary influence, even when these texts are the sources of the most-loved stories of a nation; and the fact that an amount of material of literary origin continues to be found in folklore collections is due, as Dr. Linda Dégh has observed, 'solely to the ignorance of the researchers concerning the field of cheap literature.'" And in their usual feisty manner, the Opies dismiss many of the "conjectures of the symbolists and mythologists" and proponents of "all-embracing theories" concerning the origins and meanings of fairy tales, emphasizing that "the magic in the tales (if magic is what it is) lies in people and creatures being shown to be what they really are. The beggar woman at the well is really a fairy, the beast in 'Beauty and the Beast' is really a monarch, the frog is a handsome prince, the corpse of Snow White a living princess. . . . The wonderful happens, the lover is recognized, the spell of misfortune is broken, when the situation that already exists is utterly accepted, when additional tasks or disappointments are boldly faced, when poverty is seen to be of no consequence, when unfairness is borne without indignation, when the loathsome is loved. Perhaps, after all, fairy tales are to be numbered amongst the most philosophic tales that there are."

Finally, in their most recent collection, *A Nursery Companion* (1980), the Opies bring together and reproduce in color twenty-seven nursery booklets from the Regency period—brilliant, inventive, and joyous works of limericks, metrical and alliterative alphabets, rhyming histories, grammars, tongue twisters, nursery tales, and game books that influenced and inspired, among others, John Clare, Dickens, Ruskin, and Edward Lear. (Two of the booklets, it's interesting to note, feature texts by a ten-year-old Mary Shelley and an eleven-year-old Caroline Norton.) In this collection the Opies happily rediscover for us an astonishingly modern world of children's literature that had previously either been overlooked or had remained unknown. As the editors point out: "The books that give immediate delight, and are passed on delightedly from one reader to another, are seldom the ones that are set aside for posterity. Some of the booklets reproduced here are now so scarce they are not to be found even in the largest libraries;

PUNCTUATION PERSONIFIED

THE INTERROGATIVE POINT ?

What little crooked man is this?
He's called INTERROGATION, Miss.
He's always asking this and that,
As 'What's your name?' 'Whose dog is that?'
And for your answer, he will stay
While you 'One, two, three, four' can say.

THE EXCLAMATION POINT !

or Note of Admiration

This youth, so struck with admiration,
Is of a wondering generation,
With face so long and thin and pale,
He cries 'Oh! what a wondrous tale!'
While you count four, he stops, and then,
Admiring! he goes on again.

PUNCTUATION PERSONIFIED

A DASH — CIRCUMFLEX ^
BREVE ˘   DIAERESIS ··
HYPHEN ‒   ACUTE ACCENT ´
GRAVE ACCENT ˋ   PARENTHESIS ( )

A DASH and a CIRCUMFLEX here form a hat;
A BREVE serves to mark out the face;
DIAERESIS, too, and the HYPHEN come pat,
As a breast and a neck in their place.
The arms are the ACCENTS, both GRAVE
　　and ACUTE,
And for legs the PARENTHESIS nicely may suit.

Illustration from "Punctuation Personified" (1824), in the Opies' *A Nursery Companion* and we must admit to having been assembling them for this volume for more than thirty years." And to explain the reason for the precocious blossoming of these exhilarating works, the Opies write:

> The children's books produced in the first quarter of the nineteenth century have an alertness and grace not achieved in any other period. The reader has the feeling from them, as is sometimes portrayed within them, of a period in which cultured parents possessed the inclination as well as the leisure to walk hand in hand with their children, and together look at the world around them in wonder. But the temper of the times was soon to change. The belief in progress, and the possible perfectability of man, was once again to take hold of men's minds; and, as always happens in periods of moral advancement, light-heartedness was to be frowned upon. . . . By 1832 and the no-nonsense days of the Reform Bill, the inhabitants of the nursery were once again being looked upon as little pudding-bags to be stuffed with knowledge. The wonder is, perhaps, that people had ever thought otherwise; and the suspicion cannot be avoided that, in part, nonsense had been allowed entry to top nurseries through a misapprehension.

After having resided for ten years in nearby Alton, Iona and Peter Opie, in 1959, chose their present home in West Liss (about fifty miles southwest of London)—a large, ten-room, late-Victorian ironstone house—encouraged, in part, by the knowledge that the building's walls, one-and-a-half feet thick, would allow for up to nine tons of pressure from their enormous collection of books. As they write in the preface to *The Oxford Book of Children's Verse*: "Sometimes our texts have been established only after collating four or more printings, an undertaking that would have been arduous, if not impractical, had we not (with a foresight which now amazes us) made our permanent home within a library of early children's books."

All their research is based on the study of primary material—they make use of the British Library and the Victoria and Albert Museum (among other places), but those institutions will, themselves, often call the Opies up for books or documents that *they* are missing—and to this end, as Justin G. Schiller comments, "the Opies have assembled one of the finest collections of English children's literature anywhere extant." They have also what is probably the greatest private collection of everything related to children and childhood—toys, dolls, rocking horses, marbles, children's medicines, clothes pegs, rattles, prams, etc.—from the past three centuries.

. . .

When I first arrive at the Opies' home in early May, 1981, for a four-day visit, Peter, wearing a Harris tweed jacket, greets me at the door, and, noticing that I was gazing in amazement at the library in one of the front rooms, says, "It takes five hours to see the house and the collection. So let's have lunch, talk for the next day or two, and then we'll take the tour." "The place is run like a factory," Iona announces, smiling, as she arrives to say hello, wearing a pantsuit that, like most of her clothes (she tells me later) she buys at local Save-the-Children Fund sales. "Breakfast is at eight, lunch at one, high tea at six (what the Scottish call a 'meat tea'—sandwiches or a snack on toast, tea and cakes), then a bowl of cornflakes at ten o'clock with the television news. . . . So please come into the kitchen."

> Iona (as Peter and I sit down): I'll put the kettle on.
>
> Peter: How was your train ride down from London?
>
> Jonathan: It was a bit crowded in the beginning, but at a stop called Haslemere almost everyone got off.
>
> Peter: That's the station where Tennyson used to get off, too.
>
> Iona (returning to the table): And William Allingham, the poet —he's in our children's verse anthology—used to pace up and down the platform there, thinking. It was a writer's discovery, Haslemere, and it was considered to be healthy because of all the pine trees.
>
> Peter: Tennyson moved there from his home on the Isle of Wight because, being so rural, it allowed him to get away from the crowds.
>
> Iona: Later, George Bernard Shaw moved there . . . and then some other person of a literary nature moved there, too, and called his house Undershaw because it was lower down the hill from Shaw's.
>
> Peter: It's now a hotel called Undershaw Hotel. I once thought it was Overshaw.
>
> Iona: That's for *sure!*
>
> Peter: We used to live in Alton, you know. Jane Austen's home town, as it were, was Alton—it was where her doctor and solicitor lived.
>
> Iona: And her really productive years were at Chawton, nearby. From here to Selborne is four and a half miles, and another four and a half gets you to Alton. Then, almost attached to

Alton, is Chawton. She used to go into town in a little donkey cart.

Peter: Speaking of Selborne, that's where Gilbert White lived. And *The Natural History of Selborne* is one of the books I pick up when I want to read something congenial.

Jonathan: What are the others?

Peter: Dr. Johnson's essays . . . and the essays of Robert Louis Stevenson.

Iona: We're very fond of Stevenson because he was brilliant but not at all tough; he was staggering through life as we are.

Peter: When we were doing the children's verse anthology, he was the only person *all* of whose poems we wanted to include. Well, Christina Rossetti, too.

Iona: And you know, the great sorrow of my life is that I didn't buy her own copy of *Sing-Song* . . . I wasn't quite bold enough at the time. We have our regrets. As one of the Marx Brothers said: Do you have regrets? And another one replied: Every morning for breakfast, with milk and sugar. I always liked that.

Peter: It is philosophically impossible to regret. I've got this completely worked out now. No . . . regrets. Have another orange.

Iona: And don't forget Emerson! In fact, Peter, Emerson was your companion about twenty years ago, and you've only just gone back to him.

Jonathan: It's interesting you mention Emerson since, just recently, I came across several passages from his *Journals* that touch directly on your work.

Peter: Which ones?

Jonathan: One in which he says that "children are all foreigners. We treat them as such. We cannot understand their speech or the mode of life, and so our Education is remote and accidental and not closely applied to the facts." And then two other passages in which he talks about "the uncorrupted slang of the street, the pure mud," adding: "The language of the street is always strong. . . . Cut these words and they would bleed; they are vascular and alive; they walk and run."

Peter: Those are wonderful. . . . But first of all there was Thoreau—long before Emerson.

Iona: That's right. Peter was living with Thoreau when I married him.

Jonathan: That could have been grounds for something!

Peter (laughing): And Thoreau led to Emerson. I think I was

given four volumes of Emerson by the women's liberation army . . .

Iona: That's right. When we were expecting an invasion, he had a collection of very fierce women . . .

Peter: Guerilla fighters. I had been an officer in the army, and then I was asked to train these women—teaching them to put sugar in the petrol and that sort of thing in case there was an invasion. They were very special . . .

Iona: Many of them were writers.

Jonathan: Were you one of them?

Iona: No, no, no, no. I don't think I would have taken orders from him [laughing]. Could you pass the bread?

Jonathan: So you read White, Dr. Johnson, Stevenson . . .

Peter: There are really about four . . . but mostly Gilbert White and Emerson.

At this point, Iona gets up and returns with a pot of delicious-smelling stew.

Jonathan: Ummmm!

Iona: I call it Hop-pickers' Stew. You see, this used to be great hop country, but it's more or less all gone. When we lived in Alton, the hop-pickers used to arrive in autumn . . . they were sort of Gypsy-like people, what we call "travelers."

Peter: And they used to ride into town . . .

Iona: As in *Lorna Doone* . . .

Peter: Or exactly as you see in a Western. They used to come in at a gallop—we'd hear the clattering on the High Street where we lived—fill the center of town, hitch their homes all along the marketplace, and then be told what fields they had to go out to.

Iona: We lived opposite a grocer, and he used to take his van round the hop fields in the evening, selling bread to the hop-pickers, and they used to invite him to sit down for supper with them. He said they had these wonderful iron cauldrons on an open fire with an amazing stew in which they put all different kinds of meat—hedgehogs and everything else. And every now and again, when I don't know what to cook, we have Hop-pickers' Stew. I go to my butcher in the village, and he gets very excited and gives me a lump of beef, some lamb, bits of bacon . . .

Jonathan: Is that one word for you, *hoppickers?*

Peter: Ah . . . a hyphen I think it would have.

Iona: A hyphen, yes.

Jonathan: In the States, publishers tend to take out hyphens.

Iona: We're taking out hyphens, too, but when you get the two p's coming together, it's difficult. I never know how to spell *lamp post* for some reason, and I was dying to leave out the hyphen, but it didn't work.

Peter: We had this terrible trouble with lamp post, and I don't know what we did in the end.

Jonathan: The word comes up a lot in *Street Games.*

Peter: It does, and whatever we decided to do there is what we do in the long run. [*Lamp-post* is the way it appears in the book.]

Jonathan: Think of the little decisions you have to make!

Peter: Yes, its ridiculous, it's a wonder how things ever get done.

Iona: We can spend a whole evening debating something like a hyphen. But we have to go with house style for some things, like "Reverend"—"Revd."

Peter: It's changed, it used to be "Rev."

Iona: They say it got mixed up with Revelations.

Peter: That's quite nonsense, you know.

Iona: That's quite nonsense!

Peter: But nowadays we sometimes tend to set the style. The publishers know it's going to be so much trouble with us that they leave our punctuation alone!

Iona: When we started working for the Press—*The Oxford Dictionary of Nursery Rhymes* was first published thirty years ago this year . . .

Jonathan: How did that book come about?

Peter: It all started during the war. I was two years in the army— in the Royal Fusillers and then commissioned in the Royal Sussex regiment—but being fragile, I eventually got the push (I fell off a wall—no glory). Iona and I got married during the war—she was a sergeant in the Women's Auxiliary Air Force at the time—but family pressures and the fact that she became expectant made me realize that I'd better get a job (I was then writing a book). So we got a flat in London, I went into a firm called Todd Publishing, and then the buzz bombs started—in fact, our flat got smashed in a bit. So eventually the firm was evacuated to the country in Bedfordshire.

Iona: It was a place called Waresley—a funny, little, very old village—it even had a village pump because there was no running water. And one day, Peter and I were walking alongside a cornfield, and we took a ladybird onto . . . I forget whose finger it was. But we recited the rhyme—"Ladybird, ladybird,/ Fly away home,/Your house is on fire/And your children all gone"—and we wondered where the verse came from, how old was it? We got bitten by these questions.

Peter: So come the weekend, we rushed to London to the Kensington Public Library, and nothing was satisfactory. We went from one place to another—finally, of course, to the British Museum, which always felt safe when the bombs were coming down. You couldn't believe a bomb would hit it . . . and, equally, one felt that if a bomb did come by, what a glorious thing to go up with! It would have been marvelous!

Iona: The most recent book that had information about the rhyme was J. O. Halliwell's *Nursery Rhymes of England,* which was published in 1842. That seemed a rather long time ago, and we thought that, perhaps, there was room for a new book on the origins of nursery rhymes. It seemed a much more congenial project for Peter than the other work he was doing, so we sort of drifted into it . . . but he must have seen it as something we could do together.

Peter: That story about wondering about the ladybird rhyme is the superficial level. The deep level is that we were going to have a child; being the kind of people we were, we wanted to know everything one could about children and about getting ready for this awful event that we were entirely unprepared for. One was terrified of this—at least I was. And I went up the Charing Cross Road and bought every book I could find on childbirth. Grantley Dick Reed's *Natural Childbirth* was one that made sense to me; in it, he said that childbirth was the most natural thing in the world, and his message was: Don't be worried, just have the child. So we wrote to him, visited him at his clinic in Working, became prize pupils, and went around counseling other people afterwards. [Iona and Peter have three children—James, Robert, and Letitia.]

Hitherto, I'd always written about myself, or love, or the people I'd met [Peter wrote three books of stories and philosophical essays on his own—*I Want to Be a Success* (1939), *Having Held the Nettle* (1945), and *The Case of*

Being a Young Man (1946)]; and now, suddenly, I had been brought face to face with childhood. It would have been exactly the same if I'd been in a road accident and lost both my legs—I would have then been interested in the disabled and started writing about them and their troubles. We were having a child, so our complete interest now went into the things of childhood. And everything grew from that. There were young children in the house, and when they grew bigger, we started work on *Lore and Language* because we were dealing with eight-, nine-, and ten-year-olds. But, of course, the problem has been that we've been so involved with finding out about childhood that we've never got any further.

Jonathan: After you'd realized that Halliwell's book was the last important work on nursery rhymes, how did you go about doing your research?

Peter: First of all, Halliwell *was* remarkable, and we had his findings. (Incidentally, at the London Library in the forties, there was an old gray-haired man who used to sign out your books, and he actually remembered Halliwell coming in!) Then we went through the whole of *Notes and Queries* and *The Athenæum*, all kinds of folklore and folksong journals, and then the whole of the Black Letter Ballads (the Roxburghe and Pepysian collections)—Pepys was a great collector of ephemera, by the way, he was our sort of man. In fact, we've read all of Pepys—the diaries in the old and also the new edition—it's taken us about two years going through that (Iona and I read alternate volumes).

Iona: We're waiting for the tenth volume now.

Peter: We read for any number of subjects—for any reference to children, for any reference to folklore, superstition, calendar custom, social custom. . . . What are we *not* reading for?

Iona: We're really reading for human life on an unofficial level.

Peter: Anything that anybody has not done already. . . . Anyway, to get back to "Ladybird," we looked up nursery rhymes, riddles, ballads, any kind of thing that might give us a lead. But on the way to looking up an entry, our eye often got caught by five or six other interesting items. So we had great difficulty getting to the reference, and sometimes we'd even forget the reference we were trying to get to because we were so interested in everything else!

But while doing the nursery-rhyme dictionary it occurred

to me that the next time we started another work, we'd have to start searching through these volumes all over again. And that would have been absurd—we didn't and don't want to approach life like that; you want to go through those great source books once and for all. So what we did, and do now, is to go through books making cards of anything that we think might be of interest to us in the future. It makes life a lot slower, but it does mean that we have an extraordinary number of references to all sorts of obscure things that have taken our fancy, and sometimes these things join up in one way or another.

Jonathan: There are an additional four lines to the "Ladybird" rhyme that you included in the *Dictionary*: "All except one/ And that's little Ann/And she has crept under/ The warming pan." And it's almost as if the rhyme goes from one deep level —the first four lines—to another very light one—the last four.

Peter: Quite right. The second part doesn't appear in the early versions, and has been attached. You see, sometimes the verses get rationalized: Something was said that wasn't quite understandable to a later generation, so people filled it in with words that sounded right. (The name *Ann* might originally have been something like *Abouberigann*.) This happens quite a lot, especially in the counting-out rhymes [e.g., "Eena, meena, mona, my"], which is why you can't take a literal approach with these texts before you have the earliest one.

I've always been chronologically minded—I was brought up on the *Oxford English Dictionary*—and knew that philology couldn't begin until you'd arranged your quotations chronologically: You can't look for the origin of a word until you've seen how it has developed. And people keep looking at the present-day word, phrase, or rhyme and then try to equate that version with some ancient myth or whatever. But if you trace it back and arrange it chronologically, you may find that the text was quite different. And then, conversely, you also have the situation in which, for example, the church bells are set to ring "Oranges and Lemons" because a particular church is called St. Clement's and therefore this *must* be the Oranges and Lemons church! So you make your bells agree with the myth. And that is what people constantly do.

Jonathan: To backtrack a moment, how did you and Iona find the time to do all your research?

Peter: While Iona and I were working on the *Dictionary*, I won
a literary prize for my autobiographical book *The Case of
Being a Young Man*, which was worth five hundred pounds
and a guaranteed sale of a hundred thousand copies. I was
earning eight pounds a week at that time, and that check was
a year's pay in front of me. So I quit my office job—taking on,
with Iona, the writing of an ordinary pocket dictionary—and
went on with our work.

In the beginning, one publisher seemed interested in the
nursery-rhyme book and took us to the Café Royal where he
gave us a real wigging, saying: "You know, some of the rhymes
don't have notes." And we explained that we couldn't find
anything out about them—we meant that we just knew them
ourselves or had picked them up in some uninteresting book—
and he repeated: "But they *must* have come from somewhere!"
Anyhow, we went away absolutely furious, but it was a very
useful lesson: *Everything comes from somewhere.* And from
then on everything we wrote down had an exact reference of
where and when and how we got it. You must write down
every single thing: who the person was, his or her age, where
he or she got it from

And in this way, one gradually learned to be scholarly.
[See the "Ladybird, Ladybird" entry from *The Oxford Dictionary of Nursery Rhymes*, reprinted on pp. 272–73.] Because
we were both self-educated. Thank God! Had we gone to university, we'd have known that what we were doing was absurd.
Since people didn't deal with children and things like that, it
would have been considered a nonsubject or a silly one. And
at the time, when we said we studied nursery rhymes, we were
considered an oddity. So we very quickly learned to keep absolutely quiet about it. And also, had we been to university, we
would have realized that everybody knew so much, but because we didn't know what was and wasn't permissible and
possible, we just went forward (Iona learned German and
Italian in order to work on our books). And, equally, we were
not only enthusiastic but also self-critical; we went on criticizing ourselves until we felt that there couldn't be much
wrong with what we were doing.

After a couple of years, while we were working at the
Bodleian Library, in the inner sanctum where the books are
chained to the walls, the keeper of manuscripts came up and

> Ladybird, ladybird,
>   Fly away home,
> Your house is on fire
>   And your children all gone;
> All except one
>   And that's little Ann
> And she has crept under
>   The warming pan.

Child's warning to the ladybird. Traditionally the insect is set on
a finger before being addressed. This is what the present writers
used to do, and what a woodcut of the reign of George II depicts.
When the warning has been recited (and the ladybird blown
upon once), it nearly always happens that the seemingly earth-
bound little beetle produces wings and flies away. The names by
which it is popularly known in this and other countries show
that it has always had sacred associations: 'Ladybird' (from Our
Lady's bird), 'Marygold', 'God's Little Cow', 'Bishop that
burneth'; the German 'Marienkäfer' and 'Himmelsküchlichen';
the Swedish 'Maria Nyckelpiga', the Russian 'Bózhia koróvka',
the French 'Bête à bon Dieu', the Spanish 'Vaquilla de Dios',
and the Hindu 'Indragôpa.' The rhyme is undoubtedly a relic of
something once possessed of an awful significance. It is closely
matched by incantations known in France, Germany, Switzer-
land, Denmark, and Sweden, sometimes even to the detail of the
name Ann:

> Goldchäber, flüg uf, uf dine hoche Tanne,
> Zue diner Muetter Anne.
> Si git dir Chäs und Brod,
> 's isch besser as der bitter Tod.

Another German version is:

> Himmelsküchlichen, flieg aus!
> Dein Haus brennt,
> Deine Kinder weinen alle miteinander.

And in France, where the words are also addressed to the
cockchafer:

> Vole au firmament bleu,
> Ton nid est en feu,

Les Turcs avec leur épée
Vont te tuer ta couvée.
Hanneton, vole, vole,
Hanneton, vole.

Varieties of the *Coccinella* are found in most parts of the world, and are almost everywhere regarded as friendly. To kill one is unlucky. This would seem to rule out the hypothesis that a witch or evil spirit is represented and that the rhyme is a form of exorcism. (A much-practised method of ridding oneself of witches was to tell them that their dwelling was on fire.) A theory in Germany is that the rhyme originated as a charm to speed the sun across the dangers of sunset, the house on fire symbolizing the red evening sky. In *The Rosicrucians* the beetle is compared with the Egyptian scarab and the rhyme thought to be a remnant of beliefs associated with Isis. It has also been pronounced to be a relic of Freya worship. In England country children also employ the insect for divination.

T Thumb's PSB, c. 1744, 'Lady Bird, Lady Bird, Fly away home, Your house is on fire, your children will burn' / *Nancy Cock's PSB*, c. 1780, ends 'Your children are gone' / Similar in *GG's Garland*, 1784; *T Tit's SB*, c. 1790; *Newest Christmas Box*, c. 1797; *Songs for the Nursery*, 1805; *Vocal Harmony*, c. 1806; *Northern Antiquities*, 1814; *Nurse Lovechild's DFN*, c. 1830; *Boy's Week-Day Book*, 1833. Full version appears in *Poetic Trifles* (J. G. Rusher), c. 1840. Numerous variants are given by Chambers, 1847; Northall, 1892; Eckenstein, 1906 (who quotes foreign equivalents). Also in *N & Q*; *Folk-Lore*, especially 1938; *I saw Esau*, I. and P. Opie, 1947. Emily Brontë (c. 1840) based a poem on the rhyme.
  Cf. *Deutsches Kinderbuch*, Karl Simrock, 1848, 'Marienkäferchen, fliege weg! Dein Häuschen brennt, Dein Mutterchen flennt, Dein Vater sitzt auf der Schwelle: Flieg in Himmel aus der Hölle', and other variations / *Deutsche Kinder-Reime*, Ernst Meier, 1851, 'Maikäfer, flieg! Dein Vater ist im Krieg, Deine Mutter ist in Pommerland, Pommerland ist abgebrannt' / *Deutsche Mythologie*, Jacob Grimm, 1854 / *Germanische Mythen*. W. Mannhardt, 1858, 'Maikäfer fliege fort, Dein Häuschen brennt, Dein Kreischen brennt. Die Jungen sitzen drinnen Und spinnen, Und wenn sie ihre Zahl (to Schock) nicht haben, Können sie nicht spazieren gan', and many variations / *Deutsches Kinderlied*, F. M. Böhme, 1897 [1924] / *Faune populaire de la France*, E. Rolland, 1881, 'Petite manivole, Vole, vole, vole! Ton père est à l'école, Vole, vole, vole! Il t'achète une belle robe. Vole, vole, vole, Si tu ne voles pas Tu n'en auras pas' / *Finnisch-ugrische Forschungen*, 1937 [*American Folk-Lore*].

asked us what we were doing. We told him that we were looking at the origins of nursery rhymes, and he said, "Oh, that's rather interesting . . . do you have a publisher?" We said no, and he mentioned that a great friend of his was Elizabeth Withycombe, who had just published *The Oxford Dictionary of English Christian Names*. Well, this had been our model, it was a superb and witty book, giving a brief article on each name, tracing its history, and then giving the references. He asked if we'd like to meet her, and we said we'd love to. Remember, we knew nobody at Oxford at all—either at the University or at the Clarendon Press.

So he invited us all around to coffee; Elizabeth Withycombe was very kind, saying she'd mention our project to the Press, where she had recently been working. And then we got a letter from her saying that the Press thought they might be interested in a "small corpus" on nursery rhymes done in the way we were thinking of doing it, and would we like to send the manuscript? And could she see it first? So we worked on— the whole dictionary took seven years, full time, except for an occasional job of abridging classics and things like that— and it got larger and larger because we kept finding out more stuff: Each thing we looked at led to something else. Eventually, though, we sent her the manuscript—our third draft— and she said it wouldn't do, the introduction wasn't right, pull yourself together, everything has to go into it, she told us. And her comments were very salutary.

So we redid the introduction, sent it to her again, and she delivered it to the Press. We heard nothing for six months. But during that period they had sent the manuscript to every surviving editor of the *Oxford English Dictionary*, and not one of them found a single mistake in it. (I'm not saying there weren't any, but, by good luck, they found none.) And so, finally, the Press said they'd publish it but asked us to include things like "Oranges and Lemons," "London Bridge," and "Ring-a-ring o' roses" (game rhymes we'd purposely left out in order to include them in another volume). And I remember going in to see the boss, Sir Arthur Norrington, who said: "Look here, Opie, this is going to be an Oxford book. Every single quotation has got to be verified. Every fact has got to be checked!" (This was for the Clarendon Press—the scholarly and academic part of the Oxford University Press.) We then went to see the assistant secretary, Dan Davin, and he said: "Now look here, Opie, we have books on the stocks which various professors have been doing for twenty years. And we say: 'Isn't it about time this book is ready?' and they say: 'Well, in Buenos Aires I know there's going to be a lecture on my subject, and until I see an offprint of that paper, I really can't finish it.' But you've got to set a date and say: Nothing more after that!"

So we worked another year on it, sent in the completed manuscript, and it took perhaps a year going through the Press. Also, we had one or two little struggles, such as getting illustrations into it. You see, the Press saw the book as a little side work they'd put out, and planned on printing 2,500 copies— just what the market could stand—mostly for libraries and a few interested people. Then the publishers' reps went out with the catalog, and they began getting a lot of response to the book. So the Press put the first printing up to 5,000, 7,500, then 10,000 copies—that was quite a large printing for those days.

We had just had a third child, had recently moved to Alton, and one Sunday when we were trying to get our living-room in order—we hadn't even unpacked—a great man with a red beard came to the door. I opened it, and he asked, "Is this where Mr. and Mrs. Opie live?" "Yes, it is." "Well," he asked, "could I see your father." And I said, "I beg your pardon?" "Is this where the editors of *The Oxford Dictionary of Nursery Rhymes* live?" "Yes, I'm Peter Opie." "Oh, I'm sorry," he exclaimed, "I imagined it would have been an old person who had done the *Dictionary*." And he came in and wrote an article for *The Daily Mail*, a photographer came and took pictures of us with the children, and we even went on television. And there was even a leader in *The Times* about it. The Press was tickled pink, because nothing like this had ever happened to them before. The *Dictionary* sold out that month, but if it had come out before the war, there would have been no sale—it just hit the right mood, and people started buying it for themselves. And it now sells three times as many copies as it did at the beginning because interest in the subject has grown.

But don't forget: At no time did anybody at the Press ever ask us who we were, where we came from, what our qualifications were, or anything else. They purely looked at the material. And for a while after that, they didn't even look at our manuscripts. Now they do—we like people to read the manuscript, we take every kind of advice we can because we've got no pride—you musn't have pride, because all you're trying to do is to produce the best possible work.

Jonathan: So the *Dictionary* led to *Lore and Language*?

Peter: Exactly. You see, when we were doing the nursery rhymes, we realized that there was this other stuff that was being communicated from child to child. We didn't actually know if the subject really existed, but we did distinguish child rhymes from nursery rhymes; and *that*, I think, was the first time that that had been done. So in 1947, in order to make a little money, we put out a small book entitled *I Saw Esau*—just by going to the files and using material we weren't going to use in the *Dictionary*. But we also put it out, in a sense, as a kind of scout volume. And within weeks one was getting the real stream of stuff, and we started meeting children. So we thought: This *is* extraordinary, they're all repeating the rhymes that Norman Douglas had printed in *London Street Games* [1916]—we thought the children must have been reading a cheap edition of Douglas's book. And then, after we moved from Farnham to Alton, we realized that, since the children were producing the rhymes there, too, they were probably being repeated all over the country.

We decided there would be enough to make a larger book, and after we completed the *Dictionary* we got an agreement with the Press to do a work on children's lore and games, which would include sayings and riddles and anything else we could find. Of course, once we started on it, we realized it was going to have to be a two-volume work—one on lore and language, one on games. And, of course, after finishing two chapters of *Children's Games*, we knew it was going to have to split again. And now we plan to put singing games and games with implements into two separate volumes—but, once more, each of those may be too large because there's so much material, and the second may have to divide into games with balls and games with other implements. At the moment, we think there might be a book on marbles, tipcat, hopscotch, and tops. And what we'll do with ball-bouncing in general and skipping we just don't know.

I'm sixty-two, and we're certain we have about twenty years of work just to complete the games books. And we have other projects we've been doing research for as well—one on superstitions dealt with on historical principles; then a study on the family, especially interfamily material concerning the relationship between parents and children; then we've got to write a book on the theory of folklore; and we want to do a volume on the tunes for the nursery rhymes; and, of course, a new edition of the *Dictionary of Nursery Rhymes*—when it's redone, every single rhyme will have a new article. We've been collecting material on nursery rhymes continuously for thirty years, and people have been sending us information from all over the world. But what has been so interesting is that our basic ideas about the rhymes haven't really changed. . . . And then, naturally, there is children's literature itself—a collection like *A Nursery Companion* needed doing, and there are other volumes we'd like to put together.

Jonathan: How do you get everything done?

Peter: Aside from publicity for the books when they come out, we don't appear on radio and television, and we don't do anything else.

Iona: We don't go on holidays, we don't entertain, and Peter doesn't drive—as you can imagine, we have a list of famous people who don't drive cars [smiling].

Peter: Sir Julian Huxley came here, and we were delighted to find out that Lady Huxley did the driving. . . . The whole secret of life, to my mind, is to capitalize on your disadvantages. Mine are that I can't drive, I can't sing, I can't dance. And I avoid going to parties—in fact, I dislike parties and always feel a fool at them. I was once introduced to Dorothy Sayers and immediately thought she was Agatha Christie—or was it the other way around? I'm absolutely shocking at this.

Evelyn Waugh got bored very easily, and so, if a lunch party that he was giving was going too well, he would say something to a neighbor, as rude as could be, just to have a little excitement. Because he *liked* things going wrong, unpleasantness, fights—for that then aroused his great intellect to work. It didn't work in tranquillity; and as a result of that, he had a tempestuous life.

My mother used to say, "You must get out and meet people, how else can you be a writer?" But all life is within oneself. Most people are rushing about because they're afraid of what they're carrying around in themselves. But I find that one other person is enough . . . and what an arrogance you have to have if you want to go against the herd! Most people try to look for ways to get through their days—does the day drag along or is it too short? Our days are so short that we don't know what's happened to them. So the only thing possible is to keep cutting down what one does. And stay in.

Darwin was probably the most wonderful man in the nineteenth century—he's one of the people one relates to because he was, in a sense, self-educated. I am invalidish enough, but Darwin managed to be *completely* invalidish, so much so that he never went out; he even had someone else read his famous lecture announcing the origin of the species. So one can't help but have a very great fellow feeling for him—even if, unfortunately, he didn't live *just* down the road . . . it was a little bit further away [smiling].

Iona and I stay at home, and we only operate in tranquillity. I mean, one of the reasons we're still married is that we don't like squabbling. And it would be such a nuisance to separate. It's impossible: Who would take which book and so on? So we both have our souls and work here.

After lunch is over, Peter says that he has some work to do; so Iona suggests I accompany her to her ground-floor study/office that the Opies call the Folklore Room. Here are located scores of dictionaries; reference books of all kinds on language, song, religion, and regional folklore; and magazine sets, including bound copies of a complete set of *Notes and Queries*—the weekly (now quarterly) folklore magazine originally edited by W. J. Thoms. (Correspondents—in the beginning, mostly Victorian intellectual gentlemen or clergymen—would write the magazine with queries about words, superstitions, and genealogies; and other correspondents would write back to answer.) This particular set, Iona informs me, belonged to Lewis Carroll. "It was still in Oxford when we found it," she says, "and it has his signature in violet ink in the first volume, as you can see. He got some of his best ideas from it, like the idea for the Cheshire-Cat ('the-cat-left-with-just-a-smile'). The index isn't good, and you have to double-check all the entries because the correspondents' answers weren't always correct. We've read through all the volumes—Peter would take on one and I'd read the next. We do the same with most of the multivolume sets. Right now we're doing *Punch*—he's reading 1846 and I, 1847."

But along with books, the room is filled with scores of boxes and drawers containing cards on which are written traditional phrases, proverbs, and lists of bibliographical source books on games and play in general; boxes of original children's games; and about four hundred different-colored quarto files devoted to rhymes of all kinds, as well as to calendar customs and superstitions, marbles ("We have three thousand cards with marble terms, calls, and names, plus entries on Roman marbles and medieval marbles found in the Thames"), hop-scotch, indoor and party games, ball games, activities ("The crazes come in here," Iona says, "like walking on tins, skateboard, Frisbees, and the fluff craze, which was when children started pulling little bits off each other's jumpers and making a big fluffy ball out of them!"), sports like cricket ("We have files on street cricket and on the history of real cricket to go with them, because we have to know what children are copying"), and games with implements (bat and ball, tops, tipcat).

"Remember," Iona says, "this represents seventy years of work—thirty-five for each of us. And when you do a collection of rhymes, you must include every theory there is about a particular rhyme, because if you leave one out, everybody who has that particular theory will send you a note. So it's a form of self-protection. They can't *all* be right, and yet they all have adherents. Once, we had sent to us, by a member of Oxford University, a theory about one nursery rhyme, and I looked it up in the file, and it first appeared in *Punch* as a *parody* of the kind of things university people produce. So it's a wonderful circle. Our doctor down the road was taught in medical school that 'Ring-a-ring o' roses' is about the bubonic plague; he believes it firmly. But we no longer contradict people because they get so disappointed. In fact, we think we've got the whole story of how that particular rhyme developed, and that will come in our singing games book."

Iona and I sit down by her desk, and I ask her about her partnership with her husband. "We're complete equals in terms of our personalities," she explains, "because we've done our privations. In a way, it was like the beginning of a fairy tale: When I first got married, I felt that that was the end of my life, really, because I was caught up with the usual woman's style of life. We started a family fairly soon. My mother-in-law saw that I didn't know how to run a house, so she showed me how it was done. I'm not by nature very domestic, and for about fifteen years I was trying my best to be a good mother and an efficient housewife. But I rather overdid it, trying to cook and dust better than anyone else. And I ought to have acknowledged that I wasn't either good at it or able to do both the books and domestic work. And it was bad for Peter, too, because he was a refugee in his own workroom: you can imagine trying to write with three children milling around downstairs. He used to have the oldest child, James, up for at least a half hour a day, and he would sit on Peter's knee and draw honey pots—I think the first word James learned to spell was *honey*.

"After these early domestic and maternal years—climbing the glass mountain and the trials—I found that I'd done my training: I had learned how to do research and produce books, and I was able to take over a lot of the work. So when Peter was feeling a little bit weary with the subject, I came into it, thinking, Now is my chance, now I can have the job I always wanted! And with my new enthusiasm, I sort of rushed in and made a new wave. I've taken over the work at the British Library because I love it—that blue dome is my temple of learning. And I more or less thought of the *Children's Games* book as mine—I took that research to the nth degree in a way I don't think Peter would have. Just about four days ago—to link up a couple of the things I've been saying—I was talking to a woman in the lady readers' restroom at the British Library. She told me she came from Malta—she's getting her Ph.D. here—and I spoke to her for almost an hour about her childhood; so now I have pages of stuff about what Maltese children sing and do in the street.

"Peter's the writer, but I can take a game and rough-shape it— rather like a Greek statue that was carved just so far by one craftsman and that then went to a sculptor at another mason's yard to have the fine work done on it. Well, this is what I do with a game. Then it comes back to me, and I might say that Peter's left out a detail or that he hasn't emphasized something enough; and then it goes back to him—we haven't really discussed it verbally, we've done this all on paper. And then he corrects it, we finally meet to talk about it . . . we get into the Turkish bath, as it were, and just sit there and sweat over a sentence and turn it around six different ways.

"So what a happy ending! It's an awfully smug thing to say, but I've got everything now. Even free time. When I was washing a few garments the other day, I noticed that a baby rabbit was sitting out- side eating a chestnut leaf, which is something quite new to me, because the leaves are so large and tough. And he started at the end of it, solemnly ate his whole way through this leaf—which was larger than he was, in fact—and it was wonderful. Time stood still, and I thought: I'm going to watch that rabbit consume that leaf. I stopped, and time stopped, and the rabbit ate the leaf. . . . And dust I now look at in a literary way. I love dust. I think of Elizabeth Barrett Browning surrounded by fluffy dust inches deep. And Rupert Brooke with his feathery fairy dust. It just doesn't matter to me if someone pulls out a piece of furniture and it's found to be littered with dust behind it. I feel very lucky!"

At high tea later that afternoon—back in the kitchen—Peter begins to explain to me that he has a very weak memory, quoting, with approval, Montaigne's statement that a "strong memory is commonly coupled with infirm judgment."

Peter: May I have the salt please?

Iona: Yes, you may. You know, I've spent ten years trying to teach you the difference between geraniums and fuchsias.

Peter: Actually, she doesn't quite mean that.

Iona: Don't I mean it?

Peter: What it is is that I can't remember which name belongs to which.

Iona: Oh yes, I see. He can see the difference but can't get the names.

Peter: Names mean nothing to me whatsoever. A name is merely a code word that is used to express an idea or refer to an object or something.

Iona: Hmmmm.

Peter: And this is what I have against education, you see. They say, What is the capital of Czechoslovakia? And whoever says "Prague" gets full marks. But he or she doesn't know what "Prague" means or anything, it's just a Pavlovian response to the word Czechoslovakia.

Iona: Like putting a coin in the slot.

Peter: Now someone like me . . . like a coin in the slot, exactly . . . can't remember . . .

Iona: That's right . . .

Peter: . . . you see, and that's why I don't remember.

Iona: Those poor little kids in Philadelphia who are being trained in that Better Baby Institute, run by an American ex-lieutenant-colonel! Enthusiastic parents go there to start teaching their children as soon as they're born—math, the names of composers, anything you can think of.

Jonathan: Rousseau wouldn't have approved of that institute at all.

Iona: It's the complete contrary, isn't it?

Jonathan: Even John Locke would have thought that was going too far.

Iona: I think he probably would have, yes . . . though he did think that the earlier you start teaching facts the better they're assimilated.

Peter: Words you have known since you were young you accept and use without ever analyzing them. That's Iona's idea.

Iona: You never question them again.

Jonathan: When I was young, I always confused "Up and at 'em" with "Up and Adam."

Iona: It's probably what Wellington said on some occasion.

Peter: Yes, it probably is, actually. [*Brewer's Dictionary of Phrase and Fable* attributes this "somewhat apocryphal order"—"Up, Guards, and at them!"—to Wellington as his command to the Guards at the battle of Waterloo.]

Jonathan: In *Lore and Language*, you have a section devoted to how children mishear things. Could you give me an example?

Peter: Iona had one the other day.

Iona: There are hundreds of examples, that's the trouble.

Peter: I'm afraid we can't remember.

Iona: We have no memories, we only have filing systems. Because the traffic is going through at such a rate, all we remember is from our own childhoods, and then only the ordinary things that any one lifetime has acquired in the way of memories. But everybody else's childhood is coming at us, so we can't remember all the things we hear.

Peter: That's true, we just write them down. But I also have a thing even against memory as such. If you have a memory, you tend not to be very good at creating. Pope has a line on this, which I'll give you. . . . I always keep it on me because I can't even remember what the quotations are that say that it's a disadvantage to have a good memory. If there were no writing, I'd be lost!

Jonathan: Plato disagreed with you completely. He thought the invention of writing was going to destroy memory. What did Boswell do with Johnson?

Peter: What he did was exactly what Iona does . . . or something similar to it. Boswell made any surreptitious notes he could and then went straight back home and wrote it all down. And Iona manages to do this in her playground reports . . . as long as she does it immediately afterwards.

Iona: I have a reporter's notebook with ruled lines, and the children say, You're not writing on the lines, that's not very tidy, don't you write any neater than that? And I say, No, because I'm in too much of a hurry. It's that little bit of scribble that helps me get it back later. I can decipher the scribble just for a couple of hours, and then it's gone.

Peter: The two great inventions were the wheel and writing. The wheel enabled people to take about with them more than they were able to carry, and writing enabled people to take around with them more than they could remember. . . . I thought of that just the other day.

Iona: I think that's jolly good!

Peter: We still behave as if writing hadn't been invented. We produce a book which says everything we want to say in it, and instantly everybody writes to you and asks you to lecture! You go to universities to hear third-rate people lecturing, when the first-rate professors, wherever they are in the world, have written their books on the subject.

People have not adapted yet to the age of writing. Don't think, however, that I am against the human touch or human contact: That is what life is all about—in fact, there would be no life without it. But that's quite a different thing from the passing on of knowledge. . . . And gosh, the nice thing when you're with a human being is not to keep jabbering the whole time. That's how Iona and I have managed to last for thirty-eight years.

Iona: The thing about Peter is that he has an original mind, which is one of the reasons I married him; but to add to this is his wonderful lack of memory—he can't write in clichés because he can't remember them!

Peter: I have literally looked in the *Encyclopedia Britannica* for facts in articles that we *wrote* . . . because one simply does not remember. When you're engaged in oral communication you can only carry in your ears about five words at a time. So you have to bring only one thought over at that moment, you can't carry, as you can when you're writing, several things in the background which you're also coming up to; and you can't refer back. The eye is the great form of communication.

Jonathan: I gather that you and Iona often exchange notes about your ongoing work.

Peter: If there's something important that has to be explained, we write it down and hand it to the other person. . . . Do you want anything on your bread?

Jonathan: Actually, I like it plain.

Peter: How interesting, yes!

Iona: You must always ask if you're missing something . . .

Peter: Yes, that's right . . .

Iona: . . . because A, we don't think, and B, we just go along with our own habits. But we really are kindred spirits, Jonathan, if you don't mind my complimenting you to your face, which one shouldn't do.

Peter: But are you sure it's a compliment, dear?

Iona: Well, when I was in the air force during the war, I used to get away on my own and go walking with a haversack containing only a loaf of brown bread in it. So I understand about liking plain bread.

Peter: I just now remembered the line by Alexander Pope that I couldn't recall before: "When memory prevails, the solid power of understanding fails." That's one of my favorites. And, mind you, our friend Johnson said that it wasn't important to remember everything, only to know where you could find the information.

Iona: We need an index of all the indexes!

Jonathan: Your friend Johnson? Samuel Johnson?

Peter: Yes, we say "our friend Johnson" or "our friend Godwin" William Godwin. We've read so much about Godwin and have some of his own books here . . .

Iona: Most of our friends we've never met. They're either dead long ago or we've been writing to them but haven't met them.

Peter: One knows more about William Godwin, certainly, than about one's neighbors. I'm certain I know what the secret marks in his diary mean, but that's another matter altogether.

And, you know, one knows all his family, his children . . . we've got his handwriting here . . . we know more about him than he knew himself, after all.

Jonathan: Do you like him?

Peter: Oh, yes, you can't help feeling affection for a great man like that. He became a bit of a crank. And what is such fun is that he had these great ideas about education; and then, as so often, the moment it came to the actual point, he went against the whole lot of it. His second wife brought two children, and he had two by her . . . did the Shelley girl have a full brother or sister?

Iona: No, I don't think so, I think she was by herself.

Peter: Because Mary Wollstonecraft, the mother, died. She was a lovely person. A lovely family, and one sort of feels inside them.

Iona: Poor William Godwin . . . with all the muddles he got into, and his money troubles.

Peter: And we have all the books that he published to try to make money with again.

Jonathan: Do you feel some kind of sympathetic magic by owning a copy of an author's book?

Peter: Of course, it's true that to hold in one's hand something that the author held in *his* hand is wonderful; but I don't care for ideas like magic. That it makes you tingle, yes. And even buying a first edition of an author whom you like is an expression of love, much like buying a ring for a lady: It's an expression of your affection and respect. And if I read an eighteenth-century book, I like to do so in an eighteenth-century edition, because this is how one gets close, you see.*

* One is reminded of the poem by Emily Dickinson beginning:

> A precious — mouldering pleasure — 'tis —
> To meet an Antique Book —
> In just the Dress his Century wore —
> A privilege — I think —
>
> His venerable Hand to take —
> And warming in our own —
> A passage back — or two — to make —
> to Times when he — was young — . . .

It is not pure antiquarianism, it is rather this desire to get *back* to the person—and if you have a sample of the handwriting as well, then one really is trying to understand.

Jonathan: When did you both start your amazing book collection?

Peter: A year after we got married. It began with nursery rhymes, but we were always looking to the future; and we realized that one never could be a proper worker unless one possessed the books oneself. So we went around to the antiquarian book-shops. We realized we'd probably someday work on fairy tales, and that, in turn, led to something else. To compile *A Nursery Companion*, we used the booklets from our collection—some of them are the only known copies.

Iona: When our son James was about six months old, Peter came back from work one day, and he pulled *The Gentle Warbler* out of his pocket—it was one of those little tiny chapbooks—and he was pleased I liked it because he felt it was so flippant. But both of us always collected books—all kinds of books.

Peter: Just last week we bought about a thousand cheap children's books. We go from the beginning to the end—particularly in the popular line—anything that sells a million copies.

Iona: We collect the things that the British Library doesn't. And stuff is coming in all the time—almost every day. In the past week we have got sheet music from 1856 with the earliest appearance of "Little Bo-Peep"—in fact the source of it, I think. And it was, as we suspected, a concert song. We found it at the outdoor country market in Petersfield, just nearby, where we go every week. And then on Sunday we got a German student's drinking song book with little studs on the binding to keep it out of the beer, and that has the eighteenth-century German student song that was brought to England, translated into English, and made into the English singing game "The Farmer's in His Den."

Peter: I've had the collecting fever ever since I was a child. When I was at Eton, we weren't allowed money—the currency was cigarette cards—and when I left school, I had more cards than all of the other students together. I had three secretaries, whom I paid in cards, to do any dirty work I didn't want to do myself. My school report said that I was undoubtedly going to become a millionaire, but that was quite untrue. It seemed so easy to make money that I've never had any desire to do it since. (My card collection got stolen during the school holidays, by the way!)

So come back tomorrow and you can see our collection.

The next morning, after breakfast, I arrive to take the Grand Tour of the house, with Peter as my guide. We begin in the North Library on the ground floor, which contains, as Peter puts it, "basically what anyone should have—the standard works of English literature—just so that you can get down to the real thing right away." I also notice, in passing, an enormous section of books on fables and on nineteenth-century fairy tales, a complete set of the Victorian magazine *The Boy's Own Paper*, and many works on natural history.

Across the hall is Peter's study—a large room in which is housed the Opies' main children's literature collection, and, in an enormous glass-enclosed case, their signed first editions and association and presentation copies. Peter takes out several books to show me, among them a first edition of A. A. Milne's *When We Were Very Young* signed by both the author and the illustrator E. H. Shepard who, Peter informs me with a smile, "lived just nearby"; the copy of the first American edition of *The Wind in the Willows* that Kenneth Grahame gave to his son, in which he wrote: "To Aleistair Grahame from his affectionate father Ken. Grahame/Cookham, Dean/Oct. 1908"; the signed first edition of *The Crock of Gold* that James Stephens presented to Judge Parry; and several more presentation copies of books by Lewis Carroll, Edward Lear, James Barrie, and Edith Nesbit.

"An association copy we always buy automatically," Peter tells me, "because you get nearer to the book, you've got something special, it's an individual copy. We've got books from the Darwin family, books that Emma Hamilton presented to Horatia Nelson, and one or two royal books a volume Queen Victoria gave to her daughter Beatrice, signed with her private initials. It's great fun.

"We have more than eight hundred titles published before 1800, which is nearly twice the number of the Osborne Collection in Toronto; and we have the first abridged edition of *Robinson Crusoe*—that's twenty years earlier than the copy owned by the British Library. . . . And here's Godwin's edition of *Aesop*, one of the first books he did for children, with illustrations by William Mulready—very Blakish. This copy is particularly interesting because of its inscription in the front that reads: "To Augustus Frederick of Sussex, 1806."

Now, Augustus Frederick was the child of the marriage of the Duke of Sussex, who was the son of George III, and who ran off with a commoner to Italy. Eventually, that marriage wasn't even annulled, it was just said not to have happened. So this book went into a royal household, but it was published under the name of Baldwin because Godwin was a radical philosopher and atheist—and it would have been as if the antimonarchist Willie Hamilton had given his book to Prince Charles today! . . . And finally, here's Bewick sending a book to a child: "The gift of Thomas Bewick, engraver, Newcastle to his young friend Mr. Robert Johnson, 1st January 1828." And then he added a moral at the end of the inscription: "And when cockscombs flatter and when fools adore/Learn here this lesson to be vain no more."

As Peter leads me upstairs, we pass under the framed original drawings that Randolph Caldecott did for his famous picture book *The Milkmaid*, and we enter the Knaster Room—named after Roland Knaster, "one of the great collectors whose collection came to us ten years ago"—where one finds hundreds of boxes containing books whose shape, Peter tells me, is more important than the content— "movable books, animated books, reversible books, miniature books, midget books, untearable books, turn-up books, and transformation books." Then there are boxes filled with periodicals, penny books, and comics. "We're very good on cheap picture books and circus books," Peter says, "and we have every known eighteenth-century periodical except one—and that isn't really a children's one."

Peter opens a box and takes out one of Beatrix Potter's file copies of the original edition of *Peter Rabbit*, a copy of the first Frederick Warne edition, and then a first edition of *The Tailor of Gloucester*. "We used to have the original manuscript of *Squirrel Nutkin*," he says, "and we used to read from it to our children—I trusted them, they were brought up to handle things properly—but we sold it to Leslie Linder eventually, the authority on Beatrix Potter. I thought one wouldn't mind—we were even given a facsimile of it, and I've been to see the original once or twice in exhibitions—but when you suddenly come across it, your stomach turns upside down. Linder, however, wanted it so badly; he later presented his collection to the National Book League. It's just one of those things. You never quite know what it is you love the most until you no longer have it."

The next room we visit, called The Temple, is probably the most colorful and fascinating of them all, devoted, as it is, completely to toys. And in the middle of the room are a series of display cases in which the Opies set up little exhibitions from their collection for visitors or just for themselves. "It really doesn't matter who comes to see it," Peter states, "because you learn your own stuff by putting it out."

Previous "exhibitions" have concentrated on John Newbery, Randolph Caldecott, and *Struwwelpeter*; but today, there is a display on the early history of the cinema. "Here's a praxinoscope that you spin," Peter informs me, "and then the zoetrope, which was invented in 1834 and put on the market in 1869. This particular one has sixty different pictures showing a man running around with an umbrella while it's raining pitchforks—because the original version of the famous phrase is, 'It's raining cats and dogs and pitchforks pointing downwards,' and here it is being illustrated. We also have a later version that influenced Disney, with whales, porpoises, and birds flying.

"Then you can see the Magic Disc, and right next to that you'll notice the thaumatrope, which is the earliest proper moving picture, which was invented by a man called Paris and in which you put half a picture on one side (a cage), half a picture on the other (a bird), then twist it round in such a way that you get one side following the other as quickly as possible so the bird seems to be looking inside. . . . Then you can see some flicker books and the Ombro-Cinema from 1920, made in Paris, with black stripes coming down and figures moving behind them. And over here's a Brownie camera. Mrs. Ewing wrote a book about brownies, Palmer Cox took them over and wrote and illustrated *his* books about them, and Baden-Powell got the name and idea for the Girl Guide brownies from Mrs. Ewing, too. So everything joins into something else. Almost everything joins up if you know enough, but it can be a long and tortuous chain. And some people join things up too abruptly, so that there are too many missing links.

"In this room we also have an electric car from 1903, a clockwork train from around 1860, a nineteenth-century Noah's Ark made in Bavaria, all kinds of movable toys and, in particular, sand toys. This one here features Léotard, the man who gave his name to the garments every ballerina wears. He came to England in 1852, and was the first man to perform on the flying trapeze. The toy is operated by means of sand flowing down onto a wheel, and you never see Léotard doing the same action twice. This was, in fact, Kenneth Grahame's favorite toy, and he writes about it in *Dream Days*.

"We have, really and truly, *everything*, you know—certainly anything that is a small object. We have the earliest known surviving race game, the earliest peepshow, and—from 1766—the earliest known jigsaw puzzle. It's the only copy in existence, and it's mentioned by Jane Austen in *Mansfield Park*. This one is by the man who was supposed to have invented them—J. Spilsbury, Master at Harrow. The first puzzles were maps (this one is a history of Europe), and here's another which we believe is the first *picture* jigsaw puzzle (it's of a boat called the *Royal George*). Both are in their original boxes with their labels on them; and these are the first bits of packaging that are known.*

"You see, one of the things we're interested in most is continuity. Reginald Scot's 16th-century *Discoverie of Witchcraft* is the earliest book which describes conjuring tricks. And we have here one of the horrible knives he describes that stabs you . . . and then we have a modern one made out of plastic. Here's a space juggler made in 1955, but if you want to find out how it works, you can read about it in *Rational Recreations* from 1775.

"What we're concerned with here is to collect on the physical side what we're collecting on the oral side in the books. As with the games, we're interested in classifying both the attraction and what makes the thing work. Toys have been looked at as sentimental objects, but we want to look at them 'scientifically.' We started by buying things that are mentioned in children's literature, to try to understand what was being made. If Iona sees children playing with some toy in the playground, we go and get one like it. So we've got her report and we've also got the object.

"This is the material side of *Lore and Language*, these are the physical jokes as opposed to the oral jokes: the stink bombs, things that go squeak when you sit down, joke pencils that collapse or expand or prick you when you write, joke lighters, cigarettes that explode, squirt rings, joke drinking glasses, disguises, tops from the seventeenth century, marbles with stripes of twisted glass inside. We have the earliest form of dominoes, which started to be played in France at the end of the eighteenth and the beginning of the nine-

---

* The Opies' son, Robert, is probably the most important collector of packaging in the world—including wrappers, tins, paper bags, tea packets, confectionary catalogues, etc.—and in 1975 he organized an extremely popular exhibit entitled "The Pack Age: A Century of Wrapping It Up" for the Victoria and Albert Museum. Their other son, James, is one of the leading collectors of Britain's lead soldiers. (The apple doesn't fall far from the tree!)

teenth centuries—here's a French set made by prisoners captured in
the Napoleonic Wars, out of the bones of the food they ate. We've
got knucklebones made from sheep or goats like those used by the
ancient Greeks. We've got yo-yos from the 1850s. . . . As I said, we've
got everything."

We leave this amazing room and climb up another stairway that
leads to the attic, which covers the entire house and which has been
converted into what the Opies call the Archive Room—an enormous
space filled with thousands of boxes containing everything one can
imagine that can be related to childhood: dolls from the eighteenth
century onwards; the first known Christmas card of 1843; children's
costumes, shoes, and baby clothes; children's medicines; nursery bis-
cuits and sugar; paper hats and paper bags; money boxes; clothes pegs
(both wooden and plastic); and lots of plastic toys. "Most people
hate these plastic toys," Peter says, "but they must be collected,
otherwise a whole generation will have no copies of what they played
with. And if you're reading a children's book and it refers to a certain
kind of food, we can usually produce it . . . we're the place of last
resort."

The tour over, Peter takes me downstairs, back to the children's
literature library, and leads me over to the mantel on which are standing two extraordinary-looking dolls, made, Peter tells me, by a married
couple from Portsmouth around 1825. One doll is that of a peddler
woman in a red cloak and a long dress, the other that of a peddler
man in a black frock coat, striped waistcoat and trousers, tall hat, high
collar, and cravat. On and about them are an incredible number of
tiny objects. "You can see," Peter points out, "that they're carrying
and selling chapbooks and ballad sheets and little children's books and
shuttlecock bats and balls and candles and slates and cheap textbooks
and religious artifacts and a pair of braces and gloves and framed
pictures—the cheap, the discarded, the 'unconsidered trifles.' And we
have in this house the actual things that these dolls have on their
trays, and we probably have written down everything that these two
people knew! It gives depth to one's work."

Later that afternoon, I return to Peter's study to ask him about his
own childhood. "I was born in Egypt," he begins. "My mother was a
volunteer during World War I, and went to Egypt, where she met
my father, who was an army doctor. They came back to England

after the war, and I arrived in a kit bag, which we still have upstairs. They had six months here, then they took me to India for two years, returned on my third birthday for a year and a half, and then, again, my father was sent off, this time to Malta. So my mother had to live with *her* mother—a woman whose husband had made a fortune in the Argentine, so it was through him that I had a small independent income.

"My father was killed racing horses in India; he was mad on horses, and when he was young he went to Blundell's and used to ride to school each day across the moors. It was very romantic. He was the sort of person who produced snakes out of his pocket. . . . Now, Iona's grandmother died of cholera—also in India—when Iona's father was three. So he was sent home and brought up by various relations in Scotland. He was as Scots as Scots can be. Being an orphan, and having had to look after a younger brother, he wasn't frightfully good at making contact with other people. And, strangely, he, like my father, was also a doctor—a medical researcher who helped save the cotton crop in the Sudan. He became director of the Wellcome Institute in Khartoum—the research center in tropical medicine—and he helped to discover what caused sleeping sickness. He was one of those sort of people who would sit on the roof of a building in the midday sun with no hat on and with a thermometer in his mouth in order to find out what happened. And with Iona's godfather, he produced the standard multivolume work on tropical medicine. Then, when he came home and retired, he decided again to go off, this time to a lepers' island near Trinidad; and after that he became a professor at Alexandria University.

"Iona stayed at home with her mother, but she has this 'research' in her blood. As do I. I went to India several times when I was a teenager—I did a lot of traveling, which is why I never want to move from my house now [laughing]—and when I was there I instantly wanted to know what the Indians were doing, what they were eating, how they were living, what shrines they went to. One was immediately fascinated, and so is anybody except the set who must go and have their gin and whatever are the standard things. I think that, generally, the English have been the best folklorists. In France it doesn't much exist; the Germans have been good, but they're so serious; and the Americans have difficulties because, if you'll forgive my saying so, until recently you've been an emergent nation and therefore folklore has been used to build up national prestige. Some of the Americans are teaching the subject, saying what is right and what is wrong in folklore and not just being students and observing. A folklorist should just watch and not participate.

"Normally, an anthropologist has to go to another country to do his research so that he can see it with a foreigner's eyes. We can see our children—and we only deal with state-educated children—with an unprejudiced eye because we were not part of that educational system ourselves; and we've got no prejudices as to whether the north is better than the south or whatever . . . we're complete outsiders. So again, it's making use of one's disadvantages."

"Did you know the lore and language of schoolchildren when you were a child?" I ask Peter.

"I didn't *know* it," he responds, "but when we started collecting it, I *recognized* it, and I realized that this was something I'd never known but could remember having heard it from other people. Come the end of the term, the others always knew the right things to say. But I was a spectator even when I was a child. I remember that when one went to a football match at school and everybody started cheering hard for his school, I always thought to myself, 'Well, if I had gone to that other school, I'd be cheering for that other team, and I don't really see it matters which side wins.' But boys mustn't think like that. The people who are so excellent at doing things are those who can go in *without* thinking, especially when being brave. But what gives me such terrific pleasure today is that I now know more about the childhood of the people I was with and what they were saying than they do themselves, since they've forgotten everything. It's very funny indeed: I have no memory, yet I have more memories written down, more oral lore, than possibly anybody else in the world. And this is, of course, why one does it: I'm the repository of talking, with no head of my own! Had Iona and I been the types who did remember rhymes and could produce them, the whole subject would have been so trivial that one couldn't have taken it seriously. Whereas to us, because they were always a bit mysterious and one never quite caught onto them, each time a rhyme actually got written down—one which up till then had been floating on the air and sort of half caught as it went around a corner with somebody else singing it—each time was a discovery, and marvelous, and untrivial.

"We are talking about essentially something we didn't know anything about in the first place—children in the street. And therefore, it's as if we had the advantage of going to a different country, but one where we happened to be able to speak the basic language. And we had another advantage: We'd been told that we could never have done this before World War II, because the children wouldn't have been communicative. One or two people tried, and the children apparently wouldn't talk to them, they were too afraid of the adults. How true that is I'm not quite certain, because you have to be able to learn to talk to children. When we ask them questions, they suddenly realize that we're not telling them anything, we are getting *them* to tell us something which we don't know ourselves, and they have never talked to adults in that way before. And once they suddenly realize that you are interested in *their* stuff—something *they* know about and you don't—then it becomes a person-to-person relationship.

"The interplay between and among children is best left alone. *Don't* teach them how to play their own street games—your own games, yes, but not theirs. At the end of the nineteenth century, singing games were discovered, principally by Cecil Sharp and Lady Gomme, and teachers began to teach children what they had learnt from them . . . and then to correct the children, saying that the *books* said that the children were getting them wrong. Also, adults produce these dreadful playgrounds which are just sheer lakes of cement or asphalt, and what the child is interested in are the *cracks* in the cement; he can't play his games without those.

"There's very curious evidence, which still seems to me astonishing, that in the Middle Ages, when all the world was countryside, you had children running around the churches, throwing balls against the church walls and breaking the windows, when all the while they had those lovely fields to play in. . . . That was what really brought it home to me—reading those medieval accounts of children playing, and asking myself: Why should they be playing where they're not wanted?

"I think that we look at children because they are beautiful specimens, the stuff which tells us about the rest of life before a veneer has come over them. And, if you can understand them, you can see that a certain person is actually a certain type of child. So if you want to know about the grown-up world, study children."

On my fourth and last day with the Opies, I arrive early in the morning to find Peter standing in the driveway, enjoying the beginnings of a perfect spring day. "You've seen the inside of the house," he smiles, "so I thought that today you'd see the outside. Anything in Gilbert White we have here," Peter says as we start walking to the stables, "badgers up the hill, herons flying over, plenty of hedgehogs, too many squirrels, and we're overrun with rabbits—it's like a wildlife park. We had a vixen who gave birth to fox cubs in the bramble bushes in our garden last year. We don't have a dog, and I have a theory that people who keep pet animals don't really like nature, because they drive everything away. But the contrary of that, of course, is that if you don't, then everything comes to you. Blackbirds pick bits out of the garbage, and robins fly into the outside lavatory and build nests on top of the cistern.

"But everything is lucky here. We have four-leaf clovers growing in the garden. Ladybirds hibernate here in the winter, and there are probably some up in the bedroom right now. Swallows go to Africa and come back, as I mentioned before, in the spring. And the magpies always come in pairs—one for sorrow, two for joy—and they nest in the middle of a holly tree. Also, if you'll notice, there are horseshoes on all the stable doors—not put there by us but all there for luck.

"Now I must deviate for a moment because horse shoes are fascinating. Did you see the film _Far From the Madding Crowd_? It was very carefully researched. And on the stable door there was a horseshoe, but it was put on with the U facing upwards. Now in fact, in Hardy's day, they were placed the other way around, as they are on our stable—ours were probably put there in the nineteenth century. But had they done a film with the horseshoe pointing downwards, they'd have had endless people writing in to complain that it was the wrong way around. Because sometime in the first decade of this century, someone started the story that the horseshoe should be facing with its points facing upwards because that held the luck in—a complete fabrication—but now every one has to be placed that way. So what they did in the film was wrong to a folklorist like me, but perhaps I'm the only person who noticed it. And that's an example of change. In the seventeenth and eighteenth centuries, moreover, the horseshoe used to be on the threshold, not on the door, so that the witches couldn't cross over. It's a fascinating subject—you've got this adaptation going on all the time."

"I've noticed," I said to Peter, "that in your books you continually insist that fairy tales, rhymes, and games are all subject to mutation—that they evolve as do all forms of life and adapt to changing circumstances. And this seems to be your view of folklore, too [see p. 253].

"In the past, and more or less to the present day," he replies, "people have thought of folklore as relics or vestiges of the past, and that to study folklore in the present is a way of learning about the past, that there are a finite number of things which can be found,

---

DEVELOPMENT OF A PLAYGROUND RHYME
from *The Lore and Language of Schoolchildren.*

1725

Now he acts the *Grenadier,*
Calling for *a Pot of Beer:*
Where's his Money? He's
    forgot:
Get him gone, a Drunken Sot.
<small>Lines from Henry Carey's ballad 'Namby Pamby' (1726 edn., E3–4).</small>

c. 1907

Eenty, teenty, tuppenny bun,
Pitching tatties doon the lum;
Who's there? John Blair.
What does he want? A bottle
    of beer.
Where's your money? I forgot.
Go downstairs, you drunken
    sot.
<small>Collected from schoolchildren in Edinburgh. Used for counting-out. Rymour Club, 'Miscellanea', vol. i, 1911, p. 104.</small>

1774

Whoes there
    A Granidier
What dye want
    A Pint of Beer.
Whoes there
    A Granidier
What dye want
    A Pint of Beer.
<small>'Catch, The Soldier and the Ale House Man' as noted down, with tune by Samuel Wesley when 8 years old (British Museum, MS. Adds. 34998, f. 34).</small>

c. 1910

Far are ye gaein'?
Across the gutter.
Fat for?
A pund o' butter.
Far's yer money?
In my pocket.
Far's yer pocket?
Clean forgot it!
<small>Current among children in Forfar, c. 1910. Jean C. Rodger, 'Lang Strang', 1948.</small>

1780

Who comes here?
    A Grenadier.
What do you want?
    A Pot of Beer.
Where is your Money?
    I've forgot.
Get you gone
    You drunken Sot.
<small>'Mother Goose's Melody' (1795 edn., p. 42).</small>

1916

Rat a tat tat, who is that?
Only grandma's pussy-cat.
What do you want?
A pint of milk.
Where's your money?
In my pocket.
Where is your pocket?
I forgot it.
O you silly pussy-cat.
<small>Used for skipping, 'London Street Games', 1916, p. 64.</small>

1939

A frog walked into a public
    house
And asked for a pint of beer.
Where's your money?
In my pocket.
Where's your pocket?
I forgot it.
Well, please walk out.

Used for counting-out in Swansea.

1943

Rat tat tat, who is that?
Only Mrs. Pussy Cat.
What do you want?
A pint of milk.
Where's your penny?
In my pocket.
Where's your pocket?
I forgot it.
Please walk out.

*Used for skipping at Castle Eden,
Co. Durham.*

1950

Mickey Mouse
In a public house
Drinking pints of beer.
Where's your money?
In my pocket.
Where's your pocket?
I forgot it.
Please walk out.

Used for counting-out in Alton.

1952

A monkey came to my shop
I asked him what he wanted.
A loaf, sir. A loaf, sir.
Where's your money?
In my pocket.
Where's your pocket?
I ain't got it.
Well, out you bunk.

*'Skipping for two'. Girl, 12, Market
Rasen.*

1952

A pig walked into a public
    house
And asked for a drink of beer.
Where's your money, sir?
In my pocket, sir.
Where's your pocket, sir?
In my jacket, sir.
Where's your jacket, sir?
I forgot it, sir.
Please walk out.

*Used for counting-out. Girl, 12, Clee
thorpes.*

1954

I had a little beer shop
A man walked in.
I asked him what he wanted.
A bottle of gin.
Where's your money?
In my pocket.
Where's your pocket?
I forgot it.
Please walk out.

Used for skipping in York City.

and that they are deteriorating as they come, and fast disappearing.
Now, our approach to this is almost exactly the opposite: We believe
that folklore is a living force that comes along through the ages, and
it's changing—sometimes there is more of it, sometimes less—and I
suggest there is more of it at the moment because in an era of dis-
belief there tends to be more credulity. People, especially students,
have no god, so they are looking at things like Tolkien, trying to
believe there is some magical formula.

"So I think that there is as much superstitious practice now as at anytime; and rightly so, because the realization that life is not as it appears on the surface, that there is such a thing as luck, is a way of explaining how things happen . . . unless you say that some benevolent or malevolent force is directing things. And belief in luck is one of the basic ideas in folklore. We all use our various signs for propitiousness. My great one is that if I can buy a cheap book on a stall outside a bookshop then I can expect to find something good within. And we all have many less rational beliefs than that—like children not wanting to put water in a jam jar when they're fishing until they've caught the first fish. Or not finishing a wedding dress until you're actually going to use it. One knows that if you tempt the gods too much, it's going to come down on you. We haven't a clue yet as to why things happen. And folklore is a sign of that recognition."

Iona has now come out to join us on a leisurely walk through and around the flower, vegetable, and formal gardens. She points to a one hundred-year-old thuya hedge in the front garden—a series of small trees planted together to create a hedge that changes shapes. "It looks like an elephant inside a boa constrictor," I suggest, remembering Saint-Exupéry's Little Prince. "It looks like whatever you want it to look like," Iona says, smiling. "An art teacher from Los Angeles who visited us said it reminded her of free sculpture."

"That horse chestnut tree there," Peter added, pointing, "is the biggest conker tree in the village. Some of the boys come up here and bring us blackberries in exchange for the conkers."

"Underneath it's really like a cave," I comment as I walk into the shadows, and the ground is filled with bluebells, whitebells, and something Iona says is called Parson in the Pulpit.

"The real name," Peter interjects, "is cuckoopint, and pint stands for pintle, and pintle stands for what Jonathan and I have and Iona doesn't!"

"The plant is so sexy it's unbelievable!" Iona laughs.

"It's called things like dead man's finger, priest's smock—it has more folk names, at least forty or more, than any other plant," adds Peter. "I once thought I'd look up all the names and then reel them off to Iona and then she'd think I was marvelous . . . but, of course, I have no memory."

"We've made a list of all the birds that visit us," Iona states, "and I can remember them: goldcrests, wrens, blue tits, finches, woodpeckers, barn and screech owls, starlings, swallows, martins, swifts . . . and, of course, robins. Ogden Nash once came to visit us, and one of the things he told us he'd come to England for was to see an English robin. And another visitor, Robert Graves, told us that our dark-red Prunus tree was the wrong color: 'That tree is the *wrong color!'* he asserted." "He thought it was a beech tree," Peter comments.

"We have many different kinds of trees here," Iona says. "Bay, quince, spotted laurel, sweet chestnut, rowan, and silver birches— the birches are in memory of Kornei Chukovsky, the Russian children's poet and educator, who came here and said we should have them. . . . And there are four or five different types of apple trees in the apple orchard."

As we circle back to the house, Iona suddenly trips and falls into some nettles, stinging herself. Immediately, she reaches for some dock leaves beside her and rubs her skin with them. "This is what Chaucer told you to do," Iona explains, "Out nettle, in dock, or nettle in, dock out . . . something like that. The leaves take the sting out, and they always grow with the nettles—an amazing provision by Mother Nature."

"I'm sorry you got stung," I say, "but it was quite a demonstration!"

"It was unrehearsed, too." Iona laughs. "And there," she says, pointing to some roses, "are what I call my Beatrix Potter roses. I went to Hill Top Farm in Sawrey, where she spent her last years, and the house smelled so beautiful, full of the scent of these flowers, that I searched and found roses just like them. And we have all kinds of roses here, even some that look after themselves.

"The most static things are always changing; the trees change their shape each year, and it's all very relaxed, and it becomes like us as we reach older age. Look at that ancient quince tree, which has been leaning over further and further, like an old person, for years. We were planning on planting a new one, but it provided for itself— it dropped a fruit over the wall and planted its own successor in the right place. One wanted to defend it, but it was better just to let it have its own way."

"And *our* material also generates its own material," Peter comments. "*Lore and Language* is now beginning to talk about the childhoods of men and women who are coming up to middle age. And toward the end of this century, it's going to be about the childhoods of the old people who will be consulting the book in order to write their autobiographies!"

.   .   .

It is getting time for me to catch the train back to London; but Peter, Iona, and I are still lingering in the garden, as I remind the Opies of the English writer on education Richard Mabey's discovery of what he calls the "unofficial countryside" in his own backyard: "I have counted over twenty different species of wild flower (excluding grasses) on my lawn," Mabey writes, "many of them just those plants through which, in children's games, we have our first physical intimacy with nature: dandelion seed-heads for telling the time; daisies for chaplets; buttercups under the chin; couch grass to wind into sister's hair as a Chinese Torture; ratstail plantains for guns; Lady's slippers and clovers to suck for nectar. These flowers are part of children's lives precisely because they are weeds, abundant and resilient plants that grow comfortingly and accessibly close to us. If we drive them out of their domestic refuges into ghettoes in the deep countryside they will be driven out of what remains of our folklore as well."

"We just look further and further into our one little patch," says Peter Opie.

"And we will stand up with Richard Mabey and defend these patches—these little corners, fields, and ditches," says Iona Opie.

In mid-February, 1982, I received a letter from Iona saying that Peter had died of a massive heart attack on February 5. "I am glad you managed to transcribe our conversations," she wrote me. "Peter undertook the interviewing in the same spirit as he undertook everything (while trying to limit his commitments)—with all his heart and strength. In everything he did, he tried his utmost. He had a strong will, and unlimited enthusiasm: in the end they broke his never-very-strong body."

"I happen to believe," Peter had said to me nine months earlier, "that life is nonsense, that we're an accident, that there is no life after death, and that there is no reason for one being here other than being here. Now, good nonsense is wonderful because it frees the mind, it's like one's dreams, it makes you realize that nothing matters very much. And it seems to me that if you appreciate nonsense, then you're *really* getting wise. That's the great freedom, because you can then make up your own rules."

And as I hear and see Peter Opie in my mind, I am reminded of all those people in the world—then and now—who have been, and are being, forced to live according to the rules, edicts, and dictates of others. As Osip Mandelstam wrote in one of his last poems (quoted

here in the translation by Clarence Brown and W. S. Merwin),
shortly before dying in a Russian concentration camp in 1938:

> Mounds of human heads are wandering into the distance.
> I dwindle among them. Nobody sees me. But in books
> much loved, and in children's games I shall rise
> from the dead to say the sun is shining.

Bibliography

A Reading List of Children's Books by the Authors Discussed in
Pipers at the Gates of Dawn

DR. SEUSS

Dr. Seuss's first two books were published by The Vanguard Press.
All the others are available from Random House.

And to Think That I Saw It on Mulberry Street (1937)
The 500 Hats of Bartholomew Cubbins (1938)
The King's Stilts (1939)
Horton Hatches the Egg (1940)
McElligot's Pool (1947)
Thidwick the Big Hearted Moose (1948)
Bartholomew and the Oobleck (1949)
If I Ran the Zoo (1950)
Scrambled Eggs Super (1953)
Horton Hears a Who (1954)
On Beyond Zebra (1955)
If I Ran the Circus (1956)
How the Grinch Stole Christmas (1957)
The Cat in the Hat (1957)
The Cat in the Hat Comes Back (1958)
Yertle the Turtle (1958)
Happy Birthday to You (1959)
Green Eggs and Ham (1960)
The Sneetches and Other Stories (1961)
Dr. Seuss's Sleep Book (1962)
Hop on Pop (1963)
Dr. Seuss's ABC Book (1963)
Fox in Socks (1965)
I Had Trouble in Getting to Solla Sollew (1965)
The Cat in the Hat Songbook (1967)
The Foot Book (1968)

My Book About Me (1969)
I Can Lick 30 Tigers Today and Other Stories (1969)
I Can Draw It Myself (1970)
Mr. Brown Can Moo! Can You? (1970)
The Lorax (1971)
Marvin K. Mooney, Will You Please Go Now! (1972)
The Shape of Me and Other Stuff (1973)
Did I Ever Tell You How Lucky You Are? (1973)
There's a Wocket in My Pocket (1974)
Great Day for Up! (1974)
Oh, the Thinks You Can Think (1975)
The Cat's Quizzer (1976)
I Can Read with My Eyes Shut (1978)
Oh, Say Can You Say? (1979)
Hunches in Bunches (1982)

MAURICE SENDAK

(Books illustrated and/or written by him)

Atomics for the Millions by M. C. Eidinoff and others (McGraw-Hill, 1947)
Good Shabbos, Everybody by Robert Garvey (United Synagogue Commission on Jewish Education, 1951)
The Wonderful Farm by Marcel Aymé (Harper & Row, 1951)
A Hole Is To Dig by Ruth Krauss (Harper & Row, 1953)
Maggie Rose: Her Birthday Christmas by Ruth Sawyer (Harper & Row, 1952)
The Giant Story by Beatrice de Regnier (Harper & Row, 1953)
Hurry Home, Candy by Meindert DeJong (Harper & Row, 1953)
Shadrach by Meindert DeJong (Harper & Row, 1953)
A Very Special House by Ruth Krauss (Harper & Row, 1953)
I'll by You and You Be Me by Marcel Aymé (Harper & Row, 1954)
Mrs. Piggle-Wiggle's Farm by Betty MacDonald (J. B. Lippincott, 1954)
The Tin Fiddle by Edward Tripp (Henry Z. Walck, 1954)
The Wheel on the School by Meindert DeJong (Harper & Row, 1954)
Charlotte and the White Horse by Ruth Krauss (Harper & Row, 1954)
Happy Hanukah, Everybody by Hyman and Alice Chanover (United Synagogue Commission on Jewish Education, 1955)
The Little Cow and the Turtle by Meindert DeJong (Harper & Row, 1955)
Seven Little Stories on Big Subjects by Gladys Baker Bond (The Anti-Defamation League, B'nai B'rith, 1955)
What Can You Do with a Show? by Beatrice de Regnier (Harper & Row, 1955)

The Happy Rain by Jack Sendak (Harper & Row, 1956)

The House of Sixty Fathers by Meindert DeJong (Harper & Row, 1956)

I Want To Paint My Bathroom Blue by Ruth Krauss (Harper & Row, 1956)

Kenny's Window by Maurice Sendak (Harper & Row, 1956)

The Birthday Party by Ruth Krauss (Harper & Row, 1957)

Circus Girl by Jack Sendak (Harper & Row, 1957)

Little Bear by Else Holmelund Minarik (Harper & Row, 1957)

Very Far Away by Maurice Sendak (Harper & Row, 1957)

Along Came a Dog by Meindert DeJong (Harper & Row, 1958)

No Fighting, No Biting! by Else Holmelund Minarik (Harper & Row, 1958)

Somebody Else's Nut Tree and Other Tales for Children by Ruth Krauss (Harper & Row, 1958)

What Do You Say, Dear? by Sesyle Joslin (Young Scott, 1958)

The Acrobat by Maurice Sendak (privately printed, 1959)

Father Bear Comes Home by Else Holmelund Minarik (Harper & Row, 1959)

The Moon Jumpers by Janice May Udry (Harper & Row, 1959)

Seven Tales by Hans Christian Andersen, translated by Doris Orgel (Random House, 1959)

Dwarf Long Nose by Wilhelm Hauff, translated by Doris Orgel (Random House, 1960)

Little Bear's Friend by Else Holmelund Minarik (Harper & Row, 1960)

Open House for Butterflies by Ruth Krauss (Harper & Row, 1960)

The Sign on Rosie's Door by Maurice Sendak (Harper & Row, 1960)

Let's Be Enemies by Janice May Udry (Harper & Row, 1961)

Little Bear's Visit by Else Holmelund Minarik (Harper & Row, 1961)

The Tale of Gockel, Hinkel, and Gackeliah by Clemens Brentano, translated by Doris Orgel (Random House, 1961)

What Do You Do, Dear? by Sesyle Joslin (Young Scott, 1961)

The Big Green Book by Robert Graves (Crowell-Collier, 1962)

Mr. Rabbit and the Lovely Present by Charlotte Zolotow (Harper & Row, 1962)

The Nutshell Library by Maurice Sendak. *Alligators All Around, One Was Johnny, Chicken Soup with Rice, Pierre* (Harper & Row, 1962)

Schoolmaster Whackwell's Wonderful Sons by Clemens Bretano, translated by Doris Orgel (Random House, 1962)

The Singing Hill by Meindert DeJong (Harper & Row, 1962)

The Griffin and the Minor Canon by Frank Stockton (Holt, Rinehart & Winston, 1963)

How Little Lori Visited Times Square by Amos Vogel (Harper & Row, 1963)

Nikolenka's Childhood by Leo Tolstoy (Pantheon Books, 1963)

Sarah's Room by Doris Orgel (Harper & Row, 1963)

She Loves Me, She Loves Me Not by Robert Keeshan (Harper & Row, 1963)

Where the Wild Things Are by Maurice Sendak (Harper & Row, 1963)

The Bat-Poet by Randall Jarrell (Pantheon Books, 1964)

The Bee-Man of Orn by Frank Stockton (Holt, Rinehart & Winston, 1964)

Pleasant Fieldmouse by Jan Wahl (Harper & Row, 1964)

The Animal Family by Randall Jarrell (Pantheon Books, 1965)

Hector Protector and *As I Went over the Water* by Maurice Sendak (Harper & Row, 1965)

Lullabies and Night Songs edited by William Engvick, music by Alec Wilder (Harper & Row, 1965)

Zlateh the Goat and Other Stories by Isaac Bashevis Singer, translated by the author and Elizabeth Sub (Harper & Row, 1966)

The Golden Key by George MacDonald (Farrar, Straus & Giroux, 1967)

Higglety Pigglety Pop! or There Must Be More to Life by Maurice Sendak (Harper & Row, 1967)

Poems from William Blake's "Songs of Innocence" (privately issued by The Bodley Head, London, 1967)

A Kiss for Little Bear by Else Holmelund Minarik (Harper & Row, 1968)

The Light Princess by George MacDonald (Farrar, Straus & Giroux, 1969)

In the Night Kitchen by Maurice Sendak (Harper & Row, 1970)

Fantasy Drawings by Maurice Sendak (The Rosenbach Foundation, 1970)

The Magician: A Counting Book by Maurice Sendak (The Rosenbach Foundation, 1971)

Pictures by Maurice Sendak (Harper & Row, 1971)

The Juniper Tree and Other Tales from Grimm, translated by Lore Segal and Randall Jarrell (Farrar, Straus & Giroux, 1973)

King Grisly-Beard: A Tale from the Brothers Grimm (Farrar, Straus & Giroux, 1973)

Fortunia by Mme. D'Aulnay (private press, 1974)

Really Rosie, Starring the Nutshell Kids. Scenario, lyrics, and pictures by Maurice Sendak, music by Carole King, design by Jane Byers Bierhorst (Harper & Row, 1975)

Fly by Night by Randall Jarrell (Farrar, Straus & Giroux, 1976)

Seven Little Monsters by Maurice Sendak (Harper & Row, 1976)

Some Swell Pup, or Are You Sure You Want a Dog? by Maurice Sendak and Matthew Margolis (Farrar, Straus & Giroux, 1976)

Outside over There by Maurice Sendak (Harper & Row, 1981)

WILLIAM STEIG

The first six Steig titles were published by Windmill Books,
the following ones by Farrar, Straus & Giroux.

C D B! (1968)
Roland the Minstrel Pig (1968)
Sylvester and the Magic Pebble (1969)
The Bad Island (1969)
The Bad Speller (1970)
An Eye for Elephants (1970)
Amos and Boris (1971)
Dominic (1972)
The Real Thief (1973)
Farmer Palmer's Wagon Ride (1974)
Abel's Island (1976)
The Amazing Bone (1976)
Caleb and Kate (1977)
Tiffky Doofky (1978)
Gorky Rises (1980)
Doctor De Soto (1982)

ASTRID LINDGREN

The following is a list of Astrid Lindgren's works that have been published
in English. Certain of these books have been published only in the United
States or only in England—the former are indicated by one asterisk, the
latter by two. American and British editions of those books that have been
published in both countries occasionally feature different translations and
titles; the titles listed below are those of the American editions. The dates
listed are those of the first American or British editions.

Pippi Longstocking (The Viking Press, 1950)
Pippi Goes on Board (The Viking Press, 1957)
Pippi in the South Seas (The Viking Press, 1959)
Bill Bergson Master Detective* (The Viking Press, 1952)
Bill Bergson Lives Dangerously* (The Viking Press, 1954)
Bill Bergson and the White Rose Rescue* (The Viking Press, 1965)
The Children of Noisy Village (The Viking Press, 1962)
Happy Times in Noisy Village (The Viking Press, 1963)
The Six Bullerby Children** (Methuen, 1963)
All about the Bullerby Children** (Methuen, 1970)
Mischievous Meg (The Viking Press, 1962)
Lotta on Troublemaker Street (Macmillan, 1963)
The Children on Troublemaker Street (Macmillan, 1964)

Rasmus and the Vagabond (The Viking Press, 1966)
Seacrow Island (The Viking Press, 1969)
Emil in the Soup Tureen (Follett, 1970)
Emil's Pranks (Follett, 1971)
Emil and Piggy Beast (Follett, 1973)
Karlsson-on-the-Roof (The Viking Press, 1971)
The Brothers Lionheart (The Viking Press, 1975)
Ronia, the Robber's Daughter (The Viking Press, 1983)

In addition to the above story books, Astrid Lindgren has written the texts to the following picture books, translated into English and illustrated by various artists:

Eva Visits Noriko-San (Macmillan, 1957)
Sia Lives on Kilimanjaro (Macmillan, 1959)
My Swedish Cousins (Macmillan, 1960)
Lilibet—Circus Child (Macmillan, 1961)
Brenda Brave Helps Grandmother (St. Louis: Webster, 1961)
The Tomten (Coward-McCann, 1961)
The Tomten and the Fox (Coward-McCann, 1965)
Marko Lives in Yugoslavia (Macmillan, 1962)
Christmas in the Stable (Coward-McCann, 1962)
Dirk Lives in Holland (Macmillan, 1963)
Christmas in Noisy Village (The Viking Press, 1964)
Springtime in Noisy Village (The Viking Press, 1966)
Randi Lives in Norway (Macmillan, 1965)
Simon Small Moves In** (Burke, 1965)
A Day at Bullerby** (Methuen, 1967)
Noy Lives in Thailand (Macmillan, 1967)
Matti Lives in Finland (Macmillan, 1969)
Skrallan and the Pirates (Doubleday, 1969)
Of Course Polly Can Ride a Bike (Follett, 1972)
Of Course Polly Can Do Almost Everything (Follett, 1978)
My Very Own Sister** (Methuen, 1974)
That Emil** (Hodder & Stoughton, 1973)
Emil and the Bad Tooth** (Hodder & Stoughton, 1976)
Pippi on the Run (The Viking Press, 1976)

CHINUA ACHEBE

Chike and the River (Cambridge University Press, 1966)
How the Leopard Got Its Claws (written with John Iroaganachi—New York: The Third Press, 1973)

The Drum was first published by Fourth Dimension Publishers in Nigeria in 1977. It was reprinted in *Wonders*, edited by Jonathan Cott and Mary Gimbel (Summit Books, 1980)

"The Flute"—a retelling of an African folktale—appears in *Sharing Literature with Children*, edited by Francelia Butler (David McKay Company, 1977). An earlier version of the story appeared in Achebe's novel *Arrow of God* (The John Day Company, 1967)

P. L. TRAVERS

Unless otherwise noted, all books are published by
Harcourt Brace Jovanovich.

Mary Poppins (1934)
Mary Poppins Comes Back (1935)
I Go By Sea, I Go By Land (Dell Publishing Co., 1941)
Mary Poppins Opens the Door (1943)
Mary Poppins in the Park (1952)
Mary Poppins from A to Z (1962)
The Fox at the Manger (Grosset & Dunlap, 1962)
Friend Monkey (1975)
Mary Poppins in the Kitchen (1975)
About the Sleeping Beauty (McGraw Hill, 1975)
Two Pairs of Shoes (The Viking Press, 1980)
Mary Poppins in Cherry Tree Lane (Delacorte Press, 1982)

IONA AND PETER OPIE

Unless otherwise noted, all books are published by the
Oxford University Press.

I Saw Esau (Williams & Norgate, Ltd., 1947)
The Oxford Dictionary of Nursery Rhymes (1951)
The Oxford Nursery Rhyme Book (1955)
The Lore and Language of Schoolchildren (1959)
The Puffin Book of Nursery Rhymes (Penguin Books, 1963)
Children's Games in Street and Playground (1969)
The Oxford Book of Children's Verse (1973)
The Classic Fairy Tales (1974)
A Nursery Companion (1980)

Permission Credits

Some portions of this work were previously published in *The New Yorker*, *Rolling Stone*, and *Parabola* magazine.

Grateful acknowledgment is made to the following for permission to reprint previously published material:

Atheneum Publishers, Inc.: The poem "Mounds of human heads . . ." by Osip Mandelstam is reprinted from *Selected Poems*, trans. by Clarence Brown and W. S. Merwin. Copyright © 1973 by Clarence Brown and W. S. Merwin. British Commonwealth and open market rights administered by Oxford University Press. Reprinted by permission.

Contemporary Books, Inc.: Excerpt from *Wilhelm Reich: The Evolution of His Work* by David Boadella, © 1974. Reprinted by permission of Contemporary Books, Inc., Chicago, Illinois.

Doubleday & Co., Inc., and Harold Ober Associates Incorporated: Excerpts from *Morning Yet On Creation Day* by Chinua Achebe. Copyright © 1975 by Chinua Achebe. Reprinted by permission of Doubleday & Co., Inc. and Harold Ober Associates Incorporated.

Farrar, Straus & Giroux, Inc.: Excerpts from *Character Analysis* by Wilhelm Reich, translated by Vincent B. Carfagno, copyright © 1945, 1949, 1972 by Mary Boyd Higgins as Trustee of the Wilhelm Reich Infant Trust Fund. From *Ether, God and Devil* by Wilhelm Reich, translated by Therese Pol, © copyright 1949, 1951, 1973 by Mary Boyd Higgins as Trustee of the Wilhelm Reich Infant Trust Fund. From *Listen, Little Man!* by Wilhelm Reich, translated by Ralph Manheim, translation copyright © 1974 by Mary Boyd Higgins as Trustee of the Wilhelm Reich Infant Trust Fund. From *The Murder of Christ* by Wilhelm Reich, copyright 1953 by Mary Boyd Higgins as Trustee of the Wilhelm Reich Infant Trust Fund. From *Abel's Island* by William Steig, copyright © 1976 by William Steig. From *The Amazing Bone* by William Steig, copyright © 1976 by William Steig. From *Amos and Boris* by William Steig, copyright © 1971 by William Steig. From *Bad Island* by William Steig, copyright © 1969 by William Steig. From *Caleb and Kate* by William Steig, copyright © 1977 by William Steig. From *Dominic* by William

Illustration Credits

Index

JONATHAN COTT was educated at Columbia College, the University of California, Berkeley, and the University of Essex in England. He is the author of *Stockhausen: Conversations with the Composer*; *He Dreams What Is Going On Inside His Head*, a collection of essays, interviews, and reviews; *City of Earthly Love*, a collection of poems; and *Forever Young* (eight conversations with, among others, Glenn Gould, Henry Miller, Werner Herzog, and Oriana Fallaci). He has also edited *The Roses Race Around Her Name: Poems from Fathers to Daughters*; *Beyond the Looking Glass: Victorian Fairy Tale Novels, Stories, and Poems*; and has co-edited *Wonders*, a collection of writings for children and adults, and *The Ballad of John and Yoko*. His poetry has been widely anthologized and has appeared in the *Paris Review*, *Partisan Review*, the *American Poetry Review*, and elsewhere. He has been an editor of *Rolling Stone* since its inception, and his articles and essays have appeared in that magazine and in *The New York Times*, *Parabola*, *American Review*, *New York Arts Journal*, and *The New Yorker*.